14th Conference of the Association for Machine Translation in the Americas (AMTA 2020)

AA002060

Volume 1: MT Research Track

Online
6 – 9 October 2020

Editors:

Michael Denkowski
Christian Federman

ISBN: 978-1-7138-1982-0

Printed from e-media with permission by:

Curran Associates, Inc.
57 Morehouse Lane
Red Hook, NY 12571

Some format issues inherent in the e-media version may also appear in this print version.

Copyright© (2020) by the Association for Computational Linguistics
All rights reserved.
Copyright for individual papers remains with the authors and are licensed under a Creative Commons 3.0
license, CC-BY-ND. (https://creativecommons.org/licenses/by-nd/3.0/)

Printed with permission by Curran Associates, Inc. (2021)

For permission requests, please contact the Association for Computational Linguistics
at the address below.

Association for Computational Linguistics
209 N. Eighth Street
Stroudsburg, Pennsylvania 18360

Phone: 1-570-476-8006
Fax: 1-570-476-0860

acl@aclweb.org

Additional copies of this publication are available from:

Curran Associates, Inc.
57 Morehouse Lane
Red Hook, NY 12571 USA
Phone: 845-758-0400
Fax: 845-758-2633
Email: curran@proceedings.com
Web: www.proceedings.com

The 14th Conference of The Association for Machine Translation in the Americas

www.amtaweb.org

PROCEEDINGS

Vol. 1: MT Research Track

Editors: Michael Denkowski & Christian Federman

©2020 The Authors. These articles are licensed under a Creative Commons 3.0 license, no derivative works, attribution, CC-BY-ND.

Welcome to the 14th Biennial Conference of the Association for Machine Translation in the Americas – AMTA 2020 Virtual!

AMTA conferences traditionally provide a unique opportunity for academic and commercial researchers to share their results with colleagues as well as to understand real-world user requirements. Business and government participants benefit from updates on leading-edge R&D in MT and have a chance to present and discuss their use cases. At the same time, students who attend gain a broad perspective and understanding of the fascinating field of MT.

This year's conference, however, is significant in at least two aspects. The first is that neural machine translation (NMT) has become a de facto standard in research and industry. At our last conference in March of 2018, generic NMT systems had just begun to be widely used during the preceding year, but it was later in 2018 that customizable NMT systems became widely available, enabling many companies, governments, and other organizations to benefit from an even higher level of MT quality for their specific applications. Since then, NMT customization and usage across the spectrum from individual translators to large corporations has continued to snowball.

The second aspect has been more of a difficulty than an advantage. The COVID-19 pandemic has resulted in transforming AMTA 2020 from an in-person event at a spectacular venue in Orlando, Florida to a completely online conference. While this transformation has presented many unique challenges, we now see some silver linings in this cloud. Without the need to travel and its associated costs, our attendance numbers have doubled from previous years, and participation has come from around the globe. We have been fortunate to receive tremendous support from our many sponsors, for which we are most grateful. Notably, Microsoft has provided their Teams platform to support the virtual conference sessions.

I wish to offer my sincerest thanks to our conference organizing committee, without whom this virtual conference would not have taken place. They have worked long hours to organize and prepare for this unique format, navigating uncharted waters and overcoming various roadblocks. I trust that all who attend will benefit from the results of their diligent efforts.

Steve Richardson
AMTA President

Introduction

The AMTA 2020 research track continues the conference's tradition of bringing together machine translation users, developers, and researchers from around the world. The proceedings include ten long papers, two short papers, and three open source toolkit descriptions covering a broad range of topics. Some papers introduce extensions to widely used translation models and inference algorithms. Others focus on improving MT performance for specific domains and applications, including low resource languages and speech translation. Still others explore the connections between MT and other language processing tasks such as sentiment classification and lexicon induction.

This track is made possible by the hard work and contributions of many individuals. We would like to thank Steve Richardson and all members of the conference committee for their organizational support, Alon Lavie and the rest of the steering committee for specific advice on the research track, and all of the AMTA 2020 authors and reviewers.

Sincerely,

Michael Denkowski
Christian Federmann

Research Program Committee

Boxing Chen	Alibaba
Colin Cherry	Google
Steve DeNeefe	SDL
Marcello Federico	Amazon
George Foster	Google
Matthias Huck	SAP
Philipp Koehn	Johns Hopkins University
Roland Kuhn	National Research Council of Canada
Shankar Kumar	Google
Alon Lavie	Unbabel
Lemao Liu	Tencent
Qun Liu	Huawei
Daniel Marcu	Amazon
Steve Richardson	Church of Jesus Christ of Latter-day Saints
Raymond Slyh	Air Force Research Laboratory
Christoph Tillmann	IBM
Taro Watanabe	Nara Institute of Science and Technology
Andy Way	Dublin City University
François Yvon	LIMSI/CNRS
Bing Zhao	SRI International

Contents

A New Approach to Parameter-Sharing in Multilingual Neural Machine Translation

Benyamin Ahmadnia ahmadnia@ucdavis.edu
Department of Linguistics, University of California, Davis, CA 95616, USA
School of Professional Advancement, Tulane University, New Orleans, LA 70118, USA

Bonnie J. Dorr bdorr@ihmc.us
Institute for Human and Machine Cognition (IHMC), Ocala, FL 34774, USA

Abstract

In multilingual Machine Translation (MT), the strategy of parameter-sharing not only determines how to make optimal use of the parameter space but also directly influences ultimate translation quality. In this paper, we propose an approach to parameter-sharing in multilingual MT. The core idea of this approach is employing the expert language hierarchies as a fundamental for multilingual architecture: the closer two languages are, the more parameters they share. The proposed approach finds support in observations on the role of language affinity in recent MT literature. We consider the simplest case with two sources and one target language and show the potential of this approach. Our results demonstrate that the hierarchical architecture outperforms bilingual models and multilingual model with full parameter sharing, and show how translation quality of the hierarchical model depends on linguistic distance between source languages.

1 Introduction

Low-resource languages are the languages with fewer technologies and datasets relative to some measure of their international importance (Ahmadnia and Dorr, 2019). In simple words, the languages for which bilingual corpus is sparse, requiring recourse to techniques that are complementary to data-driven MT approaches. The biggest issue with low-resource languages is the difficulty of obtaining sufficient resources. Natural Language Processing (NLP) methods that have been created for analysis of low-resource languages are likely to encounter similar issues to those faced by documentary and descriptive linguists whose primary endeavor is the study of minority languages. Parallel data in other languages can substantially benefit low-resource MT. For example, creating a multilingual model that in which multiple parallel corpora can be combined to train a single model where languages can share some parameters to help each other learn instead of training separate models for each translation direction, is a possible way to overcome the data scarcity bottleneck.

Given that languages have a lot in common, properly organized parameter-sharing strategy could compensate for the lack of training examples in low-resource language pairs. Exploiting language relatedness can substantially enhance translation quality (Tan et al., 2019). Since a lack of systematic approach which would account for the degree of relatedness between languages in a multilingual model throughout the current approaches such as full parameter-sharing (Johnson et al., 2017), or shared encoder side with language-specific decoders (Dong et al., 2015), and with respect to the fact that languages are able to share various characteristics on different levels like alphabet, morphology, semantics, we propose an approach depending on the languages' closeness which makes sense to look for shared parts on different levels. The core idea is to organize both encoder and decoder in a hierarchical fashion, reflecting the degree of relatedness between languages, such that the most related languages share the largest number of parameters.

This paper is organized as follows; Section 2 investigates the previous related work. Section 3 describes the methodology. The experimental results and analysis are covered by Section 4. Conclusions and future work are provided in Section 5.

2 Related Work

The simplest form of parameter sharing was introduced by Johnson et al. (2017) where all parameters are shared and identifier tokens are employed to distinguish between languages. This model requires more resources to capture relationships between languages.

Dong et al. (2015) investigated the translation problem as a multi-task problem with shared encoder and separate decoders for each target language. As a disadvantage of this work, the potential knowledge sharing between target languages is not considered.

Sachan and Neubig (2018) proposed a one-to-many model, where parameters are partially shared between the multiple decoders. Although this work is similar to our approach, instead of having shared parts between individual decoders, we propose creating a hierarchy of decoders.

In the aforementioned works, languages on the encoder or decoder of multilingual models are treated the same regardless of their relatedness degree but in our model, the number of shared parameters in our approach, heavily depends on the degree of kinship between languages.

3 Method Description

We aim at proposing an optimal parameter-sharing strategy between languages in a multilingual Neural MT (NMT). The core idea is to organize languages on the encoder and decoder according to their linguistic similarity. Creating a hierarchical model on each side such that the hierarchies correspond to how languages are connected in *phylogenetic* trees[1].

As an example, assume that sufficient amount of bilingual texts for the following language pairs are available: Russian-Tatar (ru-tt), Russian-Kazakh (ru-kk), Russian-English (ru-en), English-Turkish (en-tr), English-Azerbaijani (en-az), German-Turkish (de-tr), Azerbaijani-Turkish (az-tr).Figure 1 shows a detailed high-level and detailed view of the architecture for a multilingual hierarchical model that are trained using the mentioned corpora.

In Figure 1, there are four source and five target languages connected through the chain of hierarchically organized encoders and decoders. In the encoder side, all source languages have their own respective encoders e_{ru}, e_{en}, e_{de}, and e_{az}. The parameters of these encoders are not shared with any other languages since they are intended to learn language-specific features. In detail, the outputs of some encoders are stacked together and passed to the shared encoders. These encoders are: e_{en-de} and $e_{ru-en-de}$ that are shared among two or more languages so that they can capture knowledge common to these languages. Finally, there is the last encoder ($e_{ru-en-de-es}$) that is shared by all source languages which combines the outputs of all remaining encoders together.

This architecture has been designed to enable knowledge sharing between different languages on various levels. It can be seen that English and German are connected first[2]. Then, Russian is added in[3]. Next, all these languages are joined Azerbaijani[4]. Logic on the decoder

---

[1]The closer two languages are, the more parameters they share.

[2]They come from the Germanic branch of the Indo-European language family.

[3]It belongs to a different branch of the same language family.

[4]It comes from an entirely different Turkic language family.

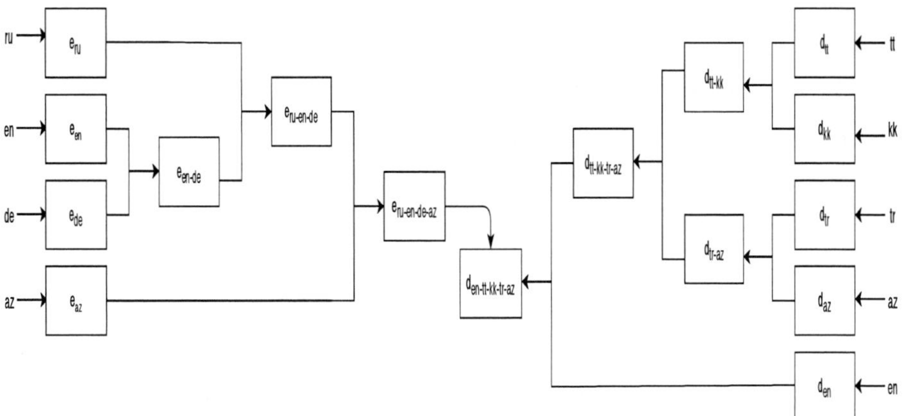

Figure 1: A high-level view of a multilingual hierarchical model. e is a shared encoder, and d is a decoder.

side is analogous—most dissimilar languages split first. We propose having the same number of parameters along any path from source to target. For example, if we compare ru-tt and az-en translation paths in Figure 1, although the latter has considerably less shared parameters, their total number should be the same for both paths. That is why some encoder blocks are longer than others, pointing that, for example, the number of parameters in e_{az} should be the same as there are cumulatively in e_{ru} and $e_{ru-en-de}$.

In NMT, model parameters are learned by maximizing the conditional probability $P(t|s)$ of reconstructing target sentence (t) given source sentence (s). In a multilingual setting, there are multiple source and target sentences $(s_1, s_2, s_3, ...), (t_1, t_2, t_3, ...)$. Then, for each available bilingual dataset (i, j), the aim is at maximizing $P(t_i|s_j)$. Assuming some parts of the model are shared, when maximizing the conditional probabilities, only those parameters are updated that depend on the path from one language to another. Considering a simple example in Figure 2. There are two possible translation paths, and individual encoder parameters $\theta_{e_1}, \theta_{e_2}$ will only be updated when the parameters for the corresponding translation path are updated.

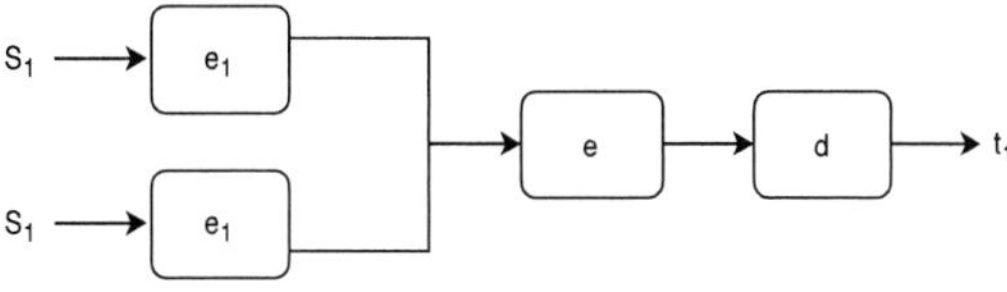

Figure 2: Simple multi-source hierarchical architecture. e_1, e_2 are individual encoders, e is a shared encoder, and d is a decoder.

As for the training procedure in a general multi-source multi-target case, there are several options. One possible way is to alternate between all translation directions in a system, but in this case, the possible concern is that the model parameters may start to oscillate between these directions. Therefore, we propose to simultaneously feed data from all source languages, stack representations at points where specific encoders merge into shared ones, and pass them through the chain of decoders down to individual decoders. There are many other decisions to be made, such as what should be the proportion between samples from different language pairs, should samples be over-sampled, should they be weighted, etc.

4 Experiments and Results

For the implementation, we selected three languages; 1) Russian (as a high-resource language from the East-Slavic subgroup within the "Indo-European" language family), 2) Kazakh, and 3) Tatar. The last two languages belong to the "Kipchak" sub-branch of the Turkic language family and hence are quite related. Kazakh and Tatar languages are far from Russian both by the number of speakers and the amount of linguistic resources, but Kazakh is a higher-resource language than Tatar in general. All three languages use the Cyrillic script.

Taking two bilingual corpora, Tatar-Russian and Kazakh-Russian. We train two separate bilingual Tatar-to-Russian and Kazakh-to-Russian translation models. Then, we employ the same corpora, and we create the multilingual model as shown in Figure 2, where Tatar and Kazakh languages are on the source side and Russian is on the target side. Both bilingual and multilingual models meet the same data, the same number of epochs, and the same number of parameters for each translation path.

To understand whether introducing a hierarchy into an encoder is beneficial, following Johnson et al. (2017), we train the model with a fully shared encoder for both source languages. We compare this model to the hierarchical model from the first set of experiments. Model architecture and size correspond to that of bilingual models. Data exposure is the same as in the hierarchical multilingual model.

Finally, to check if language relatedness indeed matters, we replace the Kazakh language with Ukrainian (the language from the same subgroup as Russian), also using the Cyrillic script. The Ukrainian language is as far from Tatar as Russian is. So, we want to test if using non-related language reduces the performance of the hierarchical multilingual model.

For Tatar-to-Russian translation, we utilized the first 300K sentence pairs from the private Tatar-Russian bilingual corpora provided by the Institute of Applied Semiotics, Academy of Sciences of the Republic of Tatarstan. For Kazakh-to-Russian translation, we acquired the bilingual corpus from WMT'19, cleaned it and used the first 700K sentence pairs. Finally, for Ukrainian-to-Russian, we took the data from JW300 dataset (Agić and Vulić, 2019) and used the 700K sentence pairs. After filtering sentences by maximum length (50 BPE (Sennrich et al., 2016) tokens) only about 250K Tatar-Russian pairs and about 450K Kazakh-Russian and Ukrainian-Russian pairs remained. Since Tatar-Russian pair is less in quantity, we reiterated them within every epoch such that on each step the system sees both languages in equal proportions. For comparability, bilingual Tatar-Russian model was exposed to the data in the same fashion, with reiterating.

Our multilingual NMT system implementation is based on Transformer architecture (Vaswani et al., 2017). We set the number of layers in individual encoders to 2, number of layers in shared encoder to 2, and the number of layers in decoder to 4. We also set the dimensional model to 256, the number of hidden layer to 1024, number of heads to 8, dropout to 0.1, and the number of epochs to 20. Bilingual models also use this architecture; the difference is that there is a single 4-layer encoder.

We trained the models with two batch sizes (128 and 256) because translation quality seems to highly depend on it. We compare bilingual models with a particular batch size to multilingual models with the same batch size. For multilingual models, half of the samples in a batch comes from the first source language and the other half—from the second. To train the hierarchical model, we simultaneously feed input data from both source languages to respective encoders and stack their outputs before passing to the shared encoder. On the decoder side, the final model outputs are compared to expected outputs for both languages (also stacked).

The results of the first set of experiments are summarized in Table 1.

BS	Dir	tt-ru	kk-ru	Multi-Hie
128	tt-ru	16.13	–	**17.39**
128	kk-ru	–	31.49	**31.58**
256	tt-ru	17.04	–	**18.23**
256	kk-ru	–	31.46	**32.37**

Table 1: BLEU scores of bilingual Tatar-Russian, Kazakh-Russian, and multilingual hierarchical models.

As seen, the hierarchical model surpassed bilingual models in both translation directions and for both batch sizes. However, the most improvements, up to 1.26 BLEU, were obtained for low-resource tt-ru translation. This suggests that both directions are able to benefit from information captured by a shared encoder, but it is more helpful to the weakest pair.

In the second set of experiments, the goal was to check whether dividing the encoder to individual and shared parts is beneficial for learning. From Table 2, we observe that in all but one case the hierarchical model performs better than the one with single encoder, and the difference is considerable especially for kk-ru direction (0.89 BLEU). This result is important because it empirically confirms our assumption about the usefulness of explicitly defining parameter sharing strategy for a multilingual model.

BS	Dir	Multi-Hie	Multi-Google
128	tt-ru	17.39	**17.40**
128	kk-ru	**31.58**	30.73
256	tt-ru	**18.23**	18.03
256	kk-ru	**32.37**	31.48

Table 2: Comparison of multilingual models: hierarchical (Multi-Hie) and with single shared encoder (Multi-Google), BLEU scores.

The third set of experiments, Table 3, shows another interesting results. Tatar language is not able to learn much from the Ukrainian language. For batch size 128, the BLEU score only decreases, and for batch size 256, it increases only by 0.07 BLEU. For the higher-resource uk-ru translation, although the scores improve, less than they did for kk-ru translation.

BS	Dir	tt-ru	uk-ru	Multi-Hie
128	tt-ru	**16.13**	–	15.99
128	uk-ru	–	17.69	**18.18**
256	tt-ru	17.04	–	**17.11**
256	uk-ru	–	18.38	**18.53**

Table 3: BLEU scores of bilingual Tatar-Russian, Ukranian-Russian, and multilingual hierarchical models.

Based on these positive results for the simple multi-source case, we conclude that the idea of introducing a hierarchy reflecting language similarity and controlling between-language parameter sharing, into multilingual architecture, has strong potential and should be explored further.

5   Conclusions and Future Work

In this paper, we proposed a hierarchical approach in multilingual NMT. The proposed approach was tested on the simple problem with two related source languages and only one target language. Our experimental results showed that the system is functioning, and in the case when source languages are related, both of them can exploit of dividing the encoder into language-specific and shared parts. We also found positive evidence supporting the assumption about the usefulness of explicitly defining parameter-sharing strategy of a multilingual model showing that parameter-sharing between related languages reaps more benefits.

As the future work, we would like to test the proposed approach on a larger set of languages on both the encoder and decoder sides of the translation model and explore different approaches to parameter-sharing.

Acknowledgements

The authors would like to express their sincere gratitude to Dr. Raul Aranovich (University of California, Davis) for all his support. The authors also would like to acknowledge the financial support received from the Linguistics Department at UC Davis.

References

Agić, Ž. and Vulić, I. (2019). JW300: A wide-coverage parallel corpus for low-resource languages. In *Proceedings of the 57th Annual Meeting of the Association for Computational Linguistics*, pages 3204–3210.

Ahmadnia, B. and Dorr, B. J. (2019). Augmenting neural machine translation through round-trip training approach. *Open Computer Science*, 9(1):268–278.

Dong, D., Wu, H., He, W., Yu, D., and Wang, H. (2015). Multi-task learning for multiple language translation. In *Proceedings of the 53rd Annual Meeting of the Association for Computational Linguistics and the 7th International Joint Conference on Natural Language Processing*, pages 1723–1732.

Johnson, M., Schuster, M., Le, Q. V., Krikun, M., Wu, Y., Chen, Z., Thorat, N., Viégas, F., Wattenberg, M., Corrado, G., Hughes, M., and Dean, J. (2017). Google's multilingual neural machine translation system: Enabling zero-shot translation. *Transactions of the Association for Computational Linguistics*, 5:339–351.

Sachan, D. S. and Neubig, G. (2018). Parameter sharing methods for multilingual self-attentional translation models. In *Proceedings of the Third Conference on Machine Translation*.

Sennrich, R., Haddow, B., and Birch, A. (2016). Neural machine translation of rare words with subword units. In *Proceedings of the 54th Annual Meeting of the Association for Computational Linguistics*, pages 1715–1725.

Tan, X., Chen, J., He, D., Xia, Y., Qin, T., and Liu, T.-Y. (2019). Multilingual neural machine translation with language clustering. In *Proceedings of the 2019 Conference on Empirical Methods in Natural Language Processing and the 9th International Joint Conference on Natural Language Processing*, pages 963–973.

Vaswani, A., Shazeer, N., Parmar, N., Uszkoreit, J., Jones, L., Gomez, A. N., Kaiser, Ł., and Polosukhin, I. (2017). Attention is all you need. In *Proceedings of the 31st Conference on Advances in Neural Information Processing Systems*, pages 5998–6008.

Investigation of Transformer-based Latent Attention Models for Neural Machine Translation

Parnia Bahar[1,2]   bahar@cs.rwth-aachen.de
Nikita Makarov[1]   nikita.makarov@rwth-aachen.de
Hermann Ney[1,2]   ney@cs.rwth-aachen.de

[1]Human Language Technology and Pattern Recognition Group, Computer Science Department, RWTH Aachen University, 52074 Aachen, Germany
[2]AppTek GmbH, 52062 Aachen, Germany

Abstract

Current neural translation networks are based on an effective attention mechanism that can be considered as an implicit probabilistic notion of alignment. Such architectures do not guarantee a high quality alignment, even though alignments can easily be used for explainable machine translation. This work describes a latent variable attention model using the transformer architecture, where we carry out an approximate marginalization over alignments. We show that the alignment quality in transformer models can be improved by introducing a latent variable for the alignments. To study the effect of the latent model, we quantitatively and qualitatively analyze the extracted alignments from the multi-head attention. We demonstrate that this method slightly improves translation quality on four WMT 2018 shared translation tasks, as well as generating more focused alignments for better interpretability.

1   Introduction

Current state-of-the-art neural machine translation (NMT) systems are based on attention models (Bahdanau et al., 2015; Luong et al., 2015; Gehring et al., 2017; Vaswani et al., 2017), where "soft attention" is used to focus on the most relevant parts of the source sequence while generating target words. This distribution can be considered as an implicit probabilistic notion of alignment as an intermediate step of the translation model. However, it does not work in the same way as its analogous alignment in conventional statistical machine translation (SMT) (Koehn and Knowles, 2017).

Contrary to SMT, where a "hard alignment" is a transparent process that defines the correspondence between source and target words, it is often challenging for the fuzzy attention mechanism to extract a comprehensible alignment. Although the context vector, a weighted sum of the input states, includes the alignment information implicitly, the alignment model does not directly influence the final translation probability of a sentence. Hence, it is often hard to determine the contribution of the attention on the output. In this work,

- we incorporate the attention model into the direct hidden Markov model (HMM) formulation in the transformer architecture such that the translation posterior distribution has a direct dependency on the source positions.

- as to the interest in alignment based approaches, we intend to investigate whether the latent-based models are able to tackle the explainability problem of alignments especially for the transformer model. Similar to how some approaches in explainable NMT use the attention (Stahlberg et al., 2018; Zenkel et al., 2019; Garg et al., 2019), we also incorporate it as a key interpretation component into our work.

From the statistical perspective, we revisit the formulation of the posterior probability of a given sentence by computing a separate translation score for every target-source word pair. Since marginalization is exponential in the order of the model, we only explore a zero-order assumption, i.e. there is no dependence between subsequent alignments. The marginalization over the latent variable becomes simple and efficient for zero-order models and can be easily applied in both training and decoding. Unlike higher order dependence (Alkhouli et al., 2016, 2018; Wang et al., 2018), no dynamic programming and no search for the alignment path is required, thus a simple beam search decoder is used. We also address the theoretical connection between our approach and IBM model 2 (Brown et al., 1993). Tackling the costly computation of the softmax for all source positions, we employ an approximation by taking the topK relevant positions. To the best of our knowledge, this work explores the first instance of a zero-order latent variable alignments using the transformer architecture in an end-to-end fashion for machine translation.

2 Related Works

Similar to IBM and HMM alignments (Brown et al., 1993; Vogel et al., 1996), there are stand-alone neural approaches based on introducing word alignments as hidden variables, such that either a full sum over the alignment path or a maximum approximation (Viterbi word alignment) is used. These models decompose the translation process into two parts, namely the alignment and lexicon models. Unlike (Wang et al., 2018, 2017) where they use two separate networks, one for the alignment and one for the lexicon model and they need to jointly train two networks batch-wise, our work is still a single network trained end-to-end similar to the transformer model. Due to first-order dependence, Wang et al. (2018) also apply the forward-backward algorithm to compute the posterior probabilities as true labels, which is not required in our model. Alkhouli et al. (2016) apply explicit hard alignments to generate a translation using a maximum approximation. Alkhouli and Ney (2017) compute attention weights using pre-defined alignments to bias soft attention toward hard alignments. Yang et al. (2013) use lexical and alignment models, where alignments have no dependence on the lexical context. Tamura et al. (2014) also introduce a lexicalized neural alignment model to generate word alignments for the phrase-based translation system. In this work, we use neither pre-computed alignments nor a phrase table.

As an extension to neural alignment models, Alkhouli et al. (2018) use the transformer architecture to train both alignment and lexicon models while augmenting the multi-head attention component with additional hard alignment information. In their work, they train two separate networks and combine them in decoding with a maximum approximation. In contrast, we train a single network and sum over source positions.

Inspired by the success of statistical alignment models, Tu et al. (2016); Cohn et al. (2016) propose fertility and coverage concepts by including dependence on previous attention weights. Zenkel et al. (2019) try to gain high quality alignments by recomputing the attention heads after each target word prediction. Peter et al. (2017); Li et al. (2018) employ the full target context to improve alignment accuracy. Given statistical alignments obtained from Giza++ toolkit (Och and Ney, 2003), there are some methods in which the soft attention weights are supervised to behave similarly to the conventional hard alignments. Chen et al. (2016); Mi et al. (2016); Liu et al. (2016); Garg et al. (2019) add an additional training objective term that is dependent on the pre-computed alignments like Giza++ to guide neural models in training.

Instead of an objective function, Alkhouli and Ney (2017) modify the attention energy computation directly to have dependence on the Giza++ alignment and perform beam search over both the lexical and alignment hypotheses. Unlike the aforementioned methods, our approach does not require any pre-computed alignments, and we do not need to search for the alignment path. It means our zero-order model can be easily applied in both training and decoding.

There are also a number of recent works in which attention is used as a latent alignment by decomposing the joint distribution between an alignment model and a lexicon model (Wu et al., 2018; Shankar et al., 2018; Bahar et al., 2020). They mainly use a recurrent neural network (RNN) parameterization. The main difference of our work, is that we explore the use of transformer models. They either use character-level output or conduct the experiments on a small training set where the vocabularies appear to be small, whilst we evaluate our experiments using relatively large vocabularies. Shankar and Sarawagi (2019) extend the prior into an explicit posterior attention distribution. Deng et al. (2018) propose a non-differentiable approach, "hard attention", where an explicit dependence of a single input to output is taken by the REINFORCE algorithm (Xu et al., 2015).

In this work, we explore the soft attention as a latent variable alignment to directly calculate the posterior probability of a sentence. Our idea is a straight-forward application of an under-used idea from IBM word-based translation modeling, and makes clever use of existing transformer components to avoid adding parameters to the model. We avoid the temptation to create a separate distortion model, and just re-use attention heads. The solution is clean and probabilistically sound.

3 Background

In machine translation, given a source sequence $f_1^J = f_1, \ldots, f_j, \ldots, f_J$ of length J, with f_j being a source word, the posterior probability of a target sequence $e_1^I = e_1, \ldots, e_i, \ldots, e_I$ of length I, is defined as $p(e_1^I | f_1^J)$. This conditional distribution, the so-called translation model, covers the alignment information between source and target words either implicitly or explicitly.

In most NMT methods, including both the recurrent-based attention (Bahdanau et al., 2015) and the transformer (Vaswani et al., 2017), the encoder scans the entire source sequence and generates a sequence of vector representation. Then, the decoder generates an output sequence conditioned on the precomputed encoder states. The posterior probability distribution of the target sequence is conditioned on the source f_1^J and the target history e_1^{i-1}, as:

$$p(e_1^I | f_1^J) = \prod_{i=1}^{I} p(e_i | e_1^{i-1}, f_1^J) = \prod_{i=1}^{I} p\Big(e_i | e_1^{i-1}, c_i\big(e_1^{i-1}, h_1^J(f_1^J)\big)\Big) \tag{1}$$

Usually, the dependence on f_1^J is modelled using a soft attention mechanism, where a weighted sum c_i of the input representations h_1^J is used inside a neural network layer. Thus, it is important to observe that there is no direct dependence on source position in Equation 1. In this equation, h_1^J is the encoder's output, and c_i is the output of an attention approach at target position i, summarizing the alignment information implicitly.

4 Latent Attention Model

Similar to (Wang et al., 2018; Wu et al., 2018; Shankar et al., 2018; Bahar et al., 2020), we introduce a word alignment as a sequence of latent variables that establishes a mapping from target position i to source position j, i.e. $i \rightarrow b_i = j$ and decompose the posterior probability distribution of target sequence into two parts: alignment and lexicon models. To do so, we marginalize out all possible alignments in Equation 2. $\sum_{b_1^I}$ considers all possible alignment paths, such that b_i aligns the target position i to the source position j. Assuming the zero-order Markov assumption to simplify the dependencies of the alignment sequences, we decompose the posterior probability into alignment and lexicon models, obtaining Equation 4. Here, we note that, assuming a first-order assumption leads to the first-order hidden Markov model. Performing the sum over all alignments would lead to a combinatorial problem. Due to the zero-order dependence, one can re-arrange the sum and the product in Equation 5 by the distributive property that leads to polynomial complexity. The mathematical proof of swapping between the sum and product can be found in (Brown et al., 1993).

Since the model combines a mixture of softmaxes, the exact marginalization over all source positions is infeasible for a large vocabulary. Hence, we choose the topK source positions with the highest alignment probabilities and compute the corresponding lexicon scores. By doing so, the computational complexity reduces to $\mathcal{O}(I \times K)$ (see Equation 6). We differentiate the topK approximation by the straight-through estimator (Bengio et al., 2013). We found empirically that $K = 6$ is enough and we only get marginal benefits for $K > 6$ (see Section 7.4 for more details).

$$p(e_1^I|f_1^J) = \sum_{b_1^I} p(e_1^I, b_1^I|f_1^J) = \sum_{b_1^I} \prod_{i=1}^{I} p(e_i, b_i|e_1^{i-1}, b_1^{i-1}, f_1^J) \tag{2}$$

$$= \sum_{b_1^I} \prod_{i=1}^{I} \underbrace{p(b_i|e_1^{i-1}, b_1^{i-1}, f_1^J)}_{\text{alignment modeling}} \cdot \underbrace{p(e_i|e_1^{i-1}, b_1^i, f_1^J)}_{\text{lexicon modeling}}$$

$$\text{(exponential complexity, } J^I) \tag{3}$$

$$= \sum_{b_i} \prod_{i=1}^{I} \underbrace{p(b_i|e_1^{i-1}, f_1^J)}_{\text{alignment model}} \cdot \underbrace{p(e_i|e_1^{i-1}, b_i, f_1^J)}_{\text{lexicon model}} \tag{4}$$

$$= \prod_{i=1}^{I} \sum_{j=1}^{J} p(b_i = j|e_1^{i-1}, f_1^J) \cdot p(e_i|e_1^{i-1}, j, f_1^J)$$

$$\text{(polynomial complexity, } I \times J) \tag{5}$$

$$\approx \prod_{i=1}^{I} \sum_{j \in topK} p(b_i = j|e_1^{i-1}, f_1^J) \cdot p(e_i|e_1^{i-1}, j, f_1^J)$$

$$\text{(polynomial complexity, } I \times K) \tag{6}$$

Relation to IBM Model 2

We note the similarity between Equation 5 and IBM model 2 (in Equation 7) as both are zero-order models with respect to the alignments, however, our model has a dependence on target history.

$$p(e_1^I|f_1^J) = \prod_{i=1}^{I} \sum_{j=1}^{J} \underbrace{p(j|i, J, I)}_{\text{alignment}} \cdot \underbrace{p(e_i|f_j)}_{\text{lexicon}} \tag{7}$$

5 Neural Parameterization

In order to parameterize the individual components of the model, we use a network similar to the multihead self-attentive transformer. In the transformer architecture both the encoder and decoder are composed of stacked layers. In the encoder, multihead self-attentive components followed by a feed forward layer are used to encode the entire source sequence, obtaining a sequence of encoder states $h_1^{(L_{enc})}, \ldots, h_j^{(L_{enc})}, \ldots, h_J^{(L_{enc})}$. Here, L_{enc} is the number of encoder layers.

The decoder contains an additional multihead attention layer, incorporating the encoder states and the decoder state $s_{i-1}^{(l_{dec}-1)}$ in each decoder layer l_{dec}. Several attention heads are

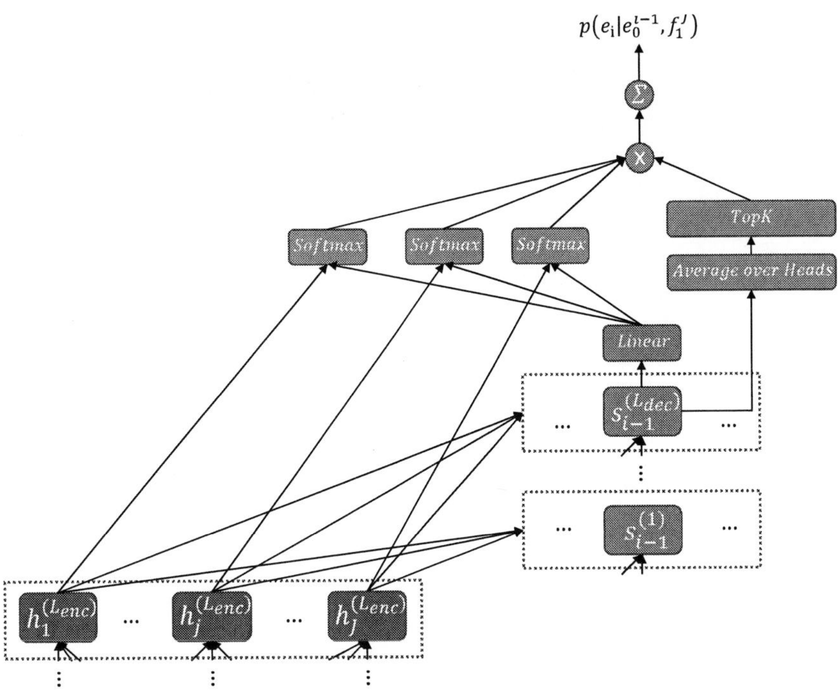

Figure 1: Overview of the transformer-based zero-order attention model. In the output layer, at each target step i, we add the decoder state $s_{i-1}^{(L_{dec})}$ with all the encoder state h_1^J (or with topK approximation only the K best ones).

used to attend to the source positions. At every decoder layer, each attention head n, computes a normalized distribution over the source positions, $\alpha_n^{(l_{dec})}(j|i)$. These weights are used to compute the context vectors. The concatenation of these context vectors are fed through a feed-forward layer to form the decoder representation $s_{i-1}^{(l_{dec})}$. The representation from the last decoder layer is then passed through a softmax layer, which provides the final distribution over the vocabulary $p(e_i|f_1^J, e_1^{i-1})$. The latent attention model has two main components. Figure 1 shows an abstract of the model architecture.

Lexicon Model: The lexicon model is fairly straightforward to implement in the transformer. As shown in Figure 1, we combine the last decoder state of the top layer with the encoder states, as well as the last target word at each time step, Therefore, we have

$$p(e_i|e_1^{i-1}, j, f_1^J) = g\left(e_{i-1}, s_{i-1}^{(L_{dec})}, h_j^{(L_{enc})}\right) \tag{8}$$

where g is a linear projection followed by the softmax. As seen in this equation, at each target step i, we add the decoder state s_{i-1} with all the encoder state h_1^J (or with topK approximation only the K best ones).

Alignment Model: On the other hand, the alignment model is not as trivial to implement. The first option is to use the existing attention weights of the transformer for the alignment, but the transformer has not only multiple attention layers, but also multiple heads per layer. The transformer's topology with multiple heads in a single layer makes the attention heads symmetrical, but the different layers might capture different alignment information (Garg et al.,

	German	English	Chinese	English
Sentences	5.9M		14.1M	
Running words	160M	157M	314M	427M
vocabularies	45k	33k	38k	32k

Table 1: Corpus statistics.

2019). To form the alignment model, we average over the attention weights across all heads within each layer of the decoder at each time step, i.e.:

$$p^{(l_{dec})}(j|e_1^{i-1}, f_1^J) = \frac{1}{N} \sum_{n=1}^{N} \alpha_n^{(l_{dec})}(j|i) \tag{9}$$

where N is the number of attention heads and l_{dec} is the decoder's lth layer. We have observed that this way the model has the ability to train the heads of selected layer (see Section 7.1). Other authors have found that the later attention layers of the transformer perform longer jumps and generally attend to more different source positions (Irie et al., 2019). Due to these properties and based on the results in Table 7.1, we focus our experiments on using the last layer's attention of the decoder, averaged over the heads, i.e.

$$p(j|e_1^{i-1}, f_1^J) = \frac{1}{N} \sum_{n=1}^{N} \alpha_n^{(L_{dec})}(j|i). \tag{10}$$

Once we compute the lexicon and alignment probabilities, we sum over j positions as stated in Equation 6 with topK approximation. The model has almost the same number of parameters as our transformer baseline. A visualization of model architecture can be seen in Figure 1.

6 Experiments

We carry out the experiments on four WMT 2018 translation tasks[1]: German↔English and Chinese↔English. The corpora statistics are shown in Table 1. We do not employ any kind of synthetic or back-translated data in this work.

For German↔English, after tokenization and true-casing using the Moses toolkit (Koehn et al., 2007), we apply byte pair encoding (BPE) (Sennrich et al., 2016) with 50k merge operations. We use the original parallel data consisting of 5.9M sentence pairs (see Table 1).

For Chinese↔English, we apply sentence pieces model (SPM) (Kudo, 2018) with an n-best size of 30 and 32k merge operations. The original bilingual data consists of almost 26M samples. We filter out the noisy data by removing illegal characters and duplication, hence we end up with 14M pairs.

For De↔En and Zh↔En, we use the newstest2015 and the newsdev2017 as the development set respectively and the newstest2017 and newstest2018 as our test sets. The models are evaluated using case-sensitive BLEU (Papineni et al., 2002) computed by the official scripts of WMT campaign, i.e. mteval-v13a[2] and case-sensitive normalized TER (Snover et al., 2006) computed by tercom[3].

For our experiments, we train both the transformer and the RNN attention models. We follow a base transformer similar to (Vaswani et al., 2017) where we use 6 layers in both the

---

[1] http://statmt.org/wmt18/

[2] ftp://jaguar.ncsl.nist.gov/mt/resources/mteval-v13a.pl

[3] http://www.cs.umd.edu/ snover/tercom/

encoder and the decoder with an internal dimension size of 512. We set the number of heads in the multi-head attention to 8. Layer normalization, dropout, and residual connections are applied. We use the same structure as our transformer baseline for the latent attention model with the almost the same number of parameters.

Given that the proposed latent method can be also applicable to the RNN attention architecture, we intend to apply this technique to the RNN attention to see if meaningful differences will be observed. However, we focus on our analysis of the difference between the transformer and the latent attention model. We train the RNN attention models similar to (Bahdanau et al., 2015), in which all words are projected into a 512-dimensional embedding space. We use a 6-layer stacked bidirectional LSTM (BLSTM) (Hochreiter and Schmidhuber, 1997) with 1024 hidden cells to compute a sequence of encoder states h_1^T. The decoder is composed of one layer LSTM of size 1024 with an additive single-head attention layer with attention feedback (Bahar et al., 2017). In the RNN latent attention model, to form the alignment model, we use the attention weights itself, $\alpha(i|j)$, as our distribution, i.e.

$$p(j|e_1^{i-1}, f_1^J) = \alpha(i|j) = \nu^\top \tanh(h_j, s_{i-1}) \tag{11}$$

For the lexicon scores, similar to the transformer modeling, we combine the decoder state with the encoder states, as well as the last output token at each time step and write

$$p(e_i|e_1^{i-1}, j, f_1^J) = g(e_{i-1}, s_{i-1}, h_j) \tag{12}$$

We note the difference between equations 12 and 13 and direct dependency on source positions instead of a summary of all inputs as a single vector c_i. To compute the lexicon probabilities, we employ a softmax over the target vocabulary, J times (or K times using the approximation), while in the attention model, we only do it once as we summarize the encoder representations using the context vector c_i without any dependence on j positions.

$$p(e_i|e_1^{i-1}, f_1^J) = g(e_{i-1}, s_{i-1}, c_i) \tag{13}$$

For RNN-based models, we use a layerwise pre-training strategy (Zeyer et al., 2018) for the first epochs. We start using only the first layer in the encoder of the model and add new layers during the training progress. We observe that the layer-wise pretraining leads to a strong RNN attention baseline. The models are trained end-to-end using the Adam optimizer with a learning rate of 0.0003, and a dropout of 10% for the transformer-based systems, and a learning rate of 0.001 and a dropout of 30% for the RNN-based attention models. We employ a learning rate scheduling scheme, where we lower the learning rate with a decay factor of 0.9 if the perplexity on the development set does not improve for several consecutive checkpoints. We remove sentences longer than 100 tokens before batching them together. All batch sizes are specified to be as big as possible to fit in memory. A beam size of 12 is used in inference. We use our in-house implementation of sequence-to-sequence modeling in RETURNN (Zeyer et al., 2018). The code[4] and the configurations of the setups are available online[5].

7 Results

7.1 Averaging Attention Heads

Our latent model is flexible to learn one of the heads, all heads within a single layer or all heads across all layers. As described in Section 5, the transformer architecture leads to have

---

[4]https://github.com/rwth-i6/returnn
[5]https://github.com/rwth-i6/returnn-experiments/

Layer	newsdev2017		newstest2017	
	BLEU	TER	BLEU	TER
1	21.9	62.7	23.4	61.2
2	22.5	61.9	23.8	60.6
3	22.6	61.9	23.8	60.6
4	21.9	62.6	23.8	60.8
5	22.5	62.0	24.2	60.3
6	22.6	61.9	24.2	60.5

Table 2: Results measured in BLEU [%] and TER [%] on the Zh→En task.

symmetrical attention heads within a layer, while different layers might learn different alignment patterns.

To examine which layer can be the most effective one for our latent attention model, we have chosen our alignment model obtained by layer-wise averaging of attention probabilities of various layers. Table 2 shows the BLEU and TER scores on the Zh→En task. As listed, for all selected layers, our model has the ability to learn a mixture of alignment and lexicon scores. For the rest of our experiments, we average over attention heads of the last layer (6th) for the latent attention model.

7.2 Translation Performance

In the second set of experiments, we compare the latent attention model with two baselines, both the transformer baseline and the RNN attention baseline. We additionally apply the RNN latent attention model on De→En and Zh→En tasks to see if the same behaviour will be observed. The results can be seen in Table 3. As shown, the latent attention model provides a small boost of 0.5% BLEU and 0.2% TER on Zh→En, 0.7% BLEU and 0.6% TER on En→Zh, 0.2% BLEU and 0.2% TER on De→En and 0.1% BLEU and 0.4% TER on En→De, on average. As expected, the transformer models give a better performance compared to the RNN attention models. Comparing the RNN latent attention model with its corresponding baseline shows very similar, yet more mixed results.

In theory, the latent model has more statistical capacity than the attention-based NMT. The attention-based NMT models are a deterministic interpolation of deterministic features (source encodings), whereas the latent attention model is a mixture model. With attention, an NMT system outputs exactly one distribution over target vocabulary per time step, whilst our model outputs J (or K when using the optimization) distributions, which are mixed probabilistically, yielding a multimodal marginal distribution. Our interpretation is that equipping a deterministic soft function with a probabilistic model might lead to better results. In this case, alignments have direct effects on the final translation scores and the lexicalized alignment model assigns more appropriate scores for the translation of target-source word pair.

In the third set of our evaluation, we compare our model with similar previous approaches. The only instance of latent model using the transformer architecture is (Alkhouli et al., 2018) where a maximum approximation is used instead of summation. Moreover, in their work, they train two independent networks whilst in our approach a single network is trained. Their model depends on pre-define alignments using GIZA++ (Och and Ney, 2003) and they hypothesis over alignments in search, whereas we do not need these steps. For De→En, our model outperforms theirs on `newstest2017` by 1.6% BLEU. We also compare with (Wang et al., 2018) where they have a full summation, however, a first-order assumption is employed. Our model consistently outperforms theirs on three tasks. We note that firstly their model is based on the RNN attention and secondly the number of parameters of their network is half of those of ours.

Task	Model	newstest2017		newstest2018	
		BLEU	TER	BLEU	TER
Chinese→English	(Wang et al., 2018)	20.2	63.7	-	-
	transformer	24.1	60.7	23.7	-
	transformer latent attention	**24.2**	**60.5**	**24.5**	-
	RNN attention	22.9	62.0	22.7	-
	RNN latent attention	22.6	61.2	23.0	-
English→Chinese	transformer	32.0	57.3	32.8	-
	transformer latent attention	**32.9**	**56.7**	**33.3**	-
	RNN attention	31.8	57.2	32.5	-
German→English	(Alkhouli et al., 2018)	32.1	-	-	-
	(Wang et al., 2018)	29.6	-	-	-
	transformer	33.5	55.1	40.4	46.8
	transformer latent attention	**33.7**	**54.9**	**40.5**	**46.7**
	RNN attention	32.6	54.9	39.6	46.8
	RNN latent attention	32.8	55.3	39.2	47.6
English→German	(Wang et al., 2018)	24.6	-	-	-
	transformer	**26.5**	64.8	39.0	50.7
	transformer latent attention	**26.5**	64.7	**39.2**	**50.1**
	RNN attention	26.3	**64.4**	38.9	50.7

Table 3: Results measured in BLEU [%] and TER [%] on the test sets. The TER computation on newstest2018 fails for Chinese sets.

7.3 Attention Analysis

As stated in the introduction, we are interested in seeing how the attention weights in the transformer could be interpreted. As the model utilizes multi-head attention, we use Equation 10 to average over the attention heads to get a single score at each time step. The effect that we have observed, which is also reported by others (Alkhouli et al., 2018; Zenkel et al., 2019; Garg et al., 2019), is that the transformer heavily attends to the frequent words like end of sentence (EOS) token, often having the highest average attention value of the sequence, as seen in the examples in Figure 2(a) and 2(e). This effect leads to worse interpretation, as well as possibly worse performance since a large portion of the processing capabilities are spent on a token with limited information value. However, the intuition behind the original multi-head attention architecture is that it learns different alignment information, if one head learns bad alignment, other heads may learn good ones.

In our figures and experiments, we add in RNN attention models as well as the latent model with RNN attention architecture to verify that the attention issues are specific to the transformer and are not inherent to the soft attention mechanism. Similar to previous observations, the RNN attention performs relatively consistently across the datasets, with generally sharper attention than the transformer baseline. As our work was motivated by the drawbacks of the transformer's attention, we focus on our analysis of the difference between the transformer and the latent attention model.

Alignment Error Rate A large factor of the motivation for the attention latent model is that the attention distributions can be interpreted as alignments. We assume that the latent attention model might produce higher quality alignments. To verify this assumption, we use the RWTH German-English Golden Alignments which provides 504 manually word-aligned sentence pairs extracted from the Europarl corpus (Vilar et al., 2006). We compare the alignment error rate

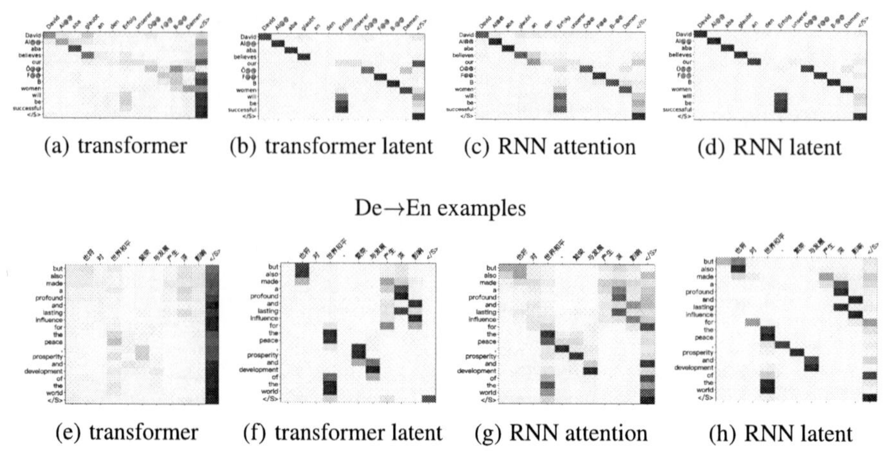

(a) transformer   (b) transformer latent   (c) RNN attention   (d) RNN latent

De→En examples

(e) transformer   (f) transformer latent   (g) RNN attention   (h) RNN latent

Zh→En examples

Figure 2: Comparison of attention distributions on different tasks. On the x-axis is the source and on the y-axis is the target.

Model	Europarl AER[%]	
	last heads	all heads
transformer	71.4	57.1
transformer latent attention	57.8	54.8
RNN attention	51.5	
RNN latent attention	49.0	

Table 4: AER [%] of different models, while the EOS and the full stop have been ignored.

(AER) of the models as a key quantitative metrics for the analysis of alignments in Table 4. To calculate the alignments for the transformer-based models, we use the maximum of the attention weights as the alignment at each time step. We interpret the alignments from the transformer baseline and the latent attention model by a) averaging over the attention heads in the last layer, and b) averaging over the attention heads of the all layers and then taking the maximum value to determine which source token corresponds to each target token.

It is important to highlight that the references are on a word level whereas the alignments from these models are sub-word based. To make the AER more comparable with traditional systems, we merge the BPEs together, where we use the average of all tokens. We also note that, the transformer baseline attends many of its heads to the most frequent tokens (e.g. EOS token, and the full stop token). To mitigate this effect on the AER, we ignore these two positions for our computations. The results show that the transformer performs significantly worse than the attention latent model on the last layer, being 71.4% vs 57.8%. On the other hand, averaging over all layers considerably improves the AER for the transformer to 57.1%, whilst only marginally improving for the latent attention model to 54.8%. This improvement implies that the transformer performs the most interpretable attention not at the last layer, but at intermediate layers. The finding is supported by the observation of other groups as well (Voita et al., 2019). The RNN Attention model performs better than both other approaches at

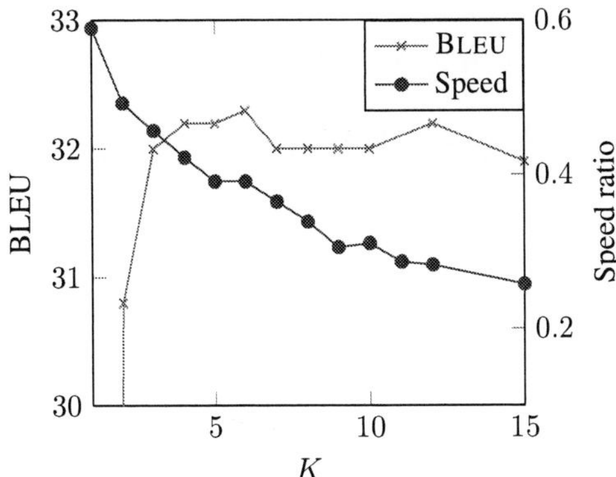

Figure 3: Speed and translation quality in BLEU vs. different values of K on the development set (`newstest2015`) of the De→En task.

51.5%, signifying that the transformer's attention is still far away from being easily interpreted as alignments. The RNN latent model is also superior its baseline by 1.5% in AER. The alignment quality of the proposed model is poorer compared to conventional alignment models such as IBM Models or other works in the literature (Zenkel et al., 2019; Garg et al., 2019). The main reason is that in our model, we do not have full dependence on the whole target sequence in contrast to the conventional alignment models neither on the current target word e_i. Since, we do left-to-right decoding, we keep the dependence only on the predecessor words for an efficient and simple search.

Qualitative Attention Analysis   A large factor of the motivation for the attention latent model is that the attention distributions can be interpreted as alignments. Based on the quantitative results, we extract some examples from `newstest2018` sets of different tasks of where the latent attention models performs better than their corresponding baseline. In Figures 2(a)-2(h), we see the examples side by side where the transformer attends to the EOS token, whereas the latent attention model has sharper attention distributions. An interesting component of these examples is that the latent attention model correctly attends to non-monotonic sub-sequences. The same behaviour can be seen for the RNN-based models, where the latent model results in a sharper distribution (cf. Figures 2(c) and 2(d) for De→En and Figures 2(g) and 2(h) for Zh→En).

Although in our model, the alignment's quality gets better both qualitatively and quantitatively, the final translation seems to be comparative with our baselines. The improvement in alignment quality does not carry over to better translations, as it is not surprising given prior work in MT (Koehn and Knowles, 2017). Thus, one important question still remains and that whether a high quality alignment is relevant and informative for the final translation quality?

7.4   Effect of K

We also plot the effect of K applied in the topK approximation versus the corresponding BLEU score, as well as the speed ratio in Figure 3 on De→En development set. As it is shown, the BLEU score goes up from 30.8 to 32.3 by changing K from 2 to 6 respectively, and then it statures without any further significant improvements. This implies that small values of K are good enough for training, and we use values around $K = 6$ for our other training runs. We also show the speed effect with respect to K. Here, the speed ratio is defined as a proportion between

Model	$K=1$	$K=2$	$K=3$	$K=6$	$K=10$	all
latent attention	30.7	31.9	32.2	32.2	32.2	32.2

Table 5: Results measured in BLEU [%] on the development set (`newstest2015`) with respect to different values of K during inference. The latent attention model has been trained using $K = 6$.

the speed of the transformer baseline and of the latent model with different K values on average of sub-epochs. Intuitively, as K increases, the training time goes up. But it is not linear with respect to K.

Similar to (Shankar et al., 2018), we also investigate whether the gain is due to the softmax bottleneck as well as to check if the larger values of K improves the performance during inference. To do so, we train the model with $K = 6$ and deploy it using different K values in inference. The results are listed in Table 5. The output has only a single softmax vector, when $K = 1$. Therefore, we assume that the latent attention model encounters the same bottleneck as the transformer. As expected, the performance drops compared to the case of $K = 6$, which means that the model gives some gains behind the ensembling. Moreover, good performance requires $K = 6$ and we do not get benefit for $K > 6$. The exact marginalization does not help as well. Applying the same K value in both training and inference meets the model's requirements.

7.5 Complexity

In order to compute the lexicon scores, we employ a softmax over the target vocabulary V, K times. The time complexity of the latent model is $\mathcal{O}(I \times K \times V)$ compared to $\mathcal{O}(I \times V)$ for the transformer. Thus, the latent attention model can become very slow for a large vocabulary. Using GPU and optimized matrix operations, the computational cost is significantly compensated by parallelization as long as everything fits in memory. The model is about 2.7 times slower than the transformer on a single GPU. Moreover, the space complexity of the model on the output layer is $\mathcal{O}(K \times V)$, rather than $\mathcal{O}(V)$ for the baseline, which requires to decrease the batch size. This concludes the necessity of multiple GPU training.

8 Conclusion and Future Work

We have investigated the use of a zero-order latent variable attention model based on both the transformer and the RNN attention architecture. The restructured model makes use of a lexicalized alignment with the aim to have more focused attention weights, leading to better explainability. Our results on four WMT 2018 translation tasks show that the model slightly outperforms over the transformer model on average over all tasks. These are the first experiments using the latent variable model on both the transformer, as well as larger vocabulary tasks in comparison to previously conducted experiments. We also believe that due to the highly similar composition of our models to previously done latent attention experiments, we can conclude that their approaches would face the same results as shown here, if applied to the transformer.

As future work, we plan to investigate the model with more elaborate dependencies, as well as further exploration on first-order dependence with respect to the alignments. Additionally, we intend to approximate the softmax for large vocabularies to further speed up the latent method. We also would like to explore how the transformer performs so well, even though it attends so much to the EOS token. Finally, we want to survey further statistical modelling approaches that improve the explainability of the transformer model.

References

Alkhouli, T., Bretschner, G., and Ney, H. (2018). On the alignment problem in multi-head attention-based neural machine translation. In *The Third Conference on Machine Translation, WMT, Belgium, Brussels, October 31 - November 1*, pages 177–185.

Alkhouli, T., Bretschner, G., Peter, J., Hethnawi, M., Guta, A., and Ney, H. (2016). Alignment-based neural machine translation. In *The First Conference on Machine Translation, WMT, Berlin, Germany, August 11-12*, pages 54–65.

Alkhouli, T. and Ney, H. (2017). Biasing attention-based recurrent neural networks using external alignment information. In *The Second Conference on Machine Translation, WMT, Copenhagen, Denmark, September 7-8*, pages 108–117.

Bahar, P., Makarov, N., Zeyer, A., Schlüter, R., and Ney, H. (2020). Exploring a zero-order direct hmm based on latent attention for automatic speech recognition. In *IEEE International Conference on Acoustics, Speech, and Signal Processing*, pages 7854–7858, Barcelona, Spain.

Bahar, P., Rosendahl, J., Rossenbach, N., and Ney, H. (2017). The rwth aachen machine translation systems for iwslt 2017. In *International Workshop on Spoken Language Translation*, pages 29–34, Tokyo, Japan.

Bahdanau, D., Cho, K., and Bengio, Y. (2015). Neural machine translation by jointly learning to align and translate. *International Conference on Learning Representations (ICLR)*.

Bengio, Y., Léonard, N., and Courville, A. C. (2013). Estimating or propagating gradients through stochastic neurons for conditional computation. *CoRR*, abs/1308.3432.

Brown, P. F., Pietra, S. D., Pietra, V. J. D., and Mercer, R. L. (1993). The mathematics of statistical machine translation: Parameter estimation. *Computational Linguistics*, 19(2):263–311.

Chen, W., Matusov, E., Khadivi, S., and Peter, J. (2016). Guided alignment training for topic-aware neural machine translation. *CoRR*, abs/1607.01628.

Cohn, T., Hoang, C. D. V., Vymolova, E., Yao, K., Dyer, C., and Haffari, G. (2016). Incorporating structural alignment biases into an attentional neural translation model. In *The 2016 Conference of the North American Chapter of the Association for Computational Linguistics: Human Language Technologies NAACL HLT, San Diego, USA, June 12-17*, pages 876–885.

Deng, Y., Kim, Y., Chiu, J., Guo, D., and Rush, A. M. (2018). Latent alignment and variational attention. In *Advances in Neural Information Processing Systems 31: Neural Information Processing Systems, NeurIPS, 3-8 December, Montréal, Canada.*, pages 9735–9747.

Garg, S., Peitz, S., Nallasamy, U., and Paulik, M. (2019). Jointly learning to align and translate with transformer models. In *The 2019 Conference on Empirical Methods in Natural Language Processing EMNLP, Hong Kong*.

Gehring, J., Auli, M., Grangier, D., Yarats, D., and Dauphin, Y. N. (2017). Convolutional sequence to sequence learning. In *Proceedings of the 34th International Conference on Machine Learning, ICML, Sydney, NSW, Australia, 6-11 August 2017*, pages 1243–1252.

Hochreiter, S. and Schmidhuber, J. (1997). Long short-term memory. *Neural Computation*, 9(8):1735–1780.

Irie, K., Zeyer, A., Schlüter, R., and Ney, H. (2019). Language modeling with deep transformers. In Kubin, G. and Kacic, Z., editors, *The 20th Annual Conference of the International Speech Communication Association (Interspeech), Graz, Austria, 15-19 September*, pages 3905–3909.

Koehn, P., Hoang, H., Birch, A., Callison-Burch, C., Federico, M., Bertoldi, N., Cowan, B., Shen, W., Moran, C., Zens, R., et al. (2007). Moses: Open source toolkit for statistical machine translation. In *The 45th annual meeting of the ACL on interactive poster and demonstration sessions*, pages 177–180.

Koehn, P. and Knowles, R. (2017). Six challenges for neural machine translation. In *The First Workshop on Neural Machine Translation, NMT@ACL, Vancouver, Canada, August 4*, pages 28–39.

Kudo, T. (2018). Subword regularization: Improving neural network translation models with multiple subword candidates. In *The 56th Annual Meeting of the Association for Computational Linguistics*, pages 66–75, Melbourne, Australia.

Li, X., Liu, L., Tu, Z., Shi, S., and Meng, M. (2018). Target foresight based attention for neural machine translation. In *2018 Conference of the North American Chapter of the Association for Computational Linguistics, NAACL-HLT, New Orleans, USA, June 1-6*, pages 1380–1390.

Liu, L., Utiyama, M., Finch, A. M., and Sumita, E. (2016). Neural machine translation with supervised attention. In *The 26th International Conference on Computational Linguistics Proceedings of the Conference COLING, Osaka, Japan, December 11-16*, pages 3093–3102.

Luong, T., Pham, H., and Manning, C. D. (2015). Effective approaches to attention-based neural machine translation. In *Proceedings of the 2015 Conference on Empirical Methods in Natural Language Processing, EMNLP, Lisbon, Portugal, September 17-21, 2015*, pages 1412–1421.

Mi, H., Wang, Z., and Ittycheriah, A. (2016). Supervised attentions for neural machine translation. In *2016 Conference on Empirical Methods in Natural Language Processing*, pages 2283–2288, Austin, Texas.

Och, F. J. and Ney, H. (2003). A systematic comparison of various statistical alignment models. *Computational Linguistics*, 29(1):19–51.

Papineni, K., Roukos, S., Ward, T., and Zhu, W.-J. (2002). Bleu: a Method for Automatic Evaluation of Machine Translation. In *The 41st Annual Meeting of the Association for Computational Linguistics*, pages 311–318, Philadelphia, Pennsylvania, USA.

Peter, J., Nix, A., and Ney, H. (2017). Generating alignments using target foresight in attention-based neural machine translation. *Prague Bull. Math. Linguistics*, 108:27–36.

Sennrich, R., Haddow, B., and Birch, A. (2016). Neural machine translation of rare words with subword units. In *The 54th Annual Meeting of the Association for Computational Linguistics ACL, Berlin, Germany, August 7-12*.

Shankar, S., Garg, S., and Sarawagi, S. (2018). Surprisingly easy hard-attention for sequence to sequence learning. In *The 2018 Conference on Empirical Methods in Natural Language Processing (EMNLP), Brussels, Belgium, October 31 - November 4*, pages 640–645.

Shankar, S. and Sarawagi, S. (2019). Posterior attention models for sequence to sequence learning.

Snover, M., Dorr, B., Schwartz, R., Micciulla, L., and Makhoul, J. (2006). A Study of Translation Edit Rate with Targeted Human Annotation. In *The 7th Conference of the Association for Machine Translation in the Americas*, pages 223–231, Cambridge, Massachusetts, USA.

Stahlberg, F., Saunders, D., and Byrne, B. (2018). An operation sequence model for explainable neural machine translation. In *The Workshop: Analyzing and Interpreting Neural Networks for NLP, Brussels, Belgium, November 1*, pages 175–186.

Tamura, A., Watanabe, T., and Sumita, E. (2014). Recurrent neural networks for word alignment model. In *The 52nd Annual Meeting of the Association for Computational Linguistics, ACL, Baltimore, USA, June 22-27*, pages 1470–1480.

Tu, Z., Lu, Z., Liu, Y., Liu, X., and Li, H. (2016). Modeling coverage for neural machine translation. In *54th Annual Meeting of the Association for Computational Linguistics ACL, Aug. 7-12, Berlin, Germany*.

Vaswani, A., Shazeer, N., Parmar, N., Uszkoreit, J., Jones, L., Gomez, A. N., Kaiser, L., and Polosukhin, I. (2017). Attention is all you need. In *Advances in Neural Information Processing Systems 30: Neural Information Processing Systems, 4-9 December 2017, Long Beach, USA*, pages 6000–6010.

Vilar, D., Popovic, M., and Ney, H. (2006). Aer: Do we need to "improve" our alignments? In *International Workshop on Spoken Language Translation*, pages 205–212, Kyoto, Japan.

Vogel, S., Ney, H., and Tillmann, C. (1996). Hmm-based word alignment in statistical translation. In *16th International Conference on Computational Linguistics, Proceedings of the Conference, COLING, Copenhagen, Denmark, August 5-9*, pages 836–841.

Voita, E., Talbot, D., Moiseev, F., Sennrich, R., and Titov, I. (2019). Analyzing multi-head self-attention: Specialized heads do the heavy lifting, the rest can be pruned. In *The 57th Annual Meeting of the Association for Computational Linguistics*, pages 5797–5808, Florence, Italy.

Wang, W., Alkhouli, T., Zhu, D., and Ney, H. (2017). Hybrid neural network alignment and lexicon model in direct hmm for statistical machine translation. In *Annual Meeting of the Assoc. for Computational Linguistics*, pages 125–131, Vancouver, Canada.

Wang, W., Zhu, D., Alkhouli, T., Gan, Z., and Ney, H. (2018). Neural hidden markov model for machine translation. In *The 56th Annual Meeting of the Association for Computational Linguistics ACL, Melbourne, Australia , July 15-20*.

Wu, S., Shapiro, P., and Cotterell, R. (2018). Hard non-monotonic attention for character-level transduction. In *The 2018 Conference on Empirical Methods in Natural Language Processing (EMNLP), Brussels, Belgium, October 31 - November 4*, pages 4425–4438.

Xu, K., Ba, J., Kiros, R., Cho, K., Courville, A. C., Salakhutdinov, R., Zemel, R. S., and Bengio, Y. (2015). Show, attend and tell: Neural image caption generation with visual attention. In *The 32nd International Conference on Machine Learning, ICML, Lille, France, 6-11 July*, pages 2048–2057.

Yang, N., Liu, S., Li, M., Zhou, M., and Yu, N. (2013). Word alignment modeling with context dependent deep neural network. In *The 51st Annual Meeting of the Association for Computational Linguistics ACL, Sofia, Bulgaria, 4-9 August*, pages 166–175.

Zenkel, T., Wuebker, J., and DeNero, J. (2019). Adding interpretable attention to neural translation models improves word alignment. *CoRR*, abs/1901.11359.

Zeyer, A., Alkhouli, T., and Ney, H. (2018). RETURNN as a generic flexible neural toolkit with application to translation and speech recognition. In *Proceedings of ACL, Melbourne, Australia, July 15-20*, pages 128–133.

Machine Translation with Unsupervised Length-Constraints

Jan Niehues   jan.niehues@maastrichtuniversity.nl
Department of Data Science and Knowledge Engineering (DKE), Maastricht University, Maastricht, The Netherlands

Abstract

We have seen significant improvements in machine translation due to the usage of deep learning. While the improvements in translation quality are impressive, the encoder-decoder architecture enables many more possibilities. In this paper, we explore one of these, the generation of constrained translation. We focus on length constraints, which are essential if the translation should be displayed in a given format.

In this work, we propose an end-to-end approach for this task. Compared to a traditional method that first translates and then performs sentence compression, the text compression is learned completely unsupervised. We address the challenge of data availability as well as investigate several methods to integrate the constraints into the model. By combining the idea with zero-shot multilingual machine translation, we are also able to perform unsupervised monolingual sentence compression.

Using the proposed approach, we are able to improve the translation quality for translation with length constraints as well as for monolingual length compression. In addition, the results are confirmed by a human evaluation.

1 Introduction

Neural machine translation (NMT) (Sutskever et al., 2014; Bahdanau et al., 2014) exploits neural networks to directly learn to transform sentences in a source language to sentences in a target language. This technique has significantly improved the quality of machine translation (Bojar et al., 2016; Cettolo et al., 2015). The advances in quality also allow for the application of this technology to new real-world applications.

While research systems tend to purely focus on a high translation quality, real-world applications often have additional requirements for the output of the system. One example is the mapping of markup information from the source text to the target text (Zenkel et al., 2019). In this work, we will focus on another use case, the generation of translations with given length constraints. Thereby, we focus on compression. That means the target length is shorter than the actual length of the translation. When translating from one language to another, the length of the source text is usually different from the length of the target text. While for most applications of machine translation this does not pose a problem, for some applications this significantly deteriorates the user experience. For example, if the translation should be displayed in the same layout as the source text (e.g. in a website), it is advantageous if the length stays the same. Another use case are captions for videos. A human is only capable of reading text up to a certain speed. For an optimal user experience, it is therefore not only important to present an accurate translation, but also to present the translation with a maximum number of words.

A first approach to address this challenge would be to use a cascade of a machine translation and sentence compression system. In this case, we would need training data to train the machine translation system and additional training data to train the sentence compression system. It is very difficult and sometimes even impossible to collect the training data for the sentence compression task. Furthermore, we need a sentence compression model with a parametric length reduction ratio. For a supervised model, we would therefore need examples with different length reduction ratios. Therefore, this work focuses on unsupervised sentence compression. Compared to related work, in this method we even do not assume to have any compressed sentences. So we need to learn how to compress sentences without having seen any compressed sentence in training.

While our work focuses on the end-to-end approach to translation combined with sentence compression, monolingual sentence compression is another important task. For example, human-generated captions are often not an accurate transcription of the audio, but in addition the text is shortened. This is due to cognitive processing constraints. The user is able to listen to more words in a given time than he or she can read in the same amount of time. When combining the length-constrained machine translation with the idea of zero-shot machine translation, the proposed method is also able to perform monolingual sentence compression. In addition, by adjusting the loss function we are able to use the same framework to perform text simplification.

The main contribution of this work is an end-to-end approach to length-constrained translation by jointly performing machine translation and sentence compression. We are able to show that for this task an end-to-end approach outperforms the cascade of machine translation and unsupervised sentence compression.

Therefore, two contributions are essential. First, by using pseudo-supervised training on standard parallel data, we are able to learn to compress without ever showing the model a compress sentence. This is achieved by making the model aware of properties (here the maximum length) that the output must fulfil. The second contribution is the adaptation of the architecture that the model is able to fulfil the properties also there is a mismatch between its influence in training and in testing. While it is straightforward to fulfil it during training, it can be difficult during decoding.

A third contribution of this work is to extend the presented approach to unsupervised monolingual sentence compression. By combining the presented approach with multilingual machine translation, we are able to also generate paraphrases with a given length constraint. The investigation shows that a system that is trained on several languages is able to successfully generate monolingual paraphrases.

2 Constrained decoding

In the targeted scenario, there is no available training data with the constraints of interest. Therefore, we need to teach the system something about the output that it cannot directly learn from the data. We investigate different methods that enable the model to fulfil the constraints without learning them from the data.

The main application is length-constrained translation. That means that we want to generate a translation with a given target length. Therefore we focus on the case of shortening the translations. While the length can be measured in words, subword tokens or letters, in the experiments we measured the length by subword tokens.

A straightforward approach is to disregard the constraints during training and search for the most probable translation respecting the constraints during decoding. We do this by restricting the search space to generate only translations with a given length. The length of the output is modeled by the probability of the end-of-sentence (EOS) token. By modifying this probability, we introduce a hard constraint that is always fulfilled.

Afterwards, we propose the length-aware model. This uses two techniques that are able to learn how to fulfil the constraints without ever seeing a sentence that was generated with the constraints. This enables us to train the model on standard parallel data.

We use pseudo-supervised training and assign the matching constraints to existing parallel data. Furthermore, by adapting the architecture, we address the train-test mismatch between the constraints in training and in decoding.

It is worth noting that the length-aware model uses the constraints as soft constraints, where translations fulfilling the constraints are preferred but other ones could also be generated. In contrast, they are modeled as hard constraints when adapting the search. In this case, only translation that fulfill the constraints are generated. Therefore, both methods can also be combined.

2.1 Restricted search space

A first strategy to incorporate the additional length constraints is to ignore them during training and restrict the inference-time search space to hypotheses that fulfill the constraint. For length constraints, this can be achieved by manipulating the end-of-sentence token probability. First, we need to ensure that the EOS token is not generated before the desired length of output J. This can be ensured by setting the probability for the end-of-sentence token to zero for all positions before the desired length and re-normalizing the probability.

$$p'(y_j|x_1,\ldots,x_I,y_1,\ldots,y_{j-1}) = \begin{cases} \frac{p(y_j|x_1,\ldots,x_I,y_1,\ldots,y_{j-1})}{1-p(EOS|x_1,\ldots,x_I,y_1,\ldots,y_{j-1})} & y_j \neq EOS \\ 0 & y_j = EOS \end{cases} \tag{1}$$

Finally, we ensure to stop the search at the desired length by setting the probability of the end-of-sentence token to one if the output sequence has reached this length.

$$p'(y_j|x_1,\ldots,x_I,y_1,\ldots,y_{j-1}) = \begin{cases} 0 & y_j \neq EOS \\ 1 & y_j = EOS \end{cases} \tag{2}$$

While this approach will guarantee that the output of the translation systems always meets the length condition (hard constraint), it also has one major drawback. Until the system reaches the constrained length, the system is not aware of how many words it is still allowed to generate. Therefore, it is not able to shorten the beginning of the sentence in order to fulfil the length constraint.

Motivated by this observation, we investigate methods to integrate the length constraint into the model and not only apply it during inference.

2.2 Length-aware model

The main idea of the length-aware model is that it should be aware of the output length through the whole decoding process. Therefore, the model needs as input in addition to the source sentence $X = x_1,\ldots,x_I$ the desired target length J. Then the model can decide what to generate based on the source text as well as only the available space given by the length constraint. However, this poses the challenge that we also need to train the model using data with constraints. These challenges are addressed by using pseudo-supervised training, where the constraints are added to existing parallel data and by integrating the length into the model. We will investigate methods to encode the length globally for the full sentence as well as methods to encode the remaining length locally at each decoding step.

2.2.1 Pseudo-supervised training

In contrast to only restricting the search space, for the length-aware model we also need the target length during training. Therefore, the first challenge we need to address when including the length constraints into the model itself is the question of training data. While there is large amounts of parallel training data, it is hard to acquire training data with length constraints. Therefore, we investigate methods to train the model with standard parallel training data. In contrast to other unsupervised methods, we are missing not only parallel data between the input and the output, but we have no data for the output. So we need to learn how to compress a sentence without ever seeing a compressed sentence.

Motivated by the success of adding the length in the use case where the output length should not be shortened but similar to the input length (Lakew et al., 2019), we perform the training by a type of pseudo-supervision. For each source sentence, in training, we also know the translation and therefore its length. The main idea is that we now assume this sentence was generated with the constraint to generate a translation with exactly the length of the given translation. Of course, this is mostly not the case. The human translator generated a translation that appropriately expresses the meaning of the source sentence and not a sentence that fulfills the length constraints.

Therefore, we have a mismatch between training and testing conditions and the learning is more difficult. While during training the given length can relatively easily be predicted by the expected length when expressing all source content in the target language, this is no longer true for testing. Due to the condition in training the system might learn to simply ignore the length information and instead generate a normal translation putting all the information of the source sentence into the target sentence. In this case, we would not have the possibility to control the target length by specifying our desired length.

2.2.2 Length representation

To address this problem, we investigate three different methods to represent the target length in the model. The motivation is thereby to ensure that the model uses the additional length information although it might not strictly necessary during training. Thereby, the training examples consist of a source sentence $X = x_1, \ldots, x_I$, a target sentence $Y = y_1, \ldots, y_J$ and the target length J.

Source embedding A first method is to model the target length globally for the whole sentence. This can be achieved by including the target length into the source sentence as an additional token. This is motivated by successful approaches for multilingual machine translation (Ha et al., 2016), domain adaptation (Kobus et al., 2017) and formality levels (Sennrich et al., 2016a). We change the training procedure to not use X as the input to the encoder of the NMT system, but instead J, X. In this way, the encoder will learn an embedding for each target length seen during training.

There are two challenges using this approach. First, the dependency between the described length J and the output Y is quite long within the model. Therefore, the model might ignore the information and just learn to generate the best translation for a given source sentence. Secondly, the representations for all possible target lengths are independent from each other. This poses a special challenge for long sentences which occur less frequently, e.g. there will be less sentence with length 63 than with length 9 and therefore the embedding of these lengths will not be learned as well as the frequent ones.

Target embedding We address the first challenge by integrating the length constraint directly into the decoder. In this case we model locally at each decoding step by encoding the number of words remaining to be generated. This is motivated by similar approaches to supervised sentence compression (Kikuchi et al., 2016) and zero-shot machine translation (Ha et al., 2017).

We incorporate the information of the number of remaining target words at each target position. For one, this should ensure that the length information is not lost during the decoding process. Secondly, by embedding smaller numbers which occur more frequently in the corpus towards the end of the sentence, the problem of rare sentence lengths does not matter that much.

Formally, at each decoder step j the baseline model starts with the word embedding of the last target word y_{j-1}. In the original transformer architecture (Vaswani et al., 2017), the positional encoding is applied on top of the embedding to generate the first hidden representation

$$h_0 = pos(emb(y_{j-1}), j). \tag{3}$$

In our proposed architecture, we include the number of remaining target words to be generated $J - j$. We concatenate h_0 with the length embedding and then apply a linear translation and a non-linearity to reduce the hidden size to the one of the original word embedding

$$h'_0 = relu(lin(cat(h_0, lenEmb(J - j)))). \tag{4}$$

The proposed architecture allows the model to consider the number of remaining target words at each decoding step. While the baseline model will only cut the end of the sentences, the model is able to shorten already at the beginning of the sentence.

Positional encoding Finally, we also address the challenge of representing sentence lengths that are less frequent. The transformer architecture introduced the positional encoding. This encodes the position within the sentence using a set of trigonometric functions. While their method encodes the position relative to the start of the sentence, we follow Takase and Okazaki (2019) to encode the position relative to the end of the sentence. Thereby, at each position we encode the number of remaining words of the sentence. Formally, we replace $h_0 = pos(emb(y_{j-1}), j)$ by $h_0^* = pos(emb(y_{j-1}), J - j)$.

2.3 Additional constraints

Besides constraining the number of words, other constraints can be implemented as easily using the same framework. In this work, we show this by limiting the number of complex and difficult words. One use case is the generation of paraphrases in simplified language. A metric to measure text difficulty, the Dale-Chall Readability metric (Chall and Dale, 1995), for example, counts such difficult words. In an NMT system, longer words are typically split into subword units by Byte Pair Encoding (BPE) (Sennrich et al., 2016b). A complex word like *marshmallow* is split into several parts, for instance *mar@@ shm@@ allow*, where @@ indicates that the word is not yet finished.

The idea to generate simpler text is now to limit the sub-word tokens that do not end a word (the ones ending on @@). This can be implemented by only counting the words that end on @@. If the target sentence would for example by *I like mar@@ shm@@ allow*, the target count would be 2.

When encoding the remaining length in the decoder, we would now not reduce it by 1 at each step, but only if the token is ending on @@. So the length sequence used in decoding would be 2 2 2 1 0.

During inference, we would now always try to generate sequences without splitted words by inputting the target length of 0. Since it is a soft constraint, the model can still generate subwords, if the other model strongly suggests that.

As for the length constrained decoding, we also would perform pseudo-supervised training and thereby be able to train our model on the default parallel data.

Reference: It might sound like it's a bad thing.
Baseline: But it might sound like
Constrained: It sounds really bad .

Table 1: Example of constrained translation

3 Evaluation

The lack of suitable data is not only a challenge for training but also for evaluation. The default approach to evaluating a machine translation system is to compare the output of the system with human translation using some automatic metric, e.g. BLEU (Papineni et al., 2002).

In our case, we would need to have a human-generated translation, which also fulfills the additional constraints. For example, translation with a length that is shortened to 80% of the input. Since this type of translation data is not available, we investigate methods to compare the length-constrained output of the system with standard human translation that do not fulfill any specific constraints.

3.1 Word matching metrics

While there is a significant amount of research in automatic metrics for machine translation (Ma et al., 2018, 2019), BLEU is still the most commonly used metric. Therefore, a first approach would be to use BLEU to compare the automatic translation with length constraints with the human translation without constraints. If we were using length constraints, this would lead to low BLEU scores due to the length penalty of the metric. But since all systems must fulfill the length constraint, the penalty would be the same for all output and we could still compare between the different outputs.

A problem of using BLEU scores as evaluation metrics in this task is illustrated by the example translations in Table 1. The baseline system only uses the length constraint for restricting the search space. In the constrained system, we are using the length constraint also as additional embeddings in the decoder. Looking at this example sentence, a human would rate the constrained translation better than the baseline translation. The problem of the latter model is that it often generates a prefix of a full translation. While this does not lead to a good constrained translation, it still leads to a relatively high BLEU score. In this case, we have one matching 4-gram, 2 tri-gram, 3 bigrams and four unigrams.

In contrast, the length-constrained model only contains words matching the reference scattered over the sentence. Therefore, in this case, we only have two unigram matches. Guided by this observation, we used different metrics to evaluate the models.

3.2 Embedding-based metrics

In order to address the challenges mentioned in the last subsection, we used metrics that are based on sentence embeddings instead of word or character-based representation of the sentence. This way it is no longer important that the words occur in the same sequence in automatic translation and reference. Based on the performance of the automatic metrics in the WMT Evaluation campaign in 2018, we used RUSE (Shimanaka et al., 2019) metric. It uses sentence embeddings from three different models: InferSent, Quick-Thought and Universal Sentence Encoder. Then the quality is estimated by an MLP based on the representation of the hypothesis and the reference translation. The hyper parameters (number of layers, hidden size, batch size, dropout rate) were optimized on the development set of the WMT Evaluation campaign and the MLP was not retrained for this task.

4 Experiments

4.1 Data

We train our systems on the TED data from the IWSLT 2017 multilingual evaluation campaign (Cettolo et al., 2017). The data contains parallel data between German, English, Italian, Dutch and Romanian. We create three different systems. The first system is only trained on the German-English data, the second one is trained on German-English and English-German data and the last one is trained on {German, Dutch, Italian, Romanian} and English data in the both directions.

The data is preprocessed using standard MT procedures including tokenization, truecasing and BPE with 40K codes. For model selection, the checkpoints performing best on the validation data (dev2010 and tst2010 combined) are averaged, which is then used to translate the tst2017 test set.

In the experiments, we address two different targeted lengths. Thereby the length of a sentence is measured by the number of subword tokens. In order to not use any information from the reference, we measure length limits relative to the source sentence length. We aim to shorten the translation to produce output that is 80% and 50% of the source sentence length. While in the first case, most information can still be conveyed, we wanted to see if the model is able to concentrate really on the important parts when shorting by half the length.

4.2 System

We use the standard transformer architecture (Vaswani et al., 2017) and increase the number of layers to eight. The layer size is 512 and the inner size is 2048. Furthermore, we apply word dropout (Gal and Ghahramani, 2016) with $p = 0.1$. In addition, layer dropout is used with $p = 0.2$ as in Pham et al. (2019). We use the same learning rate schedule as in the original work. The implementation is available on github[1]. All systems were always trained from scratch with random initialization.

4.3 Task difficulty

In an initial set of experiments, we assess the difficulty of having the additional length constraints. Therefore, we used the length of the human reference translation as a first target length. One could even argue that should make the typical machine translation easier, since some information about the translation is known. The results of this experiment are shown in Table 2. Since we do not perform compression in this experiment, the aforementioned problem with BLEU should not apply here.

Model	BLEU	RUSE
Baseline	30.80	−0.085
Only Search	28.32	−0.124
Source Emb	28.56	−0.126
Decoder Emb	27.88	−0.140
Decoder Pos	28.80	−0.138

Table 2: Using oracle length

However, the results indicate that the baseline system achieves the best BLEU score as well as the best RUSE score. All other models generate translations that perfectly fit the desired target length, but this leads to a drop in translation quality. Therefore, even if the target length

---

[1]https://github.com/jniehues-kit/NMTGMinor/tree/DbMajor

is the same as the one of the reference translation, the restriction increases the difficulty of the problem. One reason could be that the machine translation system rarely generates translations which exactly match the reference. By forcing the translation to have an exact predefined length, we are increasing the difficulty of the problem.

4.4 Length representation

In a first series of experiments for length constrained output, we analyzed the different techniques to encode the length of the output. First, we are interested in whether the different length representations are able to enforce an output that has the length we are aiming at (soft constraints). For the German to English translation task, the length of the different encoding versions are shown in Table 3. We define the length as the average difference between the targeted output given in BPE units and the output of the translation system.

First, without adding any constraints, the models generate translations that differ by 3.9 and 10.29 words from the targeted length. By specifying the length in the source side, we can reduce the length difference to half a word in the case of a targeted length of 80% and one and a half words in the case of 50% of the source length. The models using the decoder embeddings and the decoder positional encoding were able to nearly perfectly generate translation with the correct number of words.

Encoding	Avg. length difference	
	80%	50%
Baseline	3.90	10.29
Source Emb	0.55	1.40
Decoder Emb	0.07	0.16
Decoder Pos	0.09	0.19

Table 3: Avg. Length distance

Besides fulfilling the length constraints, the translations need to be accurate. Since we wanted to have a fair comparison, we evaluated the output when using a restricted search space, so that only translations with the correct number of words are generated (hard constraints). The results are summarized in Table 4

Encoding	RUSE	
	80%	50%
Baseline	−0.272	−0.605
Source Emb	−0.263	−0.587
Decoder Emb	−0.2469	−0.555
Decoder Pos	−0.2598	−0.577

Table 4: German-English translation quality

As shown in the results, we see improvements in translation quality when using the source embedding within the encoder. We have further improvements if we represent the targeted length within the decoder. In this case, we can improve the RUSE score by 2% and 5% absolute. The decoder encodings perform similarly, with small advantage for using embeddings and not positional encodings.Therefore, in the remaining of the experiments we use the embeddings.

4.5 Multi-lingual

In a second series of experiments, we combine the constrained translation approach with multi-lingual machine translation. The combination of both offers the unique opportunity to perform unsupervised sentence compression. We can treat the translation of English to English as a zero-shot direction (Johnson et al., 2017; Ha et al., 2016). This has not been addressed in traditional multi-lingual machine translation, since in this case the model will often just copy the source sentence to the target one. By adding the length constraints, we force the mode to reformulate the sentence in order to fulfil the length constraint.

The results for these experiments are shown in Table 5. In this case, we compared three scenarios. First, a model trained only on translations from German to English. Secondly, a model trained to translate from German to English and English to German. Finally, a model trained on four languages to and from English.

Model	Target Length 0.8				Target Length 0.5			
	Baseline		Dec. Emb		Baseline		Dec. Emb	
	DE-EN	EN-EN	DE-EN	EN-EN	DE-EN	EN-EN	DE-EN	EN-EN
DE-EN	-0.272		-0.247		-0.587		-0.554	
DE+EN	-0.264	-0.817	-0.223	-0.905	-0.598	-0.954	-0.523	-0.978
All	-0.225	-0.102	-0.214	0.020	-0.560	-0.525	-0.548	-0.481

Table 5: Multi-lingual systems

First of all, since the models are trained on relatively small data, we always gain when using more language pairs. Secondly, for all models training from German to English, the decoder embedding is clearly better than the baseline. Finally, to perform paraphrasing, we need a multilingual system with several language pairs. Both models trained only on the German to English and English to German data fail to generate adequate translation. In contrast, if we look at the translation from English to English for the multilingual model, the scores are clearly better than the ones from German to English. Furthermore, again, the system with decoder embeddings is clearly better than the baseline system.

In addition, we performed the same experiment with a target length of half the source length (Table 5). Although the absolute scores are significant lower since the model has to reduce the length further, the tendency is the same for this direction.

4.6 End2End vs. Cascaded

Length	Model	DE-EN	EN-EN
	End2End	-0.247	0.020
0.8	Cascade	-0.259	-0.118
	Cascade Fix. Pivot		-0.166
	End2End	-0.555	-0.481
0.5	Cascade	-0.575	-0.521
	Cascade Fix. Pivot		-0.544

Table 6: Comparison of End-to-End and Cascaded approach

In this work, we are able to combine machine translation and sentence compression. In a third series of experiments, we wanted to investigate the advantage of modelling it in an end-to-end fashion compared to a cascade of different models. We performed this investigation again for two tasks: German to English and English to English.

The cascade system for German to English, first translates the German text to English with a baseline machine translation system. In a second step, the output is compressed with the multi-lingual MT system. For the English-to-English system, the cascade system removes the zero-shot condition. Therefore, we first translate from English to German with the baseline system and then translate with length contrasted from German to English. In *cascade fix pivot* also the English to German system already fulfills the length constraint.

As shown in Table 6, in all conditions, the end-to-end approach outperforms the cascaded version. This is especially the case for the English-to-English machine translation. Compared to multi-lingual machine translation, for these tasks it seems to be beneficial to perform the zero-shot tasks instead of using a pivot language.

4.7 Simplification

Metric	DE-EN		DE+EN		All	
	Base	Simp.	Base	Simp.	Base	Simp
BPE tokens	1961	1053	1978	1041	1899	991
DCR	7.63	7.47	7.69	7.5	7.66	7.45
FRE	83.86	86.18	84.31	85.49	82.98	85.59
BLEU	30.80	30.62	32.25	31.38	32.84	31.29
RUSE	−0.085	−0.092	−0.082	−0.080	−0.042	−0.084

Table 7: Simplification

In the last series of experiments (Table 7), we investigate the ability of our method to generate simpler sentences. As described in Section 2.3, we used the proposed framework to reduce the number of rare and complex words. Again, we are using the decoder embedding to represent the amount of BPE units in the sentences. We use a system for 1 language pair, 2 language pairs and the system using 8 language pairs. First, the system is able to reduce the number of BPE tokens in the text significantly. The amount of tokens is reduced by up to 48%. Since the number of tokens is nearly kept the same, this is also reflected in a better readability. This highlights also the importance of having soft constraints. In this use case, we cannot generate reasonable translations without using rare words that get split into separate subword units. However, the proposed framework is able to reduce the amount of these words.

We measure the readability using the Dale-Chall readability formula (DCR) (Chall and Dale, 1995) and the Flesch Reading Ease (FRE) (Flesch, 1948) .[2] As shown in the table, both scores indicate that the readability is increased by the proposed method. On the other hand, we see that the translation quality is only affected slightly.

4.8 Human Evaluation

In addition to the automatic evaluation, a human evaluation of the output was performed. This evaluation was performed using the multilingual machine translation system translating from German to English. Thereby, a length constraint of 80% of the source sentence was used.

Two evaluators were asked to assign a score between 0 and 100 to the translations of 15 sentences each. In Table 8 we summarized the results. We calculate the average score of both systems as well as how often the system from one model was evaluated better than the other. First, the proposed methods were evaluated better by around 5%. Secondly, when comparing

---

[2]The scores were calculated by the tool https://github.com/mmautner/readability

the scores for the individual sentences, the proposed method generated better translations nearly three times as often as the baseline model did.

Evaluation	Baseline	Decoder Emb
Score	68%	73%
Wins	6	17

Table 8: Human Evaluation

4.9 Qualitative Results

For the length restricted system, we also present examples in Table 9. The translations were generated with the multi-lingual system using restricted search space with 0.8 times and 0.5 times the length of the source length. The length is thereby measured using the number of subword tokens.

Source:	Und, obwohl es wirklich einfach scheint, ist es tatsächlich richtig schwer, weil es Leute drängt sehr schnell zusammenzuarbeiten.
Reference:	And, though it seems really simple, it's actually pretty hard because it forces people to collaborate very quickly.
Base 0.8:	and even though it really seems simple , it is actually really hard , because it really pushes
Dec. Emb. 0.8 :	and although it really seems simple , it is really hard because it drives people to work together .
Base 0.5 :	and even though it really seems simple , it is really hard
Dec. Emb. 0. 5:	it is really hard because it drives people to work together .
Source:	Konstrukteure erkennen diese Art der Zusammenarbeit als Kern eines iterativen Vorgangs.
Reference:	Designers recognize this type of collaboration as the essence of the iterative process.
Base 0.8:	now , traditional constructors recognize this kind of collaboration as the core
Dec. Emb. 0.8	designers recognize this kind of collaboration as the core of iterative .
Base 0.5:	now , traditional constructors recognize this kind
Dec. Emb: 0.5	developers recognize this kind of collaboration .

Table 9: Examples

In the examples we see clearly the problem of the baseline model when using a restricted search space. The model mainly outputs the prefix of the long translation and does not try to put the main content into the shorter segment. In contrast, the system using the decoder embeddings is aware when generating a word how much space it still has to fill the content. Therefore, it does not just cut part of the sentence, but compress the sentence and extract the most important part of the sentence. While the first example is more concentrating on the second part of the original sentence, the second one is focusing at the beginning. Although the model reducing the length by 50% has to remove some content of the original sentence, the sentence is still understandable.

5   Related Work

The most common approach to model the target length within NMT is the use of coverage models (Tu et al., 2016). More recently, (Lakew et al., 2019) used similar techniques to generate translation with the same length as the source sentence. Compared to these works, we tried to reduce the length of the sentence by a larger margin and thereby have the situation where the training and testing conditions differ more. Furthermore, the use of multi-lingual machine translation allows also the generation of compressed sentences in the same language. This work on length-controlled machine translation is strongly related to sentence compression, where the compression is performed in the monolingual case. First approach used rule-based approaches (Dorr et al., 2003) for extractive sentence compression. In abstractive compression methods using syntactic translation (Cohn and Lapata, 2008) and phrase-based machine translation were investigated (Wubben et al., 2012). The success of encoder-decoder models in many areas of natural language processing (Sutskever et al., 2014; Bahdanau et al., 2014) motivated their successful application to sentence compression. (Kikuchi et al., 2016) and (Takase and Okazaki, 2019) investigated an approach to directly control the output length. Although their methods use similar techniques to ours, the model is trained in a supervised way. Motivated by recent success in unsupervised machine translation (Artetxe et al., 2018; Lample et al., 2018), a first approach to learn text compression in an unsupervised fashion was presented in Fevry and Phang (2018). Text compression in a supervised fashion for subtitles was investigated in Angerbauer et al. (2019).

In contrast to text compression, the combination of readability and machine translation has been researched recently. (Agrawal and Carpuat, 2019) presented an approach to model the readability using source side annotation. In contrast to our work, they concentrated on the scenario where manually created training data is available. In Marchisio et al. (2019) the authors specified the desired readability difficulty either by a source token or through the architecture by different encoders. While they concentrate on a single task and have only a limited number of difficulty classes, the work presented here is able to handle a huge number of possible output classes (e.g. in text compression the number of words) and can be applied for different tasks.

6   Conclusion

In this work, we investigated the challenge of generating translation with additional constraints. The main difficulty we addressed is the availability of training data. It is not only hard to acquire parallel data with target sides constraints, but even monolingual data which was generated respecting additional constraints is rarely available.

We address this problem by using pseudo-supervised training on standard parallel data. Instead of generating the translation with constraints, we set the constraints in a way that they are fulfilled by the existing translation. Thereby, we are able to learn to generate compressed sentences without ever seeing compressed sentences in training.

The approach results in a mismatch between training and test conditions. While in training the translation can also be correctly generated by ignoring the constraints, this is no longer the case in testing. We address this issue by adapting the architecture of the sequence-to-sequence model. A detailed evaluation using automatic and human evaluation shows the success of the presented approach.

Finally, we show the possibility to extend the presented approach to related tasks. In combination with zero-shot multi-lingual machine translation, the method is also able to perform monolingual sentence compression. Furthermore, by varying the cost function, we are able to also address other tasks like text simplification.

References

Agrawal, S. and Carpuat, M. (2019). Controlling Text Complexity in Neural Machine Translation. *arXiv:1911.00835 [cs]*. arXiv: 1911.00835.

Angerbauer, K., Adel, H., and Vu, T. (2019). Automatic Compression of Subtitles with Neural Networks and its Effect on User Experience. In *Proceedings of the 20th Annual Conference of the International Speech Communication Association (Interspeech 2019)*, pages 594–598.

Artetxe, M., Labaka, G., Agirre, E., and Cho, K. (2018). Unsupervised Neural Machine Translation. In *International Conference on Learning Representations*.

Bahdanau, D., Cho, K., and Bengio, Y. (2014). Neural Machine Translation by Jointly Learning to Align and Translate. *CoRR*, abs/1409.0.

Bojar, O., Chatterjee, R., Federmann, C., Graham, Y., Haddow, B., Huck, M., Jimeno Yepes, A., Koehn, P., Logacheva, V., Monz, C., Negri, M., Névéol, A., Neves, M., Popel, M., Post, M., Rubino, R., Scarton, C., Specia, L., Turchi, M., Verspoor, K., and Zampieri, M. (2016). Findings of the 2016 Conference on Machine Translation. In *Proceedings of the First Conference on Machine Translation: Volume 2, Shared Task Papers*, pages 131–198, Berlin, Germany. Association for Computational Linguistics.

Cettolo, M., Federico, M., Bentivoldi, L., Niehues, J., Stüker, S., Sudoh, K., Yoshino, K., and Federmann, C. (2017). Overview of the IWSLT 2017 Evaluation Campaign. In *Proceedings of the 14th International Workshop on Spoken Language Translation (IWSLT 2017)*, Tokio, Japan.

Cettolo, M., Niehues, J., Stüker, S., Bentivoldi, L., Cattoni, R., and Federico, M. (2015). The IWSLT 2015 Evaluation Campaign. In *Proceedings of the Twelfth International Workshop on Spoken Language Translation (IWSLT 2015)*, Da Nang, Vietnam.

Chall, J. and Dale, E. (1995). *Readability revisited: the new Dale-Chall readability formula*. Brookline Books.

Cohn, T. and Lapata, M. (2008). Sentence Compression Beyond Word Deletion. In *Proceedings of the 22nd International Conference on Computational Linguistics (Coling 2008)*, pages 137–144, Manchester, UK. Coling 2008 Organizing Committee.

Dorr, B., Zajic, D., and Schwartz, R. (2003). Hedge Trimmer: A Parse-and-Trim Approach to Headline Generation. In *Proceedings of the HLT-NAACL 03 Text Summarization Workshop*, pages 1–8.

Fevry, T. and Phang, J. (2018). Unsupervised Sentence Compression using Denoising Auto-Encoders. In *Proceedings of the 22nd Conference on Computational Natural Language Learning*, pages 413–422, Brussels, Belgium. Association for Computational Linguistics.

Flesch, R. (1948). A new readability yardstick. *Journal of Applied Psychology*, 32(3):p221 – 233.

Gal, Y. and Ghahramani, Z. (2016). A Theoretically Grounded Application of Dropout in Recurrent Neural Networks. In *Proceedings of the 30th International Conference on Neural Information Processing Systems*, NIPS'16, pages 1027–1035, USA. Curran Associates Inc. event-place: Barcelona, Spain.

Ha, T. L., Niehues, J., and Waibel, A. (2016). Toward Multilingual Neural Machine Translation with Universal Encoder and Decoder. In *Proceedings of the 13th International Workshop on Spoken Language Translation (IWSLT 2016)*, Seattle, USA.

Ha, T. L., Niehues, J., and Waibel, A. (2017). Effective Strategies in Zero-Shot Neural Machine Translation. In *Proceedings of the 14th International Workshop on Spoken Language Translation (IWSLT 2017)*, Tokio, Japan.

Johnson, M., Schuster, M., Le, Q. V., Krikun, M., Wu, Y., Chen, Z., Thorat, N., Viégas, F., Wattenberg, M., Corrado, G., Hughes, M., and Dean, J. (2017). Google's Multilingual Neural Machine Translation System: Enabling Zero-Shot Translation. *Transactions of the Association for Computational Linguistics*, 5:339–351.

Kikuchi, Y., Neubig, G., Sasano, R., Takamura, H., and Okumura, M. (2016). Controlling Output Length in Neural Encoder-Decoders. In *Proceedings of the 2016 Conference on Empirical Methods in Natural Language Processing*, pages 1328–1338, Austin, Texas. Association for Computational Linguistics.

Kobus, C., Crego, J., and Senellart, J. (2017). Domain Control for Neural Machine Translation. In *Procceddings of Recent Advances in Natural Language Processing (RANLP 2017)*, pages 372–378, Varna, Bulgaria.

Lakew, S. M., Di Gangi, M., and Federico, M. (2019). Controlling the Output Length of Neural Machine Translation. In *Proceedings of the 16th International Workshop on Spoken Language Translation (IWSLT 2019)*, Hong Kong. Zenodo.

Lample, G., Conneau, A., Denoyer, L., and Ranzato, M. (2018). Unsupervised Machine Translation Using Monolingual Corpora Only. In *International Conference on Learning Representations*.

Ma, Q., Bojar, O., and Graham, Y. (2018). Results of the WMT18 Metrics Shared Task: Both characters and embeddings achieve good performance. In *Proceedings of the Third Conference on Machine Translation: Shared Task Papers*, pages 671–688, Belgium, Brussels. Association for Computational Linguistics.

Ma, Q., Wei, J., Bojar, O., and Graham, Y. (2019). Results of the WMT19 Metrics Shared Task: Segment-Level and Strong MT Systems Pose Big Challenges. In *Proceedings of the Fourth Conference on Machine Translation (Volume 2: Shared Task Papers, Day 1)*, pages 62–90, Florence, Italy. Association for Computational Linguistics.

Marchisio, K., Guo, J., Lai, C.-I., and Koehn, P. (2019). Controlling the Reading Level of Machine Translation Output. In *Proceedings of MT Summit XVII*, volume 1, page 11.

Papineni, K., Roukos, S., Ward, T., and Zhu, W.-J. (2002). BLEU: a Method for Automatic Evaluation of Machine Translation. In *Proceedings of the 40th Annual Meeting on Association for Computational Linguistics - ACL '02*, page 311, Morristown, NJ, USA. Association for Computational Linguistics.

Pham, N.-Q., Nguyen, T.-S., Niehues, J., Müller, M., Stüker, S., and Waibel, A. (2019). Very Deep Self-Attention Networks for End-to-End Speech Recognition. In *Proceedings of the 20th Annual Conference of the International Speech Communication Association (Interspeech 2019)*, Graz, Austria.

Sennrich, R., Birch, A., and Haddow, B. (2016a). Controlling Politeness in Neural Machine Translation via Side Constraints. In *Proceedings of the 2012 Conference of the North American Chapter of the Association for Computational Linguistics: Human Language Technologies (NAACL-HLT 2016)*, pages 35–40, San Diego, California, USA.

Sennrich, R., Haddow, B., and Birch, A. (2016b). Neural Machine Translation of Rare Words with Subword Units. In *Proceedings of the 54th Annual Meeting of the Association for Computational Linguistics (Volume 1: Long Papers)*, pages 1715–1725, Berlin, Germany. Association for Computational Linguistics.

Shimanaka, H., Kajiwara, T., and Komachi, M. (2019). RUSE: Regressor Using Sentence Embeddings for Automatic Machine Translation Evaluation. In *Proceedings of the Third Conference on Machine Translation: Shared Task Papers*, pages 751–758, Stroudsburg, PA, USA. Association for Computational Linguistics.

Sutskever, I., Vinyals, O., and Le, Q. V. (2014). Sequence to Sequence Learning with Neural Networks. *Advances in Neural Information Processing Systems 27: Annual Conference on Neural Information Processing Systems 2014*, pages 3104–3112.

Takase, S. and Okazaki, N. (2019). Positional Encoding to Control Output Sequence Length. In *Proceedings of the 2019 Conference of the North American Chapter of the Association for Computational Linguistics: Human Language Technologies, Volume 1 (Long and Short Papers)*, pages 3999–4004, Minneapolis, Minnesota. Association for Computational Linguistics.

Tu, Z., Lu, Z., Liu, Y., Liu, X., and Li, H. (2016). Modeling Coverage for Neural Machine Translation. In *Proceedings of the 54th Annual Meeting of the Association for Computational Linguistics (Volume 1: Long Papers)*, pages 76–85, Berlin, Germany. Association for Computational Linguistics.

Vaswani, A., Shazeer, N., Parmar, N., Uszkoreit, J., Jones, L., Gomez, A. N., Kaiser, L., and Polosukhin, I. (2017). Attention Is All You Need. *CoRR*, abs/1706.0.

Wubben, S., van den Bosch, A., and Krahmer, E. (2012). Sentence Simplification by Monolingual Machine Translation. In *Proceedings of the 50th Annual Meeting of the Association for Computational Linguistics (Volume 1: Long Papers)*, pages 1015–1024, Jeju Island, Korea. Association for Computational Linguistics.

Zenkel, T., Wuebker, J., and DeNero, J. (2019). Adding Interpretable Attention to Neural Translation Models Improves Word Alignment. *arXiv:1901.11359 [cs]*. arXiv: 1901.11359.

Constraining the Transformer NMT Model with Heuristic Grid Beam Search[*]

Guodong Xie   guodong.xie@adaptcentre.ie
Andy Way   andy.way@adaptcentre.ie
Jinhua Du   jinhua.du@adaptcentre.ie
ADAPT Centre, School of Computing, Dublin City University, Dublin, Ireland
Longyue Wang*   vincentwang0229@gmail.com
Tencent AI Lab

Abstract

Constrained decoding forces a certain set words or phrases to appear in the translation results and is very useful when adapting MT to a certain domain. In recent years, the Transformer model has outperformed other neural machine translation models to become the state-of-the-art paradigm. However, constrained decoding for domain adaptation remains an open problem under the Transformer model. In this paper, we first investigate how a constrained decoding method – Grid Beam Search (GBS) – performs in the Transformer model, and then propose a source-informed heuristic method that can fully take advantage of the alignment information from the multi-head attention mechanism in Transformer to speed up the decoding in the GBS method and guide the placement of constraints during the expansion of hypotheses in GBS. Experiments on English–Chinese and English–German translation domain adaptation tasks show that the proposed method significantly outperforms the basic Transformer model in terms of BLEU and METEOR score, and prunes up to 30% hypotheses to save up to 20% decoding time compared to the GBS model while maintaining comparable translation performance.

1   Introduction

With recent advances in neural machine translation (NMT), The Transformer model (Vaswani et al., 2017) has outperformed other NMT architectures, like RNN (Luong et al., 2015) and CNN (Gehring et al., 2017), to become the state-of-the-art paradigm. The Transformer model mainly consists of layers of self-attention and a feed-forward network. It is capable of being fully parallelised and is faster both in training and inference. Its multi-layer and multi-head attention mechanism enable it to capture deep syntactic and semantic relations in sentences to produce better translation results.

Constrained decoding is an approach that exerts some constraints to a decoding process (often a beam search process) and enforces the constraints to appear in the decoding results. For translation tasks, constraints are normally some target words or phrases which are acquired in advance through domain knowledge or other methods. Constrained decoding ensures constraints partially or fully appear in the translation results by means of certain algorithms. The translation results of constrained decoding are often better than the normal decoding results, as those constraints are actually some external knowledge besides the source sentences.

---

[*] This work was done while the co-author were working with us in the ADAPT Centre at Dublin City University.

Different constrained decoding approaches have been proposed. Luong and Manning (2015), Sennrich et al. (2016a) adapted NMT systems with domain-specific data by adjusting their output vocabulary to better match the target domain. Besides, Wang et al. (2017) tried early attempts to improve translation consistency for NMT models with discourse-level context. However, these methods do not strictly enforce a constraint, so constraints are not guaranteed to appear in the output.

Anderson et al. (2017) extended beam search with a finite state acceptor (FSA) whose states mark the completed subsets of the set of constraints. However, their algorithm has an exponential complexity of $\mathcal{O}(Nk2^C)$, where n is the sentence length, k is beam size, and C is the constraint count. This results in a very slow decoding speed when the number of constraints increased.

Hokamp and Liu (2017) proposed a novel grid beam search (GBS) method that can enforce any constraints to appear in the translation results. In order to ensure the constraints are placed in the right positions in the translation results, GBS assumes that all constraints may appear at each decoding step and extends a beam vertically to grid beams. This means there are several beams at each step rather than a single beam. As a result, the number of hypotheses increases linearly according to the number of constraints. GBS can adapt a general NMT model to a domain translation task and improve the translation quality (Hokamp and Liu, 2017). Even though it has a complexity of $\mathcal{O}(NkC)$, it may expand a very large search space when the number of constrains increases, which also results in a slow and computationally expensive decoding process.

Post and Vilar (2018) proposed a fast lexically constrained decoding method with dynamic beam allocation (DBA) for NMT. This method groups together hypotheses that meet the same number of constraints into banks, and dynamically divides a fixed-size beam across these banks at each time step, which results in a complexity of $\mathcal{O}(Nk)$, so the DBA is faster and can process large constraint sets easily. The disadvantage of DBA is that the translation quality strongly depends on some factors, such as the beam size k. Their experiments show that system performance experiences a significant decrease compared to the original GBS system. DBA can be regarded as a better trade-off between translation quality and decoding time when applying constrained decoding to NMT.

There are two common problems in the above methods. First, all are based on the RNN model. Whether term constraints are necessary and whether those constraining algorithms are effective on the Transformer model are still open problems and deserve to be verified. Second, when decoding, only the constraints' own information is exploited to guide the placement of constraints, and no other information, such as source-side words, is used. An obvious deficiency of these algorithms is that all possible constraints of a sentence have to be considered at each decoding step. Furthermore, only the decoding score is used to rank and prune hypotheses in the beams. This mechanism might place a constraint in the wrong position and generate an output with a low score due to the enforced inclusion of all constraints in the output. Intuitively, a better strategy is to guide the constrained decoder to place constraints in the correct positions with the help of more useful information, so to avoid the extensive exploration of a very large search space and obtain better decoding results. As target-side constraints are actually deduced from the source sentences, if we can utilize some source-side information, we may be able to confine the search space or guide the decoding process to locate target-side constraints more accurately.

Confronting these two problems, this paper first investigates the feasibility and effectiveness of performing constrained decoding using GBS in Transformer. We then propose a source-informed heuristic method to reduce the search space of the GBS method so to speed decoding while maintaining comparable translation performance. We propose a simple but effective lexically constrained decoding strategy for Transformer, which makes use of the alignment information from the multi-head attention in Transformer to place probably correct constraints at time step t. In doing so, we can control the number of paths to expand in the GBS, and speed up the decoding process.

The main contributions of this paper include: (1) to the best of our knowledge, our work is the first to implement constrained decoding in the Transformer model and verify its performance; (2) we propose an effective and efficient method for the constrained Transformer model which fully uses source-side information from the multi-head attention in Transformer to guide the placement of constraints at each time step for a better balance between translation quality and decoding time; (3) we compare the proposed method with unconstrained Transformer and GBS Transformer via extensive experiments, and demonstrate that our model significantly outperforms the basic Transformer model in terms of BLEU (Papineni et al., 2002) and METEOR score (Denkowski and Lavie, 2014), and significantly saves up to 20% decoding time compared to the GBS model with no deterioration in performance.

2 Transformer and Grid Beam Search

2.1 Neural Transformer Model

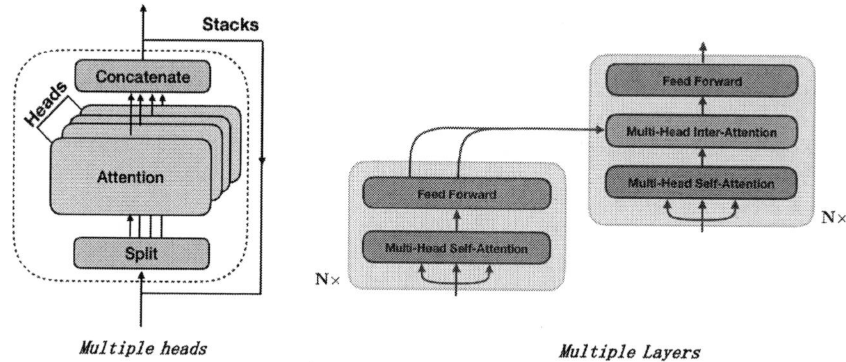

Figure 1: Transformer model

As shown in Figure 1, Transformer makes use of self-attention as the basic computational block. It uses a combination of self-attention and feed-forward layers in the encoder and additional source attention layers on the decoder side. In the standard Transformer model, the encoder is composed of a stack of $N_x = 6$ identical layers, with each layer having two sub-layers, namely a multi-head self-attention mechanism and a position-wise fully connected feed-forward network. A residual connection is employed around each of the two sub-layers, followed by layer normalisation. The decoder is also composed of a stack of $N_x = 6$ identical layers. In addition to the two sub-layers in each encoder layer, the decoder inserts a third sub-layer, which performs multi-head attention over the output of the encoder stack. Similar to the encoder, residual connections are also employed around each of the sub-layers, followed by layer normalization. Transformer's self-attention includes attention between decoder layers and the encoder's outputs, which is similar to the attention in RNN and can be regarded as alignment between source and target. Please refer to Vaswani et al. (2017) for more details.

2.2 Grid Beam Search for Constrained NMT

In normal beam search (Lowerre, 1976; Sutskever et al., 2014), the decoder maintains a beam with a fixed size k containing a set of expanded hypotheses. As mentioned, the decoding in RNN-based and Transformer NMT models is an auto-regressive process, so at each time step t, the decoder produces a distribution over the target-language vocabulary for each of these hypotheses, depending on the previous time step $t - 1$. As each beam contains k hypotheses, this produces a large matrix of dimension $k \times |V_T|$.

In order to integrate external knowledge into NMT without intervening in its learning process, constrained decoding can be adopted by NMT, which we call *constrained NMT*. By definition, constraints in constrained NMT indicate a set of pre-specified words, phrases or terms, which are acquired by automatic extraction from the corpus or via manually compilation. Constrained NMT can enforce constraints in the hypotheses and select from the set of complete hypotheses the best one that satisfies all constraints.

Hokamp and Liu (2017) formalise the notion of lexical constraints, and propose the *grid beam search* decoding algorithm which forces constraints to appear in the output. It organises the decoding process by expanding the beam of each step to grid beams which contain more than one beam. The beam count inside a grid beam corresponds to the token number of constraints. This method puts each constraint in all potential positions during decoding and it uses a kind of traversal method to find the best result.

To be specific, each beam in the grid is indexed by time step t and constraint variable c. c indicates how many constraint tokens have been covered so far by the current active hypothesis in the current beam. At each time step, only one single constraint token is covered, i.e. the set of constraints is an array of sequences, where each token can be indexed as $constraints_{ij}$, indicating $token_j$ in the $constraint_i$. $numC$ is used to represent the total number of tokens in all constraints C.

The hypotheses in a beam can be separated into two types:

(1) **open** hypotheses: the next token can be generated either from the model, or from the available constraints;

(2) **closed** hypotheses: the next token can only be generated from a currently unfinished constraint.

At each step t of the search process, the beam at **Grid**$[t][c]$ is filled with candidates which may be created in three ways:

(1) the **open** hypotheses in the beam to the left (**Grid**$[t - 1][c]$) may *generate* continuations from the model's distribution $p_\theta(y_i|x, y_0...y_{i-1})$;

(2) the **open** hypotheses in the beam to the left and below (**Grid**$[t - 1][c - 1]$) may *start* new constraints;

(3) the **closed** hypotheses in the beam to the left and below (**Grid**$[t - 1][c - 1]$) may *continue* constraints.

The beams at the top level of the grid (beams where $c = numC$) contain hypotheses which cover all constraints. Once a hypothesis at the top level generates the $\langle \text{EOS} \rangle$ token, it can be added to the set of finished hypotheses (cf. Hokamp and Liu (2017) for more detail).

3 Multi-Head Attention-Guided Source Information as Heuristics for Constrained Transformer

Our motivation to use source-side information as heuristics is that in both GBS and DBA, only the constraints' own information (often some target-side words) is used. The methods do not decide which constraint should be placed at time step t, so all available constraints need to be considered during the decoding process. The fact is that constraints extracted from the corpus or via terminology entries are bilingual, while source-side information is simply discarded in current constrained decoding methods.

Following the work of GBS in RNN-based NMT (Hokamp and Liu, 2017), we re-implement it in the Transformer model, and then take advantage of the alignment information from the multi-head attention mechanism to obtain corresponding source-side positions at time step t, and then guide the decoder to place corresponding constraints in the beam, which we call "**Heuristic GBS (HGBS)**".

3.1 Algorithm

Algorithm 1 Pseudo-code for Heuristic Grid Beam Search

1: **procedure** HEURISTIC SEARCH($model, input, constraints, maxLen, numC, k$)
2:     **if** $hyp.isOpen()$ **then** $\triangleright$ Start from Line 15 of GBS Algorithm
3:         **for** c in $constraints$ **do**
4:             **if** c not $used$ **then**
5:                 $p_A = \text{multiHeadSearch}(t, c)$
6:                 **if** $p_A >= p_{th}$ **then**
7:                     $n \leftarrow n \cup \text{model.start}(hyp, input, c)$ $\triangleright$ Only the constraint c is placed in the beam

---

When we use Pointwise Mutual Information (PMI) method (Hokamp and Liu, 2017) to extract a constraint, we actually obtain a segment pairs which contains both the source segment and target segment, which we call a "constraint pair". A Chinese–English constraint pair with source positions is shown in Table 1. There is a source sentence "传统劳动密集型产品因价格下降带来的出口值减少" whose reference target sentence is "The export value of traditional labor-intensive products decreased due to the price drop". PMI method can extract a constraint pair "劳动 密集型 产品 ||| labor intensive products" where "labor intensive products" is supposed to appear in the translation. This constraint pair is underlined in both source and target sentence in the table. The table also shows that the position of the source part of the constraint in the source sentence is 1, 2 and 3.

At time step t in decoding, before we want to take this target constraint as a candidate to start new constraints in the beam, we first retrieve the source word positions $\{1, 2, 3\}$. With this position information, we can look at the multi-head attention, and obtain the weights at time step t pointing to these three source word positions. By using these weights, we can decide whether we should start a new hypothesis of this constraint in the beam or not.

Source sentence	传统 劳动 密集型 产品 因 价格 下降 带来 的 出口 值 减少
Target sentence	The export value of traditional labor intensive products decreased due to the price drop
Target side of constraint	labor intensive products
Source side of constraint	劳动 密集型 产品
Position in source	$\{1, 2, 3\}$

Table 1: An example of a Chinese–English constraint pair

Obviously, there is a risk that if the alignment is incorrect, then we might put the constraint in the wrong place. However when hypotheses in the beam compete with each other via the model score, the possibility of generating a hypothesis with wrongly placed constraints in the output will greatly reduce.

Algorithm 1 shows the core parts of our proposed HGBS method, which is modified based on *Line 15 and 16* of the GBS Algorithm (Hokamp and Liu, 2017) by adding alignment information to guide the grid search.

3.2 Multi-Head Attention for Source-Informed Constraints

An attention function can be described as mapping a query and a set of key-value pairs to an output, where the query, keys, values, and output are all vectors. The output is computed as a weighted sum of the values, where the weight assigned to each value is computed by a compatibility function of the query with the corresponding key (Vaswani et al., 2017).

From Figure 1 we can see that there are multiple layers for the encoder and decoder, respectively. The multi-head self-attention from the last layer of the encoder is fed to each layer of the decoder to construct the soft attention alignment between the target and source positions. We found that the alignment in the last layer of the decoder works best, so we only use the alignment information from the last multi-head attention layer of the decoder to guide our constrained decoding approach.

By applying the multi-head attentions to the HGBS algorithm, we follow the steps below:

- **S1**: at each decoding step, we retrieve the attention weight distribution at the current time step t;

- **S2**: multiple weight distributions from the multi-head attention are averaged to obtain one single attention distribution;

- **S3**: taking a target constraint c as a candidate to **start** new constraints in the beam, we derive the source-word positions of its corresponding source constraint;

- **S4**: we sum up the probabilities of all links to the source word positions in **S3**. The sum is denoted as p_A;

- **S5**: if $p_A > p_{th}$, where p_{th} is a pre-defined threshold, then put c in the beam to **start** a new constraint.

- **S6**: loop from **S3** to **S6** until all available target constraints are traversed.

From Algorithm 1 and the above steps, the source-side information derived from the multi-head attention mechanism acts as a filter to remove those constraints that are not necessary to expand the hypothesis at the current time step t. The source-side alignment information helps place constraints in more reasonable positions. In this way, a number of hypotheses in GBS are pruned, and the search space decreases significantly.

4 Experiments

4.1 Translation Tasks

In our view, the most interesting finding in Hokamp and Liu (2017) is that GBS-based constrained decoding has a significant role to play in domain adaptation via terminology, which is a very important issue in application scenarios in which the translation process has to comply with specific terminology and/or style guides (Chatterjee et al., 2017).

Therefore, in order to compare the proposed **HGBS** method with **GBS**, we focus in our experiments on the domain adaptation task for constrained decoding via terminology. We use WMT English–German (EN-DE) and Chinese–English (ZH-EN) translation tasks to perform the comparison experiments.

4.2 Data

We use the same data settings for the domain adaptation experiment as in Hokamp and Liu (2017) in terms of the EN-DE task:

- the training corpus consists of 4.4 Million segments from Europarl (Koehn, 2005) and CommonCrawl (Smith et al., 2013);

- for the target domain data, the Autodesk Post-Editing corpus (Zhechev, 2012) from the domain of software localisation is used, which is quite different from the WMT data. The corpus is divided into 100,000 training sentences and 1,000 test sentences. Constraints are extracted automatically using PMI between source and target n-grams. The maximum length of a constraint or terminology is set to 5-gram as in Hokamp and Liu (2017).

For the ZH-EN translation task, in terms of the training data and testing data,

- we use LDC corpora to train the general domain Transformer, which consists of 1.25 Million segments;[*] Most sentences in this corpus come from the News domain.

- for the target domain data, we also use the Autodesk Post-Editing corpus. 159,816 sentences are extracted as the training set for PMI and constraint extraction. An additional 1,000 sentences are extracted as the test set for our constrained Transformer experiment. The maximum length for PMI constraint extraction is set to 5-grams.

All English and German sentences are preprocessed using tools from Moses (Koehn et al., 2007). Chinese sentences are segmented into words using *Jieba*,[†] a popular Python toolkit for Chinese word segmentation. Finally, the parallel pre-processed data are segmented to subwords by applying *Byte Pair Encoding* (Sennrich et al., 2016b), which is capable of encoding open vocabularies with a compact symbol vocabulary of variable-length subword units.

4.3 Systems

We use the Transformer model in the open source toolkit **THUMT** as our baseline system (Zhang et al., 2017).[‡] For the constrained Transformer model, we first reimplement the GBS method under Transformer model, which we call **GBS-T**, and we then apply our HGBS algorithm to **GBS-T** to improve its decoding speed, which we call **HGBS-T**. The evaluation metrics are case-insensitive BLEU and METEOR.

In all our experiments, we employ the base Transformer configuration with embedding size and hidden size both 512, 6 encoder and decoder layers, 8 attention heads, the standard ReLu activation function and sinusoidal positional embedding, maximum sentence length 80, batch size 4096 tokens, beam size 10. The vocabulary sizes in EN-DE are 80,711 for English and 88,990 for German. The vocabulary sizes in ZH-EN are 30,568 for Chinese and 24,585 for English. The maximum number of constraints in a sentence is 6, and the alignment threshold p_{th} is set to 0.1.[§]

4.4 Results

Table 2 shows the results of three Transformer systems in terms BLEU and METEOR score on two translation tasks. From Table 2 we can see that:

---

[*]The segments are extracted from LDC2003E07, LDC2003E14, LDC2004T07, LDC2005E83, LDC2005T06, LDC2006E24, LDC2006E34, LDC2006E85, LDC2006E92, LDC2007E87, LDC2007E101, LDC2007T09, LDC2008E40, LDC2008E56, LDC2009E16 and LDC2009E95.

[†]`https://github.com/fxsjy/jieba`

[‡]`https://github.com/thumt/THUMT`

[§]Our implementation of GBS-T and HGBS-T is available at `https://github.com/gdxie1/THUMT-GBS.git`

System	EN-DE		ZH-EN	
	BLEU	METEOR	BLEU	METEOR
Baseline	34.82	0.29	5.94	0.12
GBS-T	37.92*	0.33*	11.38*	0.23*
HGBS-T	37.13*	0.33*	11.43*	0.22*

Table 2: Comparison of three Transformer systems. $*$ indicates a significantly better result compared to the Baseline.

- GBS-T significantly outperforms the baseline on the EN-DE task by absolute 3.10 (8.9%) points and 0.04 (13.8%) points in terms of BLEU and METEOR score, respectively, and on the ZH-EN task by absolute 5.44 points and 0.11 points in terms of BLEU and METEOR score. The low Baseline score on ZH-EN confirms that the domain of the Autodesk data is significantly different from that of the LDC data. This big improvement also shows that using constrained decoding for domain adaptation via constraints is a feasible solution for the scenario of low-resource domain translation.

- HGBS underperforms GBS-T by absolute 0.79 points on EN-DE in terms of BLEU score. However, we can see that it has the same METEOR score as GBS-T. HGBS-T significantly outperforms the Baseline on EN-DE in terms of BLEU and METEOR as well, and it has a comparable performance with GBS-T.

- For ZH-EN, HGBS-T is slightly better than GBS-T in terms of BLEU, and has almost the same result as GBS-T in terms of METEOR.

From the above observations, we can conclude that (1) our HGBS-T model has a comparable translation performance to GBS-T in terms of BLEU and METEOR score; (2) our constrained Transformer model is effective for domain adaptation, especially when the domains of the training data and testing data are significantly different.

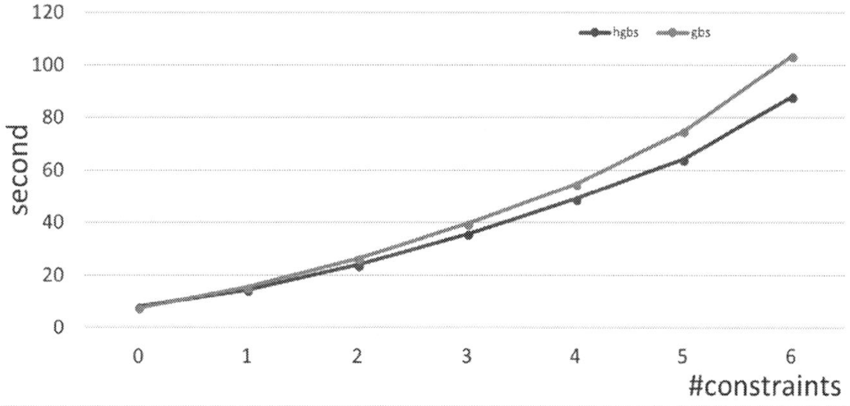

Figure 2: Comparison of decoding time consumption (seconds/constraints)

Figure 2 compares speed as a function of the number of constraints for the EN-DE task. We divide the sentences into different groups where each sentence in the same group contains the same number of constraints, and then we average decoding time over all sentences in the same group. The numbers on the vertical axis represent the average decoding time, i.e. seconds per sentence.

We can see that by using source information to prune hypotheses in the GBS, our HGBS has significantly decreased decoding time, especially when a sentence contains more than 3 constraints. In our experiments, we observed that the averaged hypotheses of each sentence in GBS-T is 4,887, while our HGBS-T has 3560, so about 30% paths are removed, as shown in Figure 3, where we can see that there is a significant decrease in the number of hypotheses in the beam that need to be expanded. As a result, in this figure, when constraints are up to 6, the average saving in decoding time can up to 20% compared to GBS.

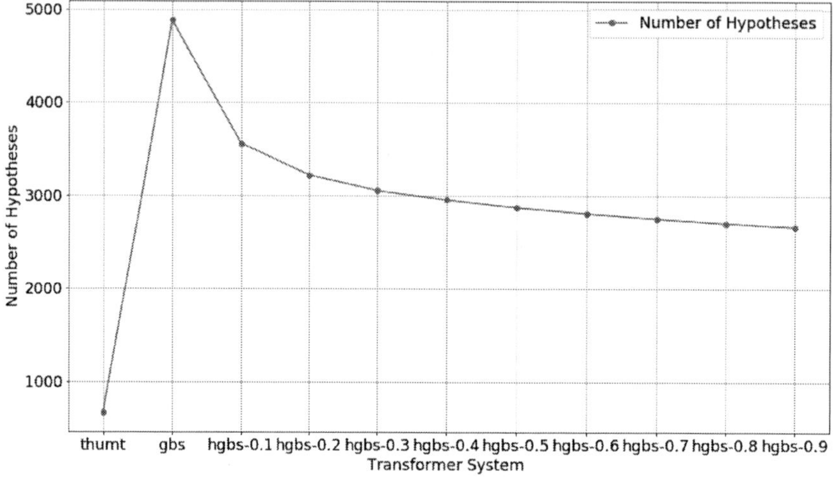

Figure 3: Comparison of number of hypotheses expanded in the decoding

4.5 Analysis

From the above experimental results, we can see that it is feasible to use the multi-head attention-guided source information for GBS in Transformer to save decoding time while maintaining comparable translation performance. To obtain this result, we carried out some experiments to look into the multi-head attention mechanism and layers of Transformer to optimise and determine some key hyper-parameters, such as the threshold p_{th}, averaging weights of the multi-head attention of the last layer to provide alignment information. In this section, we describe these experiments and provide an analysis of the results obtained.

4.5.1 Effects of Attention on Different Thresholds

Table 3 shows how the performance of HGBS changes with different settings for the alignment threshold p_{th} on the EN-DE task. The BLEU scores for HGBS-T are based on applying different thresholds p_{th} on the same test set in our experimental setting.

From Table 3, we can see that:

- our **HGBS-T** model achieves similar performance to **GBS-T** when p_{th} is set to small values. It can be seen that with the increase in threshold, translation quality decreases

Baseline	34.82								
GBS-T	**37.92**								
HGBS-T	**37.13**	36.40	36.16	35.64	35.11	34.65	34.92	35.11	35.45
Threshold p_{th}	0.1	0.2	0.3	0.4	0.5	0.6	0.7	0.8	0.9

Table 3: Performance changes with different thresholds at Layer 5

significantly. When $p_{th} = 0.6$, **HGBS-T** drops to almost the same performance as the baseline.

- based on the above observations, we set $p_{th} = 0.1$ in **HGBS-T** for all our experiments.

4.5.2 How Word Alignment Quality Affects BLEU Score

In our HGBS method, the placement of a constraint is guided by the multi-head attention information. Therefore, we infer that the quality of word alignment between the target and source is closely correlated with translation quality, i.e. a better quality word alignment will produce a higher quality of translations. In this section, we look into this issue by evaluating the word alignment of multi-head attention mechanism and measuring their correlations.

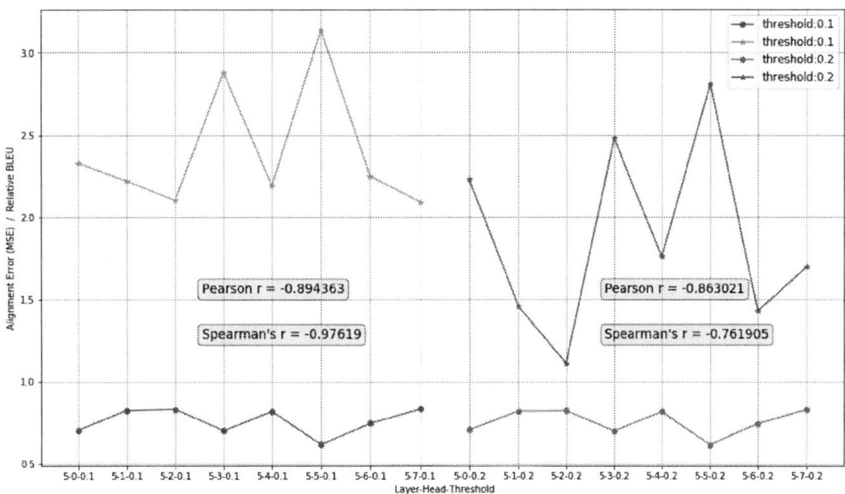

Figure 4: Correlations of the alignment error and BLEU score

To evaluate the quality of the word alignment from the multi-head attention, we use the word alignment links generated from FastAlign (Dyer et al., 2013) as the "Ground Truth". Since the word alignment from the multi-head attention is a probability distribution of the time step t in the decoder against all source words, we use Mean Square Error (MSE) as the metric to evaluate the alignment quality as in Equation (1):

$$E_{mse}(A, \alpha) = \frac{1}{T} \sum_{t=1}^{T} \sum_{i=1}^{I_t} (A_{ti} - \alpha_{ti})^2 \tag{1}$$

where A is the alignment from FastAlign, α is the alignment from the multi-head attention. T is the total time steps for the target sequence, and I_t is the number of alignment links of time step t against the source words. The alignment model of FastAlign is trained with the same EN-DE training corpus as in Section 4.2. Table 4 shows the relationship between the alignment error E_{mse} and the BLEU score with different thresholds for heads at Layer 5. "Relative BLEU" indicates that we scale the values of the column "BLEU" by subtracting an offset of 34 so that we can plot all curves in one figure in order to compare their trends. In Figure 4, the top-left curve shows the changes of relative BLEU against the changes of alignment error (bottom-left) at each head of Layer 5 when the threshold is set to 0.1. The top-right curve shows the changes of relative BLEU against the changes of alignment error (bottom-right) at each head of Layer 5 when the threshold is set to 0.2.

Layer	Head	Threshold	Alignment Error E_{mse}	BLEU	Relative BLEU
5	0	0.1	0.707	36.33	2.33
5	1	0.1	0.825	36.22	2.22
5	2	0.1	0.832	36.10	2.10
5	3	0.1	0.704	36.88	2.88
5	4	0.1	0.819	36.19	2.19
5	5	0.1	0.618	37.14	3.14
5	6	0.1	0.748	36.25	2.25
5	7	0.1	0.833	36.09	2.09
5	0	0.2	0.708	36.23	2.23
5	1	0.2	0.821	35.46	1.46
5	2	0.2	0.822	35.11	1.11
5	3	0.2	0.700	36.48	2.48
5	4	0.2	0.815	35.76	1.76
5	5	0.2	0.616	36.81	2.81
5	6	0.2	0.745	35.43	1.43
5	7	0.2	0.830	35.70	1.70

Table 4: Alignment Error and BLEU score of different heads at Layer 5 of Transformer model

We can see that for "threshold:0.1" and "threshold:0.2", the *Pearson* coefficients are -0.89 and -0.86, respectively, and the *Spearman's* coefficients are -0.98 and -0.76, respectively, which show that the BLEU score of the translations has high negative linear and monotonic correlations with the alignment errors, i.e. if the quality of word alignment is better, the translation quality is better. From this observation and analysis, regarding the proposed HGBS method, the hypothesis will be that if we can improve the quality of word alignment of multi-head attention mechanism, we would further improve translation quality and better guide the placement of constraints during the decoding to further improve translation quality.

5 Refining the model with alignmental guiding training

In order to verify the effect of alignment (or attention) on our HGBS method, we refined the Transformer model using Guided Alignment Training (Chen et al., 2016). Currently the general Transformer model normally uses 6 layers and 8 heads in each layer. We average all the attention of the 6 layers and 8 heads as a whole attention value, as the A_{ti} in Equation (1). Similar to Chen et al. (2016), we combine decoder cost and alignment cost to build the new loss function

$H(y, x, A, \alpha)$ in Equation (2):

$$H(y, x, A, \alpha) = H_D(y, x) + \omega E_{mse}(A, \alpha) \tag{2}$$

Here $H_D(y, x)$ is the normal decoder cost of the Transformer model, and ω is the weights for E_{mse}. In our experiments, we set ω as 0.05 and obtain the best performance. Our refining process is as follows: first we train a normal Transformer NMT model. Then we use $H(y, x, A, \alpha)$ as our model loss function to continue to train the model beginning from the best checkpoint. During training, all the parameters will be updated so the model will gradually output better multi-head alignment attentions. After about 200,000 more iterations, we obtain a new model refined from the alignment information. We perform this experiments in the previous section again and obtain the results shown in Table 5. We insert the previous result in the the table for convenience. From that table, we can see that the refined baseline system's performance is even

System	BLEU of EN-DE	
	not refined	refined
Baseline	34.82	34.85
GBS-T	37.92	38.16*
HGBS-T	37.13	38.12*

Table 5: Comparison of three Transformer systems after refining training. $*$ indicates a better result compared to the unrefined system.

better than the original baseline system. When we apply the GBS method and HGBS method on the refined baseline model, both produce higher BLEU scores. The GBS method obtains 0.24 increment and HGBS obtains 0.99 increment. Comparing with the refined baseline, the GBS obtains 3.31 increment and HGBS almost achieves the same performance as GBS. However on the unrefined system, HGBS obtains a lower score of 37.13 than the GBS's 37.92.

6 Conclusions and Future Work

In this paper, we first reimplement and investigate the grid beam search (GBS) method based on the Transformer model, and then propose heuristic GBS – a source-informed heuristic method guided by the multi-head attention mechanism – to speed up decoding while maintaining comparable translation performance. We compare our proposed method with unconstrained Transformer and GBS Transformer via a range of experiments on domain adaptation translation tasks, and demonstrate that our model significantly outperforms the basic Transformer model in terms of BLEU and METEOR, and at the same time significantly prunes up to 30% hypotheses and saves up to 20% decoding time with comparable results. Experimental results also show that our method is more practical for application to the scenario of low-resource domain adaptation translation compared with GBS.

In future work, we will further optimise the proposed HGBS method in terms of translation quality, decoding time and reducing the complexity by better exploiting the multi-head alignment information.

Acknowledgments

We wish to thank our erstwhile colleagues Qun Liu and Liangyou Li of Huawei Noah's Ark Lab for discussions which impacted the design of the algorithm presented in Section 3.1. We would also like to thank the three anonymous reviewers for their useful comments. This work is supported by the ADAPT Centre for Digital Content Technology which is funded under the

Science Foundation Ireland (SFI) Research Centres Programme (Grant No. 13/RC/2106) and is co-funded under the European Regional Development Fund.

References

Anderson, P., Fernando, B., Johnson, M., and Gould, S. (2017). Guided open vocabulary image captioning with constrained beam search. In *Proceedings of the 2017 Conference on Empirical Methods in Natural Language Processing*, pages 936–945, Copenhagen, Denmark.

Chatterjee, R., Negri, M., Turchi, M., Federico, M., Specia, L., and Blain, F. (2017). Guiding neural machine translation decoding with external knowledge. In *Proceedings of the Second Conference on Machine Translation*, pages 157–168, Copenhagen, Denmark.

Chen, W., Matusov, E., Khadivi, S., and Peter, J.-T. (2016). Guided alignment training for topic-aware neural machine translation. *arXiv preprint: 1607.01628*.

Denkowski, M. and Lavie, A. (2014). Meteor universal: Language specific translation evaluation for any target language. In *Proceedings of the EACL 2014 Workshop on Statistical Machine Translation*, page 376–380, Baltimore, Maryland, USA.

Dyer, C., Chahuneau, V., and Smith, N. A. (2013). A simple, fast, and effective reparameterization of ibm model 2. In *Proceedings of the 2013 Conference of the North American Chapter of the Association for Computational Linguistics: Human Language Technologies*, pages 644–648, Atlanta, Georgia.

Gehring, J., Auli, M., Grangier, D., and Dauphin, Y. (2017). A convolutional encoder model for neural machine translation. In *Proceedings of the 55th Annual Meeting of the Association for Computational Linguistics (Volume 1: Long Papers)*, pages 123–135, Vancouver, Canada.

Hokamp, C. and Liu, Q. (2017). Lexically constrained decoding for sequence generation using grid beam search. In *Proceedings of the 55th Annual Meeting of the Association for Computational Linguistics (Volume 1: Long Papers)*, pages 1535–1546, Vancouver, Canada.

Koehn, P. (2005). Europarl: a parallel corpus for statistical machine translation. In *MT Summit X, Conference Proceedings: the Tenth Machine Translation Summit*, pages 79–86, Phuket, Thailand.

Koehn, P., Hoang, H., Birch, A., Callison-Burch, C., Federico, M., Bertoldi, N., Cowan, B., Shen, W., Moran, C., Zens, R., Dyer, C., Bojar, O., Constantin, A., and Herbst, E. (2007). Moses: Open source toolkit for statistical machine translation. In *Proceedings of the 45th Annual Meeting of the ACL on Interactive Poster and Demonstration Sessions*, ACL '07, pages 177–180, Prague, Czech Republic.

Lowerre, B. T. (1976). *The Harpy Speech Recognition System*. PhD thesis, Carnegie-Mellon University, Pittsburgh PA.

Luong, M.-T. and Manning, C. D. (2015). Stanford neural machine translation systems for spoken language domains. In *Proceedings of the 12th International Workshop on Spoken Language Translation)*, pages 76–79, Da Nang, Vietnam.

Luong, M.-T., Pham, H., and Manning, C. D. (2015). Effective approaches to attention-based neural machine translation. In *Proceedings of the 2015 Conference on Empirical Methods in Natural Language Processing*, pages 1412–1421, Lisbon, Portugal.

Papineni, K., Roukos, S., Ward, T., and Zhu, W.-J. (2002). Bleu: a method for automatic evaluation of machine translation. In *Proceedings of the 40th Annual Meeting of the Association for Computational Linguistics*, pages 311–318, Philadelphia, Pennsylvania, USA.

Post, M. and Vilar, D. (2018). Fast lexically constrained decoding with dynamic beam allocation for neural machine translation. In *Proceedings of the 2018 Conference of the North American Chapter of the Association for Computational Linguistics: Human Language Technologies, Volume 1 (Long Papers)*, pages 1314–1324, New Orleans, Louisiana.

Sennrich, R., Haddow, B., and Birch, A. (2016a). Improving neural machine translation models with monolingual data. In *Proceedings of the 54th Annual Meeting of the Association for Computational Linguistics (Volume 1: Long Papers)*, pages 86–96, Berlin, Germany.

Sennrich, R., Haddow, B., and Birch, A. (2016b). Neural machine translation of rare words with subword units. In *Proceedings of the 54th Annual Meeting of the Association for Computational Linguistics (Volume 1: Long Papers)*, pages 1715–1725, Berlin, Germany.

Smith, J. R., Saint-Amand, H., Plamada, M., Koehn, P., Callison-Burch, C., and Lopez, A. (2013). Dirt cheap web-scale parallel text from the common crawl. In *Proceedings of the 51st Annual Meeting of the Association for Computational Linguistics (Volume 1: Long Papers)*, pages 1374–1383, Sofia, Bulgaria.

Sutskever, I., Vinyals, O., and Le, Q. V. (2014). Sequence to sequence learning with neural networks. In *Advances in Neural Information Processing Systems 27*, pages 3104–3112, Montreal, Canada.

Vaswani, A., Shazeer, N., Parmar, N., Uszkoreit, J., Jones, L., Gomez, A. N., Kaiser, L. u., and Polosukhin, I. (2017). Attention is all you need. In *Advances in Neural Information Processing Systems 30*, pages 5998–6008, Long Beach, CA, USA.

Wang, L., Tu, Z., Way, A., and Liu, Q. (2017). Exploiting cross-sentence context for neural machine translation. In *Proceedings of the 2017 Conference on Empirical Methods in Natural Language Processing*, pages 2826–2831, Copenhagen, Denmark.

Zhang, J., Ding, Y., Shen, S., Cheng, Y., Sun, M., Luan, H., and Liu, Y. (2017). Thumt: An open source toolkit for neural machine translation. *arXiv preprint: 1706.06415*.

Zhechev, V. (2012). Machine translation infrastructure and post-editing performance at Autodesk. In *AMTA 2012 Workshop on Post-Editing Technology and Practice (WPTP 2012)*, pages 87–96, San Diego, USA.

Machine Translation System Selection
from Bandit Feedback

Jason Naradowsky
Preferred Networks, Tokyo, Japan

narad@preferred.jp

Xuan Zhang
Kevin Duh
Johns Hopkins University, Baltimore, USA

xuanzhang@jhu.edu
kevinduh@cs.jhu.edu

Abstract

Adapting machine translation systems in the real world is a difficult problem. In contrast to offline training, users cannot provide the type of fine-grained feedback (such as correct translations) typically used for improving the system. Moreover, different users have different translation needs, and even a single user's needs may change over time.

In this work we take a different approach, treating the problem of adaptation as one of selection. Instead of adapting a single system, we train many translation systems using different architectures, datasets, and optimization methods. Using bandit learning techniques on simulated user feedback, we learn a policy to choose which system to use for a particular translation task. We show that our approach can (1) quickly adapt to address domain changes in translation tasks, (2) outperform the single best system in mixed-domain translation tasks, and (3) make effective instance-specific decisions when using contextual bandit strategies.

1 Introduction

Recent advances in machine translation have greatly improved translation quality on in-domain data (Vaswani et al., 2017). But choosing the best system to deploy for a given translation task can be difficult, as many different systems could be considered approximately state-of-the-art, and there is not a single system which is best for all situations. For instance, while neural machine translation (NMT) traditionally excels in big data scenarios, when data is scarce it is not uncommon for a statistical phrased-based translation (SMT) to be the better choice. Even different hyperparameter settings of the same model may yield systems which each excel at different translations tasks.

In this work we explore the practical question of how best to deploy and improve an MT service over time. One solution to this problem is adaptation, where the model continues to train in an online manner during deployment, and the model parameters are updated in response to new types of data. However, adapting a system in this manner has the potential to cause catastrophic forgetting (Kirkpatrick et al., 2016): the model parameters shift too much, and performance on the original translation task declines.

A second practical concern is that for translation services deployed in the real world, the degree of feedback is often limited. Users of Google Translate can rate the quality of a translation as "helpful" or "wrong", and Facebook users can use an ordinal scale from 1 to 5, but neither can realistically ask a user to provide a reference translation. Furthermore, the user provides feedback only a single time per translation, and multiple users are unlikely to ask for

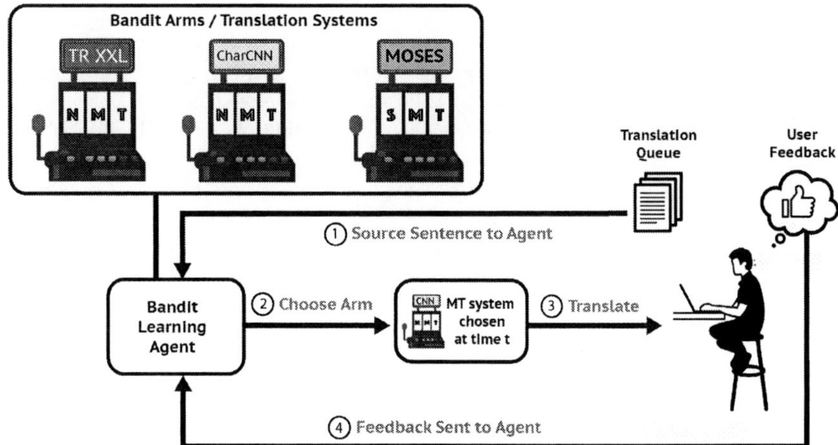

Figure 1: Basic setup: Bandit Learning Agent selects the MT system to use at time t. Based on user feedback (e.g. thumbs up/down or other signals), the bandit learning agent adapts to the stream of successive source sentences. The goal is to adapt quickly from limited user feedback.

translations of the same text. To what extent can we leverage such feedback to quickly adapt our system to the user's translation needs?

Here we turn to *bandit learning*, a class of strategies for learning a decision policy in an online setting from such limited feedback. We assume access to a number of pre-trained machine translation systems, which vary in terms of architecture, training data, and optimization method. The policy must then determine which translation system to use for a given source sentence. In contrast to adaptation, the parameters of each translation system are fixed, preventing the possibility of catastrophic forgetting.

The bandit learning setup is illustrated in Figure 1. We assume no prior knowledge of the domain(s) of sentences that the user wants to translate. Source sentences are fed to the system in sequence, and at each time step the bandit learning agent chooses one pre-built MT system to generate translations. The user provides simple feedback for each translation (such as a thumbs up/down), and the goal of the agent is to converge to the best MT system as quickly as possible.

We compare several bandit methods across three data domains (and mixtures of these domains), and find that:

- Even simple bandit algorithms can quickly adapt to new domains, and converge to choosing optimal/near-optimal systems after a few hundred examples.

- For the case of contextual bandits, where we can condition on a particular source sentence when making a decision, simple features derived from sentence length, vocabulary, and BERT, are effective. In comparison to an oracle which chooses the single best arm for a given test set, our contextual system can vastly outperform it on mixed-domain settings.

- The methods are robust to different forms of simulated human feedback proposed in the machine translation literature.

We present bandit-based translation system selection as a viable alternative to deploying or adapting a single MT system.

2 Bandit Learning

We now provide a brief overview of bandit algorithms. Borrowing terminology from casino slot-machines, which are sometimes referred to as "one-armed bandits", a bandit problem presents the gambler with a choice: given a bandit with multiple arms, which should be pulled to maximize overall earnings? Assume that each arm has its own payoff distribution. Even though this distribution is not observed, the gambler may start preferring a particular arm over time, associating it with higher reward than others.

Formally, let there be a K-arm bandit, where each arm corresponds to an action. At each timestep t, an agent must choose an action k, corresponding to selecting an arm $1 \leq k \leq K$. Each arm k is associated with a reward r_k^t, where higher values are desired. The agent's goal is to minimize cumulative regret (the amount of reward lost by making suboptimal decisions) over the course of T timesteps:

$$Regret = \sum_t^T (\max_{k' \in K} r_{k'}^t) - r_\pi^t \tag{1}$$

where r_π^t denotes the reward of the arm chosen by the agent's policy, π. Note the agent does not necessarily minimize regret in the sense that it is an objective function to optimize. It does not have access to the oracle action nor the value $(\max_{k'} r_{k'}^t)$; instead, the agent receives information only on the arm it chooses (r_π^t). Intuitively, one can imagine that the agent needs to try different actions in order build up a profile of rewards for each arm.

Thus a K-arm bandit is a classic exploration vs. exploitation problem. Exploring new or infrequent actions improves our understanding of their effects, and may lead us to discover better strategies. However, doing so comes at the cost of not exploiting the actions we currently believe to be the best. There are many established algorithms for solving bandit problems, each approaching this trade-off in a different way. We introduce some of these methods later in Section 4.3, before applying them to the practical problem of simulated human-in-the-loop translation system selection.

3 Translation Bandits

We now define online translation system selection as a bandit learning problem. In our formulation, each arm is a translation system, i.e., pulling a bandit arm is equivalent to selecting a pre-trained translation system and applying it to a given source sentence. Learning takes place across a series of rounds, and our goal is to continually adapt the choice of translation system to changing user needs (represented by the source domain), thereby maximizing user satisfaction.

We assume that the source sentences that need to be translated are in a queue, and we process them in sequential order. The bandit selection process (at time t) is as follows:

1. Observe a source sentence s^t

2. (Optionally) Compute features $\phi(s^t)$

3. Choose a MT system $k^t = \pi(s^t)$ and generate a translation $g^t = k^t(s^t)$ for the user

4. The user gives feedback in the form of a reward r_π^t based on the quality of the translation. This can be, for example, a thumbs up/down rating. In our *simulation* experiments, we compute reward as $e^t = SentenceBLEU(s^t, g^t)$ based on reference translation g^t and perturb it to approximate coarse, noisy human feedback.[1]

---

[1] We compute sentence-level BLEU because rewards are defined per example for standard bandits. Nevertheless, our final evaluation is in terms of corpus-level BLEU. Note that we use perturbed SentenceBLEU only as a way to simulate human feedback; we do not assume sentence-level feedback to be consistent with corpus-level metrics.

5. Update selection policy π

Contextual Bandits   One of the major distinctions between classes of bandit algorithms is whether the policy can condition its decision on a time-specific observation. Methods which do are referred to as *contextual bandits*, and are able to make more nuanced, instance-specific decisions. In other words, whereas simple bandits attempt to learn which arm is best, contextual bandits also learn *when* it is best. However, this necessitates computing a feature representation from the source sentence (Step 2).

Simulated Feedback   In a real world deployment, user satisfaction is obtained directly from the user, but for the purpose of conducting this study in a tractable and repeatable manner, we simulate the human-in-the-loop. In this simulated setting we have access to reference translations, and can compute the true SentenceBLEU score (Step 4). However, using such a metric would not be a realistic approximation of real user feedback. Previous work (Nguyen et al., 2017) identified several ways in which human judgements may differ from more traditional continuous MT evaluation metrics:

- (1) *granularity* (thumbs-up vs. thumbs-down, or scoring on a 1-5 scale)

- (2) *variance* (different users may rate the same output differently)

- (3) *skew* (a user might be a harsher critic in general, and be prone to giving lower scores on average than other users)

In the experiments, we simulate use feedback by transforming raw SentenceBLEU scores into lower *granularity* bins on a 1-5 rating scale (Step 4). In Section 5.3 we further assess the effect of different simulated feedback to bandit learning.

4   Experiments

We aim to study the effectiveness of bandit algorithms on the task of MT system selection, across a variety of domains (and domain mixtures). Here we introduce the MT systems, the datasets used to train them, and the bandit algorithms used to learn the system selection policy.

4.1   Datasets

Our experiment data consists of three different tasks, translating from German to English:

1. The **General-Domain** task includes data from a range of domains, and is meant to be reflective of the kind of data used in public deployed systems. Specifically, we include Open-Subtitles2018 (Lison and Tiedemann, 2016) and WMT 2017 (Bojar et al., 2017), which contains data from e.g. parliamentary proceedings (Europarl, UN), political/economic news, and web-crawled parallel corpus (Common Crawl). After filtering out long sentences ($>$80 tokens), we obtain a training set of 28 million sentence pairs.

2. The **TED** task focuses on translating captions from TED Talks, which contains specialized vocabulary in various professional fields (e.g. technology, entertainment, design) in the form of monologue speeches. We use the WIT3 data distribution (Cettolo et al., 2012) with the train/dev/test splits provided by Duh (2018).

3. The **WIPO** task focuses on patent translation, which contains even more specialized jargon, written in a formal style. We use the COPPA V2.0 distribution (Junczys-Dowmunt et al., 2016). We held out 3000 random sentences each for dev and test, leaving 821 thousand sentences as training data.

	GENERAL		TED		WIPO		ALL	
	BLEU↑	TER↓	BLEU↑	TER↓	BLEU↑	TER↓	BLEU↑	TER↓
nmt-general	**29.4**	**50.5**	34.2	42.6	36.0	49.3	33.9	48.7
smt-general	23.9	54.9	30.7	45.8	26.7	56.9	26.5	53.8
smt-ted	16.5	62.3	28.7	47.9	12.0	69.5	15.6	61.6
nmt-ted	16.5	67.3	31.5	46.3	8.4	90.1	14.0	69.8
nmt-cont-ted	27.5	53.0	**39.3**	**38.2**	29.5	61.5	30.2	52.6
smt-wipo	9.9	79.3	9.7	77.5	51.2	36.0	35.2	66.6
nmt-wipo	6.6	101.2	7.7	92.1	61.9	25.4	39.0	77.8
nmt-cont-wipo	8.0	99.4	10.0	88.3	**62.3**	**25.0**	39.6	76.0

Table 1: Overview of translation performance (DE → EN) for the eight systems which constitute the arms of the bandit. Three architectures (nmt, nmt-cont, and smt) are trained and evaluated across three different domains. Typically NMT with continued training (nmt-cont) is the highest performing system on in-domain data, but other systems offer more consistent performance.

4.2 MT Systems

The training and development data described above are used to build machine translation systems. Bandit experiments are run on the test data, which has 1982, 3000, and 5504 sentences for the TED, WIPO, and General tasks respectively. All data is tokenized by the Moses tokenizer (Koehn et al., 2007), then split into subwords by BPE (Sennrich et al., 2016) independently with 30k merge operations for the English and German sides.

Neural machine translation Models are built with Sockeye (Hieber et al., 2017), using common settings for LSTM seq2seq models (Bahdanau et al., 2015): 2 layer encoder, 2 layer decoder, 512 hidden nodes, 512 word embedding sizes.

Statistical machine translation Models are built with Joshua (Post et al., 2013). This represents a strong phrase-based SMT model with GIZA++ alignments, 4-gram language model, and MIRA-based discriminative tuning.

Systems For each task, we train SMT and NMT models from scratch using only the training data in the respective domains, resulting in 6 models: {nmt,smt}-{general,ted,wipo}. Additionally we include two improved NMT models for WIPO and TED (nmt-cont-{ted,wipo}), which starts with nmt-general as initializaton and fine-tunes on WIPO or TED training data. This continued training process usually achieves strong translation performance in the target domain, but shows increased risk of catastrophic forgetting in the original general domain task (Luong and Manning, 2015; Thompson et al., 2019). This brings the total number of systems (also the number of bandit arms, K) to 8. The baseline performance of each system on the test sets in each domain is shown in Table 1.

Metrics The bandit learning agents are updated on-the-fly on the aforementioned test sets, using perturbed/granularized sentence-level BLEU as feedback. However, for final evaluation we collect all the resulting translations and compute corpus-level BLEU (Papineni et al., 2002) (implemented via SacreBLEU (Post, 2018)) and TER (Snover et al., 2006). We experiment with different ways to mix the test sets to illustrate different scenarios for bandit learning. For error analysis, we computed regret as in Eq. 1.

	GENERAL			**TED**			**WIPO**			**AVG**		
	R↓	B↑	T↓	R↓	B↑	T↓	R↓	B↑	T↓	R↓	B↑	T↓
random	16.9	17.9	70.9	20.8	24.7	59.3	32.2	36.7	52.4	23.3	26.4	60.9
best-arm-oracle	5.9	29.4	50.5	6.2	39.3	38.2	4.5	62.3	25.0	5.5	43.7	37.9
oracle	2.2	31.6	49.9	1.8	42.1	37.2	2.3	61.7	24.1	2.1	45.1	37.0
epsilon-greedy	9.3	26.2	56.9	11.9	34.1	45.2	12.6	54.8	32.6	11.3	38.3	44.9
ucb	9.9	25.4	56.7	13.2	32.7	46.8	9.3	58.0	29.8	10.8	38.7	44.4
linucb	**7.5**	**28.0**	**52.6**	**9.7**	**36.5**	**42.2**	**5.3**	**61.7**	**25.7**	**7.5**	**42.1**	**40.2**

Table 2: Results on the in-domain test sets. Evaluation is measured in terms of average regret (R), BLEU (B), and TER (T). Lower scores are better for regret and TER; higher scores are better for BLEU.

4.3 Bandit Methods

We compare the three bandit methods:

- **Epsilon-Greedy** The agent either exploits the arm with highest average reward with probability $1 - \epsilon$, or chooses randomly (uniformly) with probability ϵ (Sutton and Barto, 1998). Intuitively, the agent maintains a running average of each arm's rewards; it greedily chooses the one with the highest reward, but occasionally tries a random arm in order to improve its estimate of the running average.

- **Upper Confidence Bound (UCB)** An ϵ-greedy strategy is prone to obvious pitfalls. For instance, if the optimal action performs poorly early on, it may take many iterations to correct the agent's behavior. Alternatively, the agent can avoid becoming over-confident in its action reward estimates by establishing an upper confidence bound on each. This encourages the model to explore actions which may have low empirical estimates of reward, if they have been tried infrequently. The particular UCB algorithm we use in this work is UCB1 (Auer et al., 2002).

- **Lin-UCB** Recall that in contextual bandits, the learner is presented with a feature vector, here derived from the source sentence. The agent may use these feature vectors, along with the rewards of arms played in the past, to make a more informed choice of which arm to play at the current time step. Over time, the aim of the learner is to collect enough information about how the context vectors and rewards relate to each other, so that it can predict the next best arm to play by looking at the feature vectors.

  LINUCB extends the principles of UCB to the contextual bandit scenario, using a linear model to predict the action (Li et al., 2010). We explore various features for this system (results in Sec. 5.4)

We also introduce three baseline systems: RANDOM, ORACLE, which always chooses the optimal translation system, and BEST-ARM-ORACLE, which chooses single best system (the one which has the highest BLEU across the entire test set).

5 Results

5.1 Overview: Comparison of Bandit Algorithms

We begin by assessing the relative strengths of bandit algorithms on the translation system selection task, and examine how closely performance on the regret-based objective function

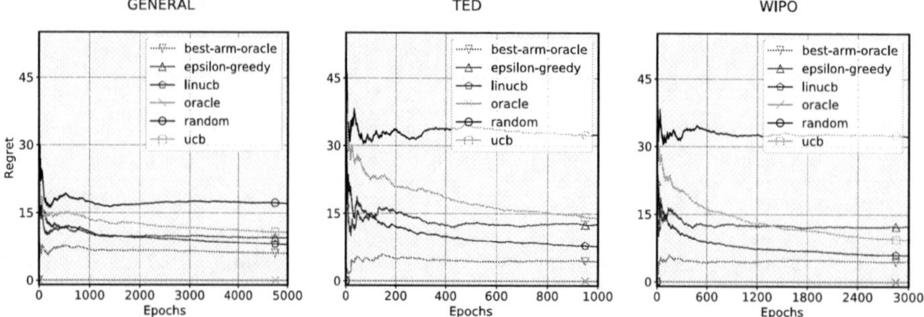

Figure 2: Comparison of cumulative regret in bandit algorithms across domains. The relative ordering of the algorithms is consistent across all three domains, with epsilon-greedy adapting early, before eventually being surpassed by linucb, which converges closer to the best-arm oracle. Note that cumulative regret lags behind changes in policy. Systems begin to find reasonable policies around epoch 50, marked by the sharp negative trajectory in cumulative regret.

corresponds to changes in translation evaluation measures like BLEU and TER. In these experiments we run each algorithm on the full test data for each of the three domains. As shown in Table 1, the highest-performing system for each domain is always an in-domain variant of neural translation. In this setting a good algorithm should quickly learn which arms are trained on in-domain data, and to exploit these as much as possible.

Fig. 2 illustrates the overall performance of EPSILON-GREEDY, UCB, and LINUCB, with respect to two oracles and a random baseline. We find that EPSILON-GREEDY is the fastest to converge. As the ϵ parameter balances exploration and exploitation, this behavior is somewhat within our control. Our results are obtained with $\epsilon = 0.3$. Empirically we observe that performance is quite robust to changes in ϵ, and values in the range 0.2 to 0.4 result in negligible performance differences (comparable to changing the random seed). In comparison, UCB performance follows a promising trajectory, but takes many more rounds to converge. For the goal of tailoring translations based on user feedback, executing thousands of interactions is likely an exorbitant requirement.

Turning to LINUCB, the contextual bandit algorithm, note the large gap between ORACLE and BEST-ARM-ORACLE performance. This is representative of the potential for additional performance gains when using a contextual method, even the data comes from a single domain. Perhaps unsurprisingly then, we find that LINUCB typically outperforms other bandit algorithms in later epochs, often closely approximating the performance of the BEST-ARM-ORACLE. However, LINUCB also performs well in early epochs, and is often the best performing system after 100 epochs. Strong early performance means there may be little compromise to using a contextual approach like LINUCB, even in single domain translation tasks.

It is also worth pointing out the small discrepancy between the cumulative regret and BLEU. For instance, this is evident in the general domain results, where LINUCB has lower cumulative regret, but a lower BLEU score. While these two metrics are highly correlated in our experiments, there is a margin of disagreement and the ranking of systems can sometimes flip when comparing across these metrics.

5.2 Adapting to new Domains

A more realistic scenario may be a mixed-domain task, in which the user's translation needs are not fixed, but change over time. We simulate this scenario by mixing data from each of the

	R↓	B↑	T↓
random	24.6	31.4	46
best-arm-oracle	17.9	34.2	42
oracle	0.0	57.9	32
epsilon-greedy	20.5	34.4	43
ucb	22.8	33.8	44
linucb	**17.4**	**46.9**	**41**

Table 3: Performance on randomly shuffled data. All bandit systems are able to adapt to new domains quickly enough to achieve performance comparable to choosing the single best system, but the contextual bandit significantly outperforms it.

three domains in different ratios. The main question we want to ask is: can the bandit algorithms outperform the BEST-ARM-ORACLE system? Doing so would be represent a clear advantage over deploying any single system.

We present the performance of these systems in Table 3. The results show that as the data is increasingly mixed, the contextual bandit, LINUCB, significantly outperforms any single system. When data is completely shuffled, this amounts to a gain of more than 12 BLEU over the single best system, a relative improvement of over 37%. This is also true of simpler bandits, and EPSILON-GREEDY also outperforms the single-best system, but by a narrower margin.

Heatmaps of the algorithm decisions (Figure 3) provide some insight into the behavior of these systems. In fully randomized sequences, we observe that after 100-200 iterations of learning, LINUCB is able to closely mimic the behavior of the ORACLE system, ultimately converging to a similar distribution over decisions.[2] EPSILON-GREEDY converges to predominantly choosing the second-best arm as a safe bet, while UCB, which adjusts its policy more slowly, never exhibits clear decision trends.

Even in less mixed scenarios (3), top), results show that LINUCB is an effective system. As the domain changes between TED and WIPO, LINUCB closely tracks the ORACLE decisions, even within the first 50 iterations, making the system a promising option for real-world deployment.

5.3 Simulated Bandit Feedback

In order to ascertain how sensitive bandit translation system selection is to the nature of simulated feedback, we explore different types of of constructing feedback. Recall the ways in which human feedback may differ from continuous metrics as identified in Nguyen et al. (2017) are granularity, variance, and skew.

To simulate granular feedback, we bin SentenceBLEU scores into one of 5 equally-sized bins. For variance in the feedback score, we sample the score from a Gaussian (with a variance shrinking parameter of 1.0) that is updated after each evaluation. For skew, we simulate a harsher critic which biases the output towards scores in a lower range (a skew of 0.25).[3] For the sake of comparison we also include a scaling function, which simply scales the BLEU score into a suitable [0,1] loss range. This serves as an "oracle" of what performance we might expect if we were somehow able to ask users to provide a fine-grained score like BLEU.

Table 4 shows the effect of the four simulated feedback styles (GRANULAR, VARIANCE,

---

[2]From the ORACLE heat map, we see that all 8 arms/systems are chosen at some point; this shows that even though we may have prior knowledge that one system is generally better than another, it is still useful to include all systems if selection is performed at the sentence level.

[3]Experiments in the previous section used granular feedback method.

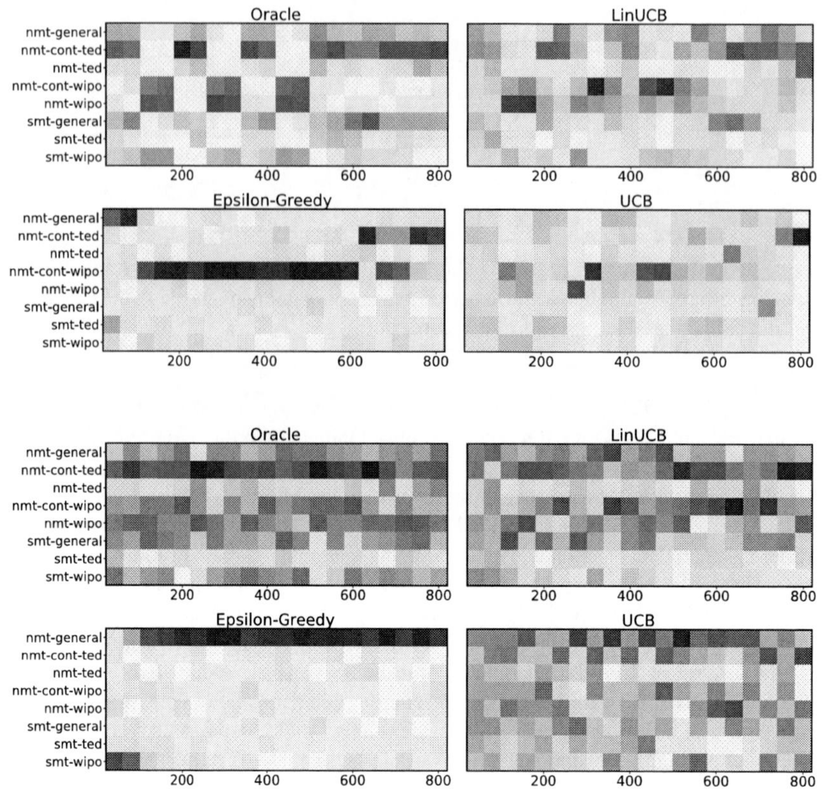

Figure 3: Decision heatmaps for shuffled data depicting the behavior of bandit algorithms across time. Each column of the heatmap represents the distribution over the choices made by the agent during that interval of training (red squares correspond to actions taken more frequently). In the top four plots we cycle the data domain every 100 examples. In the bottom four plots, the data is drawn randomly from each of the three domains. For clarity, we omit presenting heatmaps of the best-arm-oracle system, which is nmt-cont-ted in both scenarios.

SCALE, and SKEW) in a mixed data setting. We find that the nature of feedback has little overall effect on system performance. Altering the BLEU score to simulate SKEW was notably the most detrimental, but the remaining methods all performed similarly. Surprisingly we observe no significant difference between SCALE, which is essentially the full continuous BLEU metric, and other distortions to the feedback score.

5.4 Features for Contextual Bandits

Contextual bandit methods make use of feature vectors when choosing an action. In the context of translation, we can construct this vector from useful information in the source sentence. We experiment with three types of features:

- OOV, whether the source sentence contains a high proportion of out-of-vocabulary words.

- LEN, the length of the source sentence binned into five ranges of five (1-5, 6-10, ..., >25).[4]

---

[4]We use only the length feature for LINUCB in earlier in-domain experiments (Table 2).

	SCALE			VARIANCE			GRANULAR			SKEW		
	R↓	B↑	T↓	R↓	B↑	T↓	R↓	B↑	T↓	R↓	B↑	T↓
epsilon-greedy	19.3	35.0	42	21.6	37.5	44	19.0	37.3	42	19.7	33.1	43
ucb	13.3	50.1	38	13.3	50.7	38	13.1	50.2	38	12.3	51.0	38
linucb	14.1	48.9	39	13.5	48.9	39	13.6	48.5	39	15.6	45.2	40

Table 4: Effects of simulated feedback method on performance.

- BERT, features taken from a pre-trained language model (Devlin et al., 2019). Specifically, we ran the multilingual BERT base-size model out-of-the-box[5] in inference mode and extract the final layer of the transformer encoder. These embeddings are averaged across all tokens in the sentence. Since the evaluation datasets used in this study are small, on the order of thousands of examples, LINUCB has difficulty learning quickly when using large feature vectors. Therefore we take only the first 50 embedding dimensions as features.

A constant bias feature is used to establish a baseline. Table 5 shows the results. As evident by comparing against the BIAS feature results, all feature types provide useful information to the system selection task, though length and BERT features prove to be much more effective than vocabulary-based features.

	R↓	B↑	T↓
All	13.6	47.7	40
OOV	19.2	33.0	42
LEN	16.8	45.9	41
BERT	**13.3**	**48.1**	**40**
BIAS	19.0	31.8	42

Table 5: Ablation of contextual bandit features, on the randomly mixed-domain data.

6 Related Work

Multi-domain machine translation Our problem setting is closely related to multi-domain machine translation, where the data comes as a stream of sentences from a mixture of domains unknown to the model (Farajian et al., 2017; Huck et al., 2015). Typically using a single model, various extensions allow the system to cater more specifically to different types of source sentences. Such extensions may include data concatenation, model stacking, data selection and multi-model ensemble (Sajjad et al., 2017). One way is to pre-compute a domain label for each sentence using a dedicated classifier or model (Kobus et al., 2017; Tars and Fishel, 2018).

In neural models such adaptations can also be done in the learned representations. Britz et al. (2017) use a discriminator network on top of the encoder to distinguish between domains and pretend a domain token to the target sequence. Gu et al. (2019) employ a shared encoder-decoder and also private models to capture both domain-invariant and domain-specific knowledge, which are then combined to generate the target sequence. Such approaches can also be more nuanced, such as focusing on domain-specific words, and adjusting the training objective to emphasize their importance (Zeng et al., 2018).

---

[5] https://github.com/google-research/bert

A natural question is what advantage bandit system selection has over the alternative strategy of using of a domain classifier to determine which system to use. One advantage of bandit selection is that it provides a unifying framework for online learning all aspects of problem. If a domain classifier is useful, the classifier's predictions can be used as a feature in the bandit algorithm, and the extent to which that feature is useful (or useful together with other information) will also be learned. Otherwise, the domain classifier features themselves can be incorporated into a contextual bandit policy where they can be access directly.

A second consideration is that the domains encountered in deployment may not be so well-defined and aligned to the translation systems as they are in our experimental setup. Imagine a specialized domain that is not similar to the training domain of any system. In these cases, other attributes of the model, such as its architecture or optimization strategy, may become more important. This is a situation the bandit approach is well-suited for.

Bandits in NLP Due to the high cost of sourcing human annotations for NLP tasks, developing tractable training methods for learning from simple feedback has long been a desirable goal. Learning NLP tasks (machine translation, sequence labeling, text classification) from bandit feedback has been studied previously (Lawrence et al., 2017; Sokolov et al., 2016), and has been extended to train typical NLP architectures, such as neural sequence-to-sequence models (Kreutzer et al., 2017).

Bandits have also been applied previously in MT, even as the topic of a dedicated shared task (Sokolov et al., 2017). Within the context of bandit-driven MT, the focus has been on adapting an existing system, limited to simulated bandit feedback. Sokolov et al. (2016) used actual losses (BLEU) and pairwise ranking. Nguyen et al. (2017), also used bandit learning but to adapt a single neural MT system. Our approach is significantly different, in that it focuses on the use of a bandit-trained policy for selection, rather than adaptation or in-domain training.

7 Conclusion and Future Work

As MT systems become widely deployed, catering translation output to user needs, whether through adaptation or system selection, will become an increasingly important problem. In this work we showed that existing bandit algorithms are surprisingly effective at quickly adapting output to user needs, when the problem is phrased as one of selection. Contextual bandit system selection methods frequently outperform the use of a single translation system, establishing this technique as promising solution for dynamically adapting to user translation needs.

While we did not explore more recent bandit methods, including Bayesian bandits, or hierarchical bandits, intuitively such methods would be a good fit for a large scale version of this study. We assume arms are independent from one another, but they have dependencies both in terms of their architectures and in terms of their training data. One may also have prior knowledge of likely domains/arms, which can be incorporated in more advanced bandit methods.

We note that there are many kinds of deployment scenarios, depending on factors such as (a) the number of domains, (b) how much each domain drifts, and (c) whether feedback comes from a single user or multiple users. We have presented a proof-of-concept to show the potential effectiveness of bandits, but the exact scenarios where these methods are most appropriate still require more exploration. For example, the non-contextual bandit setup described here is appropriate for a computer-assisted translation application where one professional human translator post-edits sentences from long document translations. Here the number of post-edits can serves as implicit feedback, and bandit methods like Epsilon-Greedy are likely to converge in time (before the end of document) for the translator to start seeing benefits.[6] On the other hand,

---

[6] An interesting extension is to collect the resulting post-edited translations in order to adapt a personalized MT

the contextual bandit setup might be beneficial for an online MT service provider, where independent and unrelated translation requests may be interleaved. This can be viewed as another way to implement fast adaptation, but then one also needs to compare with the aforementioned multi-domain methods to decide the most suitable solution.

8 Acknowledgements

We thank the anonymous reviewers for their valuable comments. Artwork used in Fig.1 comes from TheNounProject[7], and the artists John Caserta, alifrio, and Herbert Spencer.

References

Auer, P., Cesa-Bianchi, N., and Fischer, P. (2002). Finite-time analysis of the multiarmed bandit problem. *Machine Learning*, 47(2-3):235–256.

Bahdanau, D., Cho, K., and Bengio, Y. (2015). Proceedings of the international conference on learning representations (iclr). In *Neural Machine Translation by Jointly Learning to Align and Translate*.

Bojar, O., Chatterjee, R., Federmann, C., Graham, Y., Haddow, B., Huang, S., Huck, M., Koehn, P., Liu, Q., Logacheva, V., Monz, C., Negri, M., Post, M., Rubino, R., Specia, L., and Turchi, M. (2017). Findings of the 2017 conference on machine translation (WMT17). In *Proceedings of the Second Conference on Machine Translation*, pages 169–214, Copenhagen, Denmark. Association for Computational Linguistics.

Britz, D., Le, Q., and Pryzant, R. (2017). Effective domain mixing for neural machine translation. In *Proceedings of the Second Conference on Machine Translation*, pages 118–126, Copenhagen, Denmark. Association for Computational Linguistics.

Cettolo, M., Girardi, C., and Federico, M. (2012). Wit^3: Web inventory of transcribed and translated talks. In *Proceedings of the 16th Conference of the European Association for Machine Translation (EAMT)*, pages 261–268, Trento, Italy.

Devlin, J., Chang, M.-W., Lee, K., and Toutanova, K. (2019). BERT: Pre-training of deep bidirectional transformers for language understanding. In *Proceedings of the 2019 Conference of the North American Chapter of the Association for Computational Linguistics: Human Language Technologies, Volume 1 (Long and Short Papers)*, pages 4171–4186, Minneapolis, Minnesota. Association for Computational Linguistics.

Duh, K. (2018). The multitarget ted talks task. http://www.cs.jhu.edu/~kevinduh/a/multitarget-tedtalks/.

Farajian, M. A., Turchi, M., Negri, M., and Federico, M. (2017). Multi-domain neural machine translation through unsupervised adaptation. In *Proceedings of the Second Conference on Machine Translation*, pages 127–137, Copenhagen, Denmark. Association for Computational Linguistics.

Gu, S., Feng, Y., and Liu, Q. (2019). Improving domain adaptation translation with domain invariant and specific information. In *Proceedings of the 2019 Conference of the North*

---

engine, which can then be one of many arms in the bandit, or to allow multiple human translators to share their translation memories.

[7] https://thenounproject.com/

American Chapter of the Association for Computational Linguistics: Human Language Technologies, Volume 1 (Long and Short Papers), pages 3081–3091, Minneapolis, Minnesota. Association for Computational Linguistics.

Hieber, F., Domhan, T., Denkowski, M., Vilar, D., Sokolov, A., Clifton, A., and Post, M. (2017). Sockeye: A toolkit for neural machine translation. *arXiv preprint arXiv:1712.05690*.

Huck, M., Birch, A., and Haddow, B. (2015). Mixed-domain vs. multi-domain statistical machine translation. In *MT Summit 2015*.

Junczys-Dowmunt, M., Pouliquen, B., and Mazenc, C. (2016). Coppa v2. 0: Corpus of parallel patent applications building large parallel corpora with gnu make. In *4th Workshop on Challenges in the Management of Large Corpora Workshop Programme*.

Kirkpatrick, J., Pascanu, R., Rabinowitz, N., Veness, J., Desjardins, G., Rusu, A. A., Milan, K., Quan, J., Ramalho, T., Grabska-Barwinska, A., Hassabis, D., Clopath, C., Kumaran, D., and Hadsell, R. (2016). Overcoming catastrophic forgetting in neural networks. cite arxiv:1612.00796.

Kobus, C., Crego, J., and Senellart, J. (2017). Domain control for neural machine translation. In *Proceedings of the International Conference Recent Advances in Natural Language Processing, RANLP 2017*, pages 372–378, Varna, Bulgaria. INCOMA Ltd.

Koehn, P., Hoang, H., Birch, A., Callison-Burch, C., Federico, M., Bertoldi, N., Cowan, B., Shen, W., Moran, C., Zens, R., et al. (2007). Moses: Open source toolkit for statistical machine translation. In *Proceedings of the 45th annual meeting of the ACL on interactive poster and demonstration sessions*.

Kreutzer, J., Sokolov, A., and Riezler, S. (2017). Bandit structured prediction for neural sequence-to-sequence learning. In *Proceedings of the 55th Annual Meeting of the Association for Computational Linguistics (Volume 1: Long Papers)*, pages 1503–1513. Association for Computational Linguistics.

Lawrence, C., Sokolov, A., and Riezler, S. (2017). Counterfactual learning from bandit feedback under deterministic logging : A case study in statistical machine translation. In *Proceedings of the 2017 Conference on Empirical Methods in Natural Language Processing, EMNLP 2017, Copenhagen, Denmark, September 9-11, 2017*, pages 2566–2576.

Li, L., Chu, W., Langford, J., and Schapire, R. E. (2010). A contextual-bandit approach to personalized news article recommendation. In *Proceedings of the 19th International Conference on World Wide Web*, WWW '10, pages 661–670, New York, NY, USA. ACM.

Lison, P. and Tiedemann, J. (2016). OpenSubtitles2016: Extracting large parallel corpora from movie and TV subtitles. In *Proceedings of the Tenth International Conference on Language Resources and Evaluation (LREC'16)*, pages 923–929, Portorož, Slovenia. European Language Resources Association (ELRA).

Luong, M.-T. and Manning, C. D. (2015). Stanford neural machine translation systems for spoken language domain. In *International Workshop on Spoken Language Translation*, Da Nang, Vietnam.

Nguyen, K., Daumé III, H., and Boyd-Graber, J. (2017). Reinforcement learning for bandit neural machine translation with simulated human feedback. In *Proceedings of the 2017 Conference on Empirical Methods in Natural Language Processing*, pages 1464–1474, Copenhagen, Denmark. Association for Computational Linguistics.

Papineni, K., Roukos, S., Ward, T., and Zhu, W.-J. (2002). BLEU: A method for automatic evaluation of machine translation. In *Association for Computational Linguistics*.

Post, M. (2018). A call for clarity in reporting BLEU scores. In *Proceedings of the Third Conference on Machine Translation: Research Papers*, pages 186–191, Belgium, Brussels. Association for Computational Linguistics.

Post, M., Ganitkevitch, J., Orland, L., Weese, J., Cao, Y., and Callison-Burch, C. (2013). Joshua 5.0: Sparser, better, faster, server. In *Proceedings of the Eighth Workshop on Statistical Machine Translation*, pages 206–212, Sofia, Bulgaria. Association for Computational Linguistics.

Sajjad, H., Durrani, N., Dalvi, F., Belinkov, Y., and Vogel, S. (2017). Neural machine translation training in a multi-domain scenario. In *Proceedings of the 14th International Workshop on Spoken Language Translation (IWSLT)*.

Sennrich, R., Haddow, B., and Birch, A. (2016). Neural Machine Translation of Rare Words with Subword Units. In *Proceedings of the 54th Annual Meeting of the Association for Computational Linguistics*, Berlin, Germany. Association for Computational Linguistics.

Snover, M., Dorr, B., Schwartz, R., Micciulla, L., and Makhoul, J. (2006). A study of translation edit rate with targeted human annotation. In *Conference of the Association for Machine Translation in the Americas (AMTA)*.

Sokolov, A., Kreutzer, J., Lo, C., and Riezler, S. (2016). Learning structured predictors from bandit feedback for interactive NLP. In *Proceedings of the 54th Annual Meeting of the Association for Computational Linguistics (Volume 1: Long Papers)*, pages 1610–1620, Berlin, Germany. Association for Computational Linguistics.

Sokolov, A., Kreutzer, J., Sunderland, K., Danchenko, P., Szymaniak, W., Fürstenau, H., and Riezler, S. (2017). A shared task on bandit learning for machine translation. In *Proceedings of the Second Conference on Machine Translation*, pages 514–524. Association for Computational Linguistics.

Sutton, R. S. and Barto, A. G. (1998). *Reinforcement Learning: An Introduction*. MIT Press, Cambridge, MA, USA.

Tars, S. and Fishel, M. (2018). Multi-domain neural machine translation. In *The 21st Annual Conference of the European Association for Machine Translation (EAMT)*, volume abs/1805.02282, Alacant, Spain.

Thompson, B., Gwinnup, J., Khayrallah, H., Duh, K., and Koehn, P. (2019). Overcoming catastrophic forgetting during domain adaptation of neural machine translation. In *Proceedings of the 2019 Conference of the North American Chapter of the Association for Computational Linguistics: Human Language Technologies, Volume 1 (Long and Short Papers)*, pages 2062–2068, Minneapolis, Minnesota. Association for Computational Linguistics.

Vaswani, A., Shazeer, N., Parmar, N., Uszkoreit, J., Jones, L., Gomez, A. N., Kaiser, L., and Polosukhin, I. (2017). Attention is all you need. In *Neural Information Processing Systems (NeurIPS)*.

Zeng, J., Su, J., Wen, H., Liu, Y., Xie, J., Yin, Y., and Zhao, J. (2018). Multi-domain neural machine translation with word-level domain context discrimination. In *Proceedings of the 2018 Conference on Empirical Methods in Natural Language Processing*, pages 447–457, Brussels, Belgium. Association for Computational Linguistics.

Generative latent neural models for automatic word alignment

Anh Khoa Ngo Ho

François Yvon

Université Paris-Saclay, CNRS, LIMSI

Bât. 508, rue John von Neumann, Campus Universitaire, F-91405 Orsay

anh-khoa.ngo-ho@limsi.fr

francois.yvon@limsi.fr

Abstract

Word alignments identify translational correspondences between words in a parallel sentence pair and are used, for instance, to learn bilingual dictionaries, to train statistical machine translation systems or to perform quality estimation. Variational autoencoders have been recently used in various of natural language processing to learn in an unsupervised way latent representations that are useful for language generation tasks. In this paper, we study these models for the task of word alignment and propose and assess several evolutions of a vanilla variational autoencoders. We demonstrate that these techniques can yield competitive results as compared to Giza++ and to a strong neural network alignment system for two language pairs.

1   Introduction

Word alignment is one of the basic tasks in multilingual Natural Language Processing (NLP) and is used to learn bilingual dictionaries, to train statistical machine translation (SMT) systems (Koehn, 2010), to filter out noise from translation memories (Pham et al., 2018) or in quality estimation applications (Specia et al., 2017). Word alignments can also be viewed as a form of possible explanation of the often opaque behavior of a Neural Machine Translation (Stahlberg et al., 2018). Word alignment aims to identify translational equivalences at the level of individual lexical units (Och and Ney, 2003; Tiedemann, 2011) in parallel sentences.

Successful alignment models either rely on bilingual association measures parameterizing a combinatorial problem (eg. an optimal matching in a bipartite graph); or on probabilistic models, as represented by the IBM Models of Brown et al. (1993) and the HMM model of Vogel et al. (1996). All these models use unsupervised learning to estimate the likelihood of alignment links at the word level from large collections of parallel sentences.

Such approaches are typically challenged by low-frequency words, whose co-occurrences are poorly estimated; they also fail to take into account context information in alignment; finally, they make assumptions that are overly simplistic (eg. that all alignments are one-to-many or many-to-one), especially when the languages under focus belong to different linguistic families. Even though their overall performance seem fair for related languages (eg. French-English), there is still much room for improving. Indeed, the error rate of automatic alignments tools such as `Giza++` (Och and Ney, 2003) or `Fastalign` (Dyer et al., 2013), even for high resource languages, is still well above 15-20%; and the situation is much worse in low-resource settings (Martin et al., 2005; Xiang et al., 2010; McCoy and Frank, 2018).

As for most NLP applications (Collobert et al., 2011), and notably for machine translation (Cho et al., 2014; Bahdanau et al., 2015), neural-based approaches offer new opportunities to reconsider some of these issues. Following up on the work of eg. (Yang et al., 2013; Alkhouli et al., 2016; Wang et al., 2018), we study ways to take advantage of the flexibility of neural networks to design effective variants of generative word alignment models.

Our main source of inspiration is the model of Rios et al. (2018), who consider variational autoencoders (Kingma and Welling, 2014; Rezende et al., 2014) to approach the unsupervised estimation of neural alignment models. We revisit here this model, trying to analyze the reasons for its unsatisfactory performance and we extend it in several ways, taking advantage of its fully generative nature. We first generalize the approach, initially devised for IBM model 1, to the HMM model; we then explore ways to effectively enforce symmetry constraints (Liang et al., 2006); we finally study how these models could benefit from monolingual data. Our experiments with the English-Romanian and English-French language pairs show that our best model with symmetry constraints is on par with a conventional neural HMM model; they also highlight the remaining deficiencies of these approaches and suggest directions for further developments.

2 Neural word alignment variational models

The standard approach to probabilistic alignment (Och and Ney, 2003) is to consider *asymmetric* models associating each word in a source sentence $f_1^J = f_1 \dots f_J$ of J words with exactly one word from the target sentence $e_0^I = e_0 \dots e_I$ of $I + 1$ words.[1] This association is governed by unobserved alignment variables $a_1^J = a_1 ... a_J$, yielding the following model:

$$p(f_1^J, a_1^J | e_0^I) = \prod_j^J p(a_j | a_1^{j-1}, f_1^{j-1}, e_0^I) p(f_j | a_1^j, f_1^{j-1}, e_0^I) \tag{1}$$

Two versions of this model are considered here: in the IBM model 1 (Brown et al., 1993), the alignment model $p(a_j | a_1^{j-1}, f_1^{j-1}, e_0^I)$ is uniform; in the HMM model of Vogel et al. (1996), Markovian dependencies between alignment variables are assumed and a_j is independant from all the preceding alignment variables given a_{j-1}. In both models, f_j is conditionally independent to any other variable given a_j and e_1^I. Under these assumptions, both parameter estimation and optimal alignment can be performed efficiently with dynamic programming algorithms. In this approach, e_1^I is not modeled.

2.1 A fully generative model

We now present the fully generative approach introduced by Rios et al. (2018). In this model, the association between a source word f_j and a target word e_i is mediated by a shared latent variable y_i, assumed to represent the joint underlying semantics of mutual translations. In this model, the target sequence e_1^I is also modeled, yielding the following generative story:[2]

1. Generate a sequence y_0^I of d-dimensional random embeddings by sampling independently from some prior distribution e.g. Gaussian

2. Generate e_1^I conditioned on the latent variable sequence y_1^I

3. Generate $a_1^J = a_1 ... a_J$ denoting the alignment from f_1^J to y_0^I

4. Generate f_1^J conditioned on y_0^I and a_1^J

---

[1] As is custom, target sentences are completed with a "null" symbol, conventionally at index 0.

[2] We omit the initial step, consisting in sampling the lengths I and J and the dependencies wrt. these variables.

This yields the following decomposition of the joint distribution of f_1^J and e_1^I, where we marginalize over latent variables y_0^I and a_1^J:

$$p(f_1^J, e_1^I) = \int_{y_0^I} p(y_0^I) p_\theta(e_1^I|y_1^I) \Big(\sum_{a_1^J} p_\theta(a_1^J) p_\theta(f_1^J|y_0^I, a_1^J) \Big) dy_0^I \tag{2}$$

Directly maximizing the log-likelihood to estimate the parameters is in general intractable, especially when neural networks are used to model the generation of f_1^J and e_1^I. The standard approach in neural generative models (Kingma and Welling, 2014) is to introduce a variational distribution q_ϕ for the latent variables and to optimize the so-called evidence lower-bound (ELBO). Following (Rios et al., 2018) we consider tractable alignment models and use the variational distribution only for modeling y_0^I conditioned on e_1^I. This yields the following objective:

$$J(\theta, \phi) = - \mathbb{E}_{q_\phi(y_1^I)}(\log p_\theta(e_1^I|y_1^I)) - \mathbb{E}_{q_\phi(y_0^I)}([\log \sum_{a_1^J} p_\theta(a_1^J) p_\theta(f_1^J|y_0^I, a_1^J))$$
$$+ \mathrm{KL}[q_\phi(y_0^I|e_1^I)||p(y_0^I)] \tag{3}$$

where $\mathbb{E}_p(f)$ denotes the expectation of f with respect to p, and KL is the Kullback-Leibler divergence. Objective (3) is a sum of three terms that are referred respectively as the *reconstruction cost*, the *alignment cost* and *KL divergence cost*. The last term can be computed analytically when the prior and the variational distributions are Gaussian and we thus assume the following parameterization $q_\phi(y_1^I|e_1^I) = \prod_i N(y_i|u_i, s_i)$, where the mean u_i and the diagonal covariance matrix $\mathrm{diag}(s_i)$ are deterministic functions of e_1^I. As is custom, the expectations in equation (3) are approximated by sampling values of y_i as $y_i = u_i + s_i \cdot \epsilon_i$, where ϵ_i is drawn from a white Gaussian noise. The reparameterization trick removes the sampling step from the generation path, and makes the whole objective differentiable (Kingma and Welling, 2014).

2.2 Introducing Markovian dependencies

The experiments in (Rios et al., 2018) only consider basic assumptions regarding the alignment model $p_\theta(a_1^J)$, corresponding to IBM model 1. Our first variation of this model considers a richer transition model assuming Markovian dependencies, for which the exact marginalization of alignment variables implied by equation (3) remains tractable with the forward algorithm. The alignment cost is the expectation of the source given the latent variables:

$$\mathbb{E}_{q_\phi(y_0^J)}([\log \sum_{a_1^J} \prod_{j=1}^J p_\theta(f_j|y_{a_j}) p_\theta(a_j|a_{j-1})]) \tag{4}$$

As is usual with HMM variants of alignment models, we parameterize the transition distribution $p_\theta(a_j|a_{j-1})$ on the distance (jump) between the values of a_j and a_{j-1} (Och and Ney, 2003). This model is referred to below as HMM+VAE.

2.3 Towards symmetric models: a parameter sharing approach

A first benefit of having a fully generative model (in both alignment directions), which jointly models f_1^J and e_1^I, is that it becomes easy to encourage these models to share information and to improve their joint performance. Our alignment models involves two decoders, one for the source and one for the target (in each direction). These components are used to compute a distribution over vocabulary words given a d-dimensional variable, and are conceptually similar.

Our first step is thus to simultaneously train the alignment models in both directions, making sure that they use the same decoder respectively for f_1^J and e_1^I. This means that the same network computes $p_\theta(e_1^I|y_1^I)$ (when e_1^I is in the target) and $p_\theta(e_1^I|y_0^J, a_1^J)$ when e_1^I is the source.

There is only one encoder computing the variational parameters in each direction, and these remain distinct in this approach. Our joint objective function now comprises six terms including two reconstruction costs, two alignment costs and two KL divergence costs. From this, we see that a first benefit of this method is computational as it greatly reduces the number of parameters to train. We also expect that it will yield two additional benefits: (a) to help improve the alignment model, which is more difficult to train for lack of observing the "right" alignment variables; in comparison the reconstruction of the target sentence is almost obvious, as each e_i is generated from the right y_i; (b) to make the alignments more symmetrical, thereby facilitating their interpretation and their recombination. This model is denoted $+\text{VAE}+\text{SP}$ below.

2.4 Enforcing agreement in alignment

The idea of training two asymmetrical models opens new ways to control the level of agreement between alignments, an idea already considered eg. in (Liang et al., 2006; Graça et al., 2010). Following the former approach, we implement this idea by adding an extra cost that rewards agreement between asymmetric alignments. For non null alignment links, this cost is based on the alignment posterior distributions and is defined as:

$$\sum_{i>0,j>0} |p(a_j = i|f_1^J, e_1^I) - p(b_i = j|f_1^J, e_1^I)|, \tag{5}$$

where b_1^J is the alignment variables introduced when e_1^I is the source of the alignment, and f_1^J is the target. Both for the IBM-1 and for the HMM variants, these posterior distributions can be computed effectively, in the latter case using the forward-backward algorithm.

In the case of the null links, the agreement term should reward configurations where one source word is aligned with the null symbol in one direction, and is not aligned to any target word in the other direction. This yields the following additional term (for the canonical source to target direction, the reverse term is analogous):

$$\sum_{j=1}^{J} |1 - p(a_j = 0|f_1^J, e_1^I) - \sum_{i=1}^{I} p(b_i = j|f_1^J, e_1^I)| \tag{6}$$

For this model ($+\text{VAE}+\text{SP}+\text{AC}$), the objective function comprises nine terms, each with its own dynamics, which makes optimization more difficult due to the heterogeneity between costs.

2.5 Training with monolingual data

Leaving the alignment module aside, the model can be used as a simple autoencoder which can be (pre)trained monolingually. We use supplementary monolingual sentences $\dot{e}_1^M$ that just go through the encoding-decoding process, and add an extra monolingual reconstruction term J_{mono} in the objective (3):

$$J_{\text{mono}}(\theta, \phi) = -\mathbb{E}_{q_\phi(\dot{y}_1^M)}(\log p_\theta(\dot{e}_1^M|\dot{y}_1^M)) + \text{KL}[q_\phi(\dot{y}_1^M|\dot{e}_1^M)||p(\dot{y}_1^M)] \tag{7}$$

where $\dot{y}_1^M$ is the latent variable associated to $\dot{e}_1^M$. Alternatively, we consider training the alignment model monolingually. We implement this idea by adding a random noise to the target sentence, to make it more similar to a source sentence and amenable to alignment. In this case, the extra reconstruction term is:

$$J_{\text{mono}}(\theta, \phi) = -\mathbb{E}_{q_\phi(\ddot{y}_0^N)}([\log \sum_{\ddot{a}_1^M} p_\theta(\ddot{a}_1^M)p_\theta(\dot{e}_1^M|\ddot{y}_0^N, \ddot{a}_1^M)) + \text{KL}[q_\phi(\ddot{y}_0^N|\ddot{e}_1^N)||p(\ddot{y}_0^N)] \tag{8}$$

where $\ddot{e}_1^N$ is a noisy version of $\dot{e}_1^M$, $\ddot{y}_1^N$ is the latent variable for $\ddot{e}_1^N$, and $\ddot{a}_1^M$ denotes the alignment variables betwen $\dot{e}_1^M$ and $\ddot{y}_0^N$. In our experiments, we only use IBM Model 1 as our alignment model.

3 Experiments

3.1 Datasets

Our experiments use two standard benchmarks from the 2003 word alignment challenge (Mihalcea and Pedersen, 2003), respectively for aligning English with French and Romanian. We consider two different settings: for French, we use a large training corpus of parallel sentences from the Europarl corpus Koehn (2005). In the case of Romanian, we use the SETIMES corpus used in WMT'16 evaluation,[3] which correspond to a more challenging scenario where the training data is limited in size. Additional experiments with monolingual data use the Romanian data from News Crawl 2019 ($\sim$ 6M sentences)[4]. Basic statistics for these corpora are in Table 1.

Corpus	# sent. in train	# sent. in test	# tokens in test		# non-null links
			Eng.	For.	
En-Fr	$\sim$1.9M	447	7 020	7 761	17 438
En-Ro	$\sim$260K	246	5 455	5 315	5 988

Table 1: Basic statistics for the data

These corpora are preprocessed, lowercased and tokenized with standard tools from the Moses toolkit.[5] Following notably (Garg et al., 2019), we perform the alignment between subword units generated by Byte-Pair-Encoding (Sennrich et al., 2015), implemented with the SentencePiece model (Kudo and Richardson, 2018) and computed independently[6] in each language with 32K merge operations. This makes the training less computationally demanding and greatly mitigates the rare-word problem, which is a major weakness of historical count-based model. Our results and analyses are however based on word-level alignments. Subword-level alignments are converted into word-level alignments as follows: a link between a source and a target word exists if there is at least one link alignment between their subwords.

3.2 Implementation

Our models are close in structure to the model proposed by Rios et al. (2018), and are made of three main components: an encoder to generate the latent variables y_0^I from e_1^I, and two decoders to respectively reconstruct e_1^I and f_1^J, with the help of the alignment model.

The encoder is composed of a token embedding layer (128 units), two LSTM layers (each comprising 64 units), and dense output layers to independently generate the mean vectors $(u_1 \ldots u_I)$ vectors and the diagonal of the covariance matrices $(s_1 \ldots s_I)$. The latent variable y_1^I has 64 units.[7] Our encoder is formally defined as:

$$\overrightarrow{h_i} = RNN(\overrightarrow{h_{i-1}}, E(e_i)) \qquad s_i = \text{softplus}(W_s h_i + b_s)$$
$$\qquad \qquad \qquad u_i = W_u h_i + b_u$$
$$h_i = W_h \, \text{concat}(\overrightarrow{h_i}, \overleftarrow{h_i}) \qquad y_i = u_i + s_i \cdot \epsilon_i$$

where $E(e_i) \in \mathbb{R}^{128}$ is the embedding of word e_i, ϵ is a noise variable $\epsilon \sim N(0,1)$ and softplus $= \log(1 + \exp(x))$ is an activation function returning a value positive. The vector y_0 is independently generated from a pseudo-sentence made of one dummy token; it is identical

---

[3] http://statmt.org/wmt16

[4] See http://statmt.org/wmt19

[5] https://github.com/moses-smt/mosesdecoder

[6] We differ there from Garg et al. (2019) who use a joint BPE vocabulary.

[7] In our BPE baseline experiments with En:Ro, we found that 64 hidden units were sufficient to obtain the best AER score after 10 iterations. As for the other meta-parameters, we decided to stick with these baseline values.

for all target sentences. Note that the decoder model does not try to reconstruct this token. The reconstruction decoder is given by:

$$p_\theta(e_i|y_i) = [\text{softmax}(W_v y_i + b_v)]_{e_i},$$

and the alignment model with emission and transition components is:

$$p_\theta(f_j|e_{a_j}) = [\text{softmax}(W_v y_{a_j})]_{f_j}$$
$$p_\theta(a_j - a_{j-1}) = [\text{softmax}(W_\Delta y_{a_{j-1}})]_{a_j - a_{j-1}}$$

where $W_v \in \mathbb{R}^{64 \times V}, b_v \in \mathbb{R}^V$, with V the target vocabulary size. $W_\Delta \in \mathbb{R}^{64 \times 301}$ with jump values in the interval $[-150, +150]$.

For experiments with monolingual data, our noise model follows the technique in (Lample et al., 2017). We randomly delete input words with probability $p_{wd} = 0.1$. We then slightly shuffle the sentence, where the difference between the position before and after shuffling each word is smaller than 4.

In all cases, our optimizer is Adam (Kingma and Ba, 2014) with an initial learning rate of 0.001; the batch size is set to 100 sentences. We use all training sentences of length lower than 50. All parameters of the `Giza++` and `Fastalign` baselines are set to their default values. `IBM-1+NN` and `HMM+NN` correspond to basic neuralizations of the IBM models as in (Rios et al., 2018; Ngo-Ho and Yvon, 2019) for both word-level and BPE-level. These models are trained by maximizing the likelihood with the expectation-maximization algorithm. We train all models for 10 iterations. Results with symmetric alignments use the grow-diag-final (GDF) heuristic proposed in (Koehn et al., 2005).

3.3 Evaluation protocol

We use the alignment error rate (AER) (Och, 2003), accuracy, F-score, precision and recall as measures of performance. AER is based on a comparison of predicted alignment links (A) with a human reference including sure (S) and possible (P) links, and is defined as an average of the recall and precision taking into account the sets P and S. AER is defined as:

$$AER = 1 - \frac{|A \cap S| + |A \cap P|}{|A| + |S|}$$

where A is the set of predicted alignments. Note that the Romanian-English reference data only contains sure links; in this case AER and F-measure are deterministically related.

3.4 Results

The top part of Table 2 reports the AER score of the IBM-1 baselines: the count-based model (`IBM-1 Giza++`) and the two neural variants, operating at the word (`IBM1+NN`) and subword (`IBM-1+BPE`) levels. We also report the performance of three VAE variants (`IBM1+VAE+BPE, IBM1+VAE+BPE+SP, IBM-1+VAE+BPE+SP+AC`). A first observation is neural baselines are better than Giza++, and that using BPE units brings an additional gain.

The basic model (`IBM-1+VAE`) falls short to match these results and proves way worse than the two neural version of the IBM-1 model. These results are in line with the findings of Rios et al. (2018), who report similar difference in performance. Sharing the parameters between directions greatly improves this baseline with a reduction in AER of about 8 points (En-Fr) and 6 points (En-Ro) for both directions, as well as for symmetrization. The reconstruction model, which is well trained in one direction, helps to improve the emission model in the reverse direction. We observe that the gain is more significant when the morphologically rich language is on the target side: this is were the emission model is the weakest and benefits most from parameter sharing. Adding an extra agreement cost fails to produce markedly better alignments for Fr-En; we however observe a gain of about 2 AER points for the symmetricized alignments in En-Ro. Overall, our best VAE model outperform the neural baseline in the large training condition (English-French); we do not see this for the other language pair, where the performance remains much below the neural baseline.

Model	English-French			English-Romanian		
`IBM-1`	En-Fr	Fr-En	GDF	En-Ro	Ro-En	GDF
`Giza++`	40.0	33.9	25.1	56.0	53.5	51.1
`IBM1+NN`	27.9	27.2	17.8	46.3	44.9	38.3
`IBM1+NN+BPE`	25.7	24.0	**14.6**	**43.4**	**40.4**	**34.4**
`IBM1+VAE+BPE`	33.4	34.3	24.9	56.3	55.6	51.3
`+SP`	**22.1**	23.8	16.8	49.3	51.4	45.2
`+AC`	22.8	**23.6**	17.8	49.1	49.2	43.3

Table 2: AER scores for `IBM-1` models. The best result in each column is in boldface.

The effect of adding a transition component in these models is less clear, as shown in Table 3, where we report the performance of HMM-based variants. Both symmetrization strategies prove again very effective to improve the basic VAE model, and our best system (+AC) achieves AER scores that are close, yet slightly inferior, to the `HMM+NN+BPE` baseline. One possible issue that we do not fully solve via symmetrization is related to the null word, which, as explained above, is not part of the reconstruction model, and which does not improve with joint learning.

Model	English-French			English-Romanian		
HMM	En-Fr	Fr-En	GDF	En-Ro	Ro-En	GDF
`Fastalign`	15.1	16.2	14.2	33.3	32.9	30.4
`HMM Giza++`	11.9	11.9	**8.5**	33.3	36.3	32.4
`HMM+NN`	11.8	11.1	9.7	**30.6**	40.1	34.3
`HMM+NN+BPE`	**9.8**	**10.4**	9.1	34.4	**29.3**	**29.4**
`HMM+VAE+BPE`	18.9	12.9	13.9	50.2	38.6	42.7
`+SP`	12.9	12.2	11.7	37.5	38.0	37.0
`+AC`	11.4	10.8	9.6	35.5	38.8	35.1

Table 3: AER scores for variants of the HMM model and for `Fastalign`.

4 Error Analysis

4.1 Balancing the terms in the VAE objective

One well-known issue of VAEs for text applications is *posterior collapse* (Bowman et al., 2016; Higgins et al., 2017), where the variational distribution collapses towards the prior distribution. This is because the KL term can get arbitrarily small, with a moderate effect on the reconstruction cost, assuming a strong reconstruction model (a recurrent network in typical applications). We also encountered this problem in our setting, but the interpretation is a bit different: when the KL term goes to zero, all words in the dictionary become indistinguishable and the reconstruction costs reaches its maximum, corresponding to the entropy of the uniform distribution of the target vocabulary. The difference in dynamics between these scores is observed in Figure 1 (left), where we apply weights equal to α, β and γ respectively to the reconstruction cost, the alignment cost and the KL divergence term. This effect is mitigated if we proportionally decrease the weight of the KL term (middle). This second graph reveals the need to also better balance the importance of the other two terms. Using larger weights for the reconstruction term ($\alpha = 10$) and even more for the alignment term ($\beta = 50$), we keep the KL divergence high and make sure that the optimization focuses on decreasing the two other terms [8].

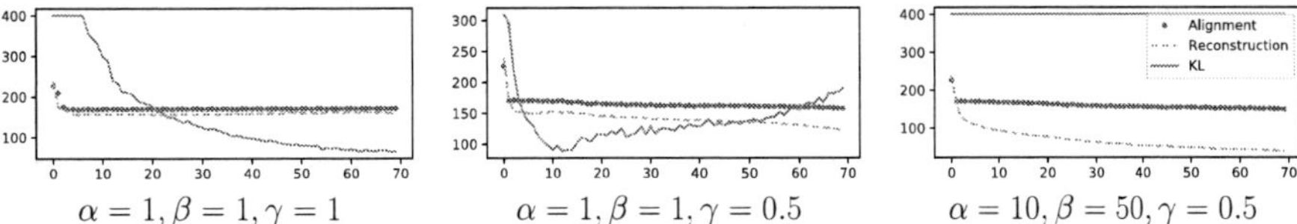

$$\alpha = 1, \beta = 1, \gamma = 1 \qquad \alpha = 1, \beta = 1, \gamma = 0.5 \qquad \alpha = 10, \beta = 50, \gamma = 0.5$$

Figure 1: Visualizing the three terms of the ELBO for Romanian-English. The weights of the reconstruction cost, alignment cost and KL divergence are set to α, β, γ respectively.

4.2 Unaligned words

In asymmetrical models, the number of links that are generated is constant and equal to the total number of "source" words. A source word is deemed unaligned when it is linked to the special NULL token on the target side; a target word is unaligned when it emits no source word. We perform an in-depth analysis of these special links. Results for the alignment from French into English are in Table 4; we observe similar trends for the other direction and for the other language pair. We compute the alignment accuracy as the proportion of words (on both sides) for which the binary decision (aligned or non-aligned) is correct; we also report the precision and recall for unaligned words. Results in Table 4 show that the number of unaligned words varies in great proportion, with a minimum of about 3000 words (HMM+NN) and a maximum of nearly 6600 (IBM1+VAE+BPE and HMM+VAE+BPE). For this language pair, the reference contains 821 unaligned words. They also demonstrate the inability of all models to correctly predict null links, the best model achieving a precision of only 13.1%.

Model	# Unaligned	Accuracy	Precision	Recall
IBM1+NN	3836	74.0	8.7	49.7
IBM1+NN+BPE	3633	75.8	10.1	54.4
IBM1+VAE+BPE	6596	57.4	7.5	73.2
+SP	5621	64.2	9.0	75.1
+AC	5622	64.3	9.1	76.0
HMM+NN	2994	80.4	13.1	58.1
HMM+NN+BPE	4835	70.7	12.2	87.5
HMM+NN+BPE+Joint	4843	70.3	11.6	83.5
HMM+VAE+BPE	6591	58.6	8.7	84.9
+SP	6581	59.0	9.1	89.3
+AC	5579	65.5	10.4	86.0

Table 4: Evaluation of null-alignment links when aligning French with English.

Predicting so many unaligned words is extremely detrimental to the performance of the two basic VAE models for which we observe a very poor recall for non-null links, which is hardly compensated by the good precision scores. We see here clearly the effect of the symmetrization constraints (especially for the HMM model) where the reward associated with symmetric

---

[8] In our baseline experiment with English-Romanian (From http://www.statmt.org/wpt05/), using these weights resulted in an acceptable AER scores and seemed appropriate for our further experiment; a small exploration of the hyper-parameter space showed that these results were stable.

predictions reduces the tendency to align French words with the NULL English, and to leave too many English words unaligned. Even there (HMM+VAE+BPE+SP+AC), the number of predicted non-null links is about half as what we see for HMM+NN: as it predicts much more links than the others, this model also as an clear edge when it comes to post-hoc symmetrization, since the "grow-diag-final" heuristics heavily depends on the size of the intersection. Note that this problem has a much stronger overall effect in English-Romanian than in English-French. This is because the English-Romanian test set only contains sure links, which means that a low recall for aligned words directly impacts the AER. We do not see this for the French-English data, which contain many possible links that have no impact on recall (Fraser and Marcu, 2007).

Incidentally, we also observe a null-word problem for HMM+NN+BPE; presumably splitting words in small units that are unrelated across languages can also make the model prefer the null alignment over links between actual words. These results clearly point out one deficiency of the current approach: for lack of having a proper model for the latent representation of the NULL token, the VAE-based approach tends to leave too many words unaligned.

4.3 Symmetrization and agreement

We now study the effects of sharing parameters across alignment directions. We consider the English-Romanian test, for which the relationship between precision, recall and AER is straightforward. Detailed scores for all IBM-1 models are in Table 5. We see the clear benefits of sharing parameters, which contributes a jump of both precision, recall and F-measure compared with the baseline VAE. Models SP and SP+AC generate more alignment links (about +500 links) than the baseline model. This enhancement helps to outperform Giza++ but is insufficient to surpass the conventional neural network models, especially when using BPE. Numbers in Table 5 show that the gain in recall is largest in the direction En-Ro: this is because the better reconstruction of English words boosts the translation model.

Model	Precision			Recall			F-measure		
IBM-1	En-Ro	Ro-En	GDF	En-Ro	Ro-En	GDF	En-Ro	Ro-En	GDF
Giza++	58.8	49.9	73.8	35.1	43.5	36.5	43.9	46.4	48.8
+NN	57.7	60.0	75.7	50.0	50.9	51.9	53.6	55.1	61.6
+NN+BPE	63.9	64.1	80.4	50.6	55.6	55.3	56.5	59.5	65.5
+VAE+BPE	56.6	53.9	79.5	35.4	37.6	35.0	43.6	44.3	48.6
+SP	60.6	57.8	76.2	43.5	41.8	42.7	50.7	48.5	54.8
+AC	61.3	58.9	76.9	43.5	44.6	44.8	50.8	50.8	56.6

Table 5: Precision, recall and F-measure of IBM-1 models for English-Romanian

We now measure more directly the level of agreement between the two alignment directions for English-French (Table 6). We note that the model integrating agreement costs (+SP+AC) leads to a higher number of agreements in comparison to the other VAE-based models, and also yields the best scores in terms of intersection AER.

4.4 Training with monolingual data

A last extension concerns the use of monolingual data in the low-resource condition. To compute the performance of the reconstruction model (R-ACC), we compute the proportion of words for which the model's prediction actually corresponds to the correct word. Experiments are performed with English-Romanian.[9] Results in Table 7 show that +Mono helps improve the reconstruction model, which attains almost perfect reconstruction accuracy in both directions,

---

[9] The Romanian corpus is from News Crawl 2019, the English corpus is from Europarl, and corresponds to the English side of the English-French data.

Model HMM	# Agree	Ratio En-Fr	Ratio Fr-En	AER (inter)
Giza++	4683	72.6	75.5	7.5
+NN	4771	73.2	76.7	7.4
+NN+BPE	4040	75.0	80.2	10.4
+VAE+BPE	3160	69.1	76.0	18.7
+SP	3586	86.2	86.5	13.0
+AC	3989	83.6	84.8	10.1

Table 6: Agreement between alignments in two directions for English-French, in terms of the number of alignment links, its ratio to the total number of alignment links predicted by the model and the AER of the "intersection" heuristic.

suggesting that the autoencoder is overfitting. The gain brought by monolingual data is found only for IBM-1, for the direction Ro-En (-3.6 AER). The extra-task of denoising the input (+Mono+Noise) further improves the AER compared to the parameter sharing approach.

Model	English-Romanian		Romanian-English	
+VAE+BPE+SP	R-ACC	AER	R-ACC	AER
IBM-1	84.6	49.3	93.0	51.4
+Mono	98.1	49.1	98.1	47.8
+Noise	98.4	48.8	97.9	47.6
HMM	95.5	37.5	97.5	38.0
+Mono	98.5	37.9	98.1	38.0
+Noise	98.8	36.3	97.5	36.5

Table 7: Training with a monolingual corpus (+Mono) and the noise model (+Noise) on English-Romanian data. R-Acc is the accuracy of the reconstruction model.

5   Related work

The majority of recent approaches to neural word alignment fall into two categories: heuristic and probabilistic. A representative heuristic approach is (Legrand et al., 2016), which learns association scores between source and target word embeddings without any underlying probabilistic model. This simple approach is used to clean up translation memories in (Pham et al., 2018). More recently (Sabet et al., 2020) directly takes pre-trained non-contextual and contextual multilingual representations (Devlin et al., 2019) as their association scores, deriving individual word alignments by solving an optimal matching problem.

Early work on probabilistic neural alignment is (Yang et al., 2013), where a feed-forward neural network is used to replace the count-based translation model of a HMM-based aligner. This approach is further developed in (Tamura et al., 2014) where a recurrent network helps to capture contextual dependencies between alignment links. This early work aims to improve the alignment quality for phrase-based MT. As discussed above, the work of (Rios et al., 2018) also considers neural versions of IBM models, with the goal to improve word representations through cross-lingual transfer in low-resource contexts. Alignment is also the main focus of (Ngo-Ho and Yvon, 2019) which reviews a whole set of alternative parameterizations for neural IBM-1 and HMM models, varying the word embeddings (word and character based), the context-size in the translation model and the parameterization of the distortion model.

A much more active line of research tries to improve neural MT by exploiting the conceptual similarity between alignments and attention (Koehn and Knowles, 2017). Cohn et al.

(2016) modify the attention component to integrate some biases that are useful in alignements: a preference for monotonic alignements, for reduced fertility values, etc. They also propose, following (Liang et al., 2006), to enforce symmetrization constraints, an idea also explored in (Cheng et al., 2016); The same methodology is studied in (Luong et al., 2015; Yang et al., 2017), with the objective to introduce dependencies between successive attention vectors. The work of Peters et al. (2019) also aims to enhance the attention component of a sequence-to-sequence, by enforcing sparsity via the sparse-max operator.

The work reported in (Alkhouli et al., 2016; Wang et al., 2017) explores ways to explicitly introduce alignments in NMT. They study various neuralizations of the standard generative alignment models, and also consider ways to exploit weak supervision from count-based models. This line of research is pursued by (Kim et al., 2017; Deng et al., 2018), where attention vectors are handled as structured latent variables in NMT; in this study, variational autoencoders are used represent the alignment structure. Finally, Garg et al. (2019) propose to jointly learn alignment and translation in a multi-task setting, thereby improving a Transformer-based model.

When compared to heuristic approaches, an obvious defect of IBM models is their directionality, which means that they deliver asymmetric alignments. Attempts to remedy this problem, while preserving the sound probabilistic underlying models have been many. Liang et al. (2006) propose to jointly train EM in both directions, enforcing directional link posteriors to agree as much as possible through an additional agreement term; this work is generalized in (Liu et al., 2015). Graça et al. (2010) use a different technique and enforce symmetry via additional constraints on the posterior link distribution.

Since their introduction in (Bowman et al., 2016), VAE models of text generation have been developed in multiple ways, and applied to many NLP tasks, in particular to Machine Translation (Zhang et al., 2016). This approach generalizes the basic VAE approach by making the latent variable and the target sentence conditionally dependent from the observed source. One major difference with our work in that the model includes one latent variable per sentence, where we consider one for each target word.

6 Conclusion and outlook

In this paper, we have revisited the proposal of Rios et al. (2018) and explored variants of the variational autoencoder models for the unsupervised estimation of neural word alignment models. Our study has confirmed the previous findings and highlighted two promising aspects of this model. First, it is a full model of the joint distribution, which makes it easy and natural to introduce symmetrization constraints, as we have shown by proposing two such extensions. With these constraints, we were experimentally able to close the gap with strong baselines implementing neural variants of the conditional HMM models in the large data condition. Second, it opens new alleys to also incorporate monolingual data during training, which might especially prove useful in low-resource scenarios.

One remaining problem in this approach is the prediction of the null links, which is quite problematic in an encoder-decoder approach. We have shown in particular that the VAE model is strongly inclined to under-generate alignment links, which is detrimental to the overall AER performance. Symmetrization is a first answer to this problem, which however only partly fixes the issue. Another difficult problem with this model is controlling the optimization problem, a difficult task when the objective functions combines multiple terms with varying dynamics. More work is needed there to design better optimization strategies, with a better balance between the various sub-objectives.

Acknowledgements

This work has been made possible thanks to the Saclay-IA computing platform.

References

Alkhouli, T., Bretschner, G., Peter, J.-T., Hethnawi, M., Guta, A., and Ney, H. (2016). Alignment-based neural machine translation. In *Proc. WMT*, pages 54–65, Berlin, Germany.

Bahdanau, D., Cho, K., and Bengio, Y. (2015). Neural machine translation by jointly learning to align and translate. In *Proc. ICLR*, San Diego, CA.

Bowman, S. R., Vilnis, L., Vinyals, O., Dai, A., Jozefowicz, R., and Bengio, S. (2016). Generating sentences from a continuous space. In *Proc. CoNLL*, Berlin, Germany.

Brown, P. F., Pietra, V. J. D., Pietra, S. A. D., and Mercer, R. L. (1993). The mathematics of statistical machine translation: Parameter estimation. *Comput. Linguist.*, 19(2).

Cheng, Y., Shen, S., He, Z., He, W., Wu, H., Sun, M., and Liu, Y. (2016). Agreement-based joint training for bidirectional attention-based neural machine translation. In *Proc. IJCAI*, New York, NY.

Cho, K., van Merrienboer, B., Bahdanau, D., and Bengio, Y. (2014). On the properties of neural machine translation: Encoder–decoder approaches. In *Proc. SSST workshop*, Doha, Qatar.

Cohn, T., Hoang, C. D. V., Vymolova, E., Yao, K., Dyer, C., and Haffari, G. (2016). Incorporating structural alignment biases into an attentional neural translation model. In *Proc. NAACL-HTL 2016*, San Diego, CA.

Collobert, R., Weston, J., Bottou, L., Karlen, M., Kavukcuoglu, K., and Kuksa, P. (2011). Natural language processing (almost) from scratch. *J. Mach. Learn. Res.*, 12.

Deng, Y., Kim, Y., Chiu, J., Guo, D., and Rush, A. M. (2018). Latent alignment and variational attention. In *Proc. NIPS*, Montréal, Canada.

Devlin, J., Chang, M.-W., Lee, K., and Toutanova, K. (2019). BERT: Pre-training of deep bidirectional transformers for language understanding. In *Proc. NAACL*, pages 4171–4186, Minneapolis, MN.

Dyer, C., Chahuneau, V., and Smith, N. A. (2013). A simple, fast, and effective reparameterization of IBM model 2. In *Proc. NAACL*, Atlanta, GO.

Fraser, A. and Marcu, D. (2007). Measuring word alignment quality for statistical machine translation. *Comput. Linguist.*, 33(3):293–303.

Garg, S., Peitz, S., Nallasamy, U., and Paulik, M. (2019). Jointly learning to align and translate with transformer models. In *Proc. IJCNLP-EMNLP*, Hong Kong, China.

Graça, J. V., Ganchev, K., and Taskar, B. (2010). Learning tractable word alignment models with complex constraints. *Comput. Ling.*, 36(3).

Higgins, I., L.M, A.P, C.B, X.G, M.B, M, S., and L, A. (2017). Beta-VAE: Learning basic visual concepts with a constrained variational framework. In *Proc. ICLR*, Toulon, France.

Kim, Y., Denton, C., Hoang, L., and Rush, A. M. (2017). Structured attention networks. In *Proc. ICLR*, Toulon, France.

Kingma, D. P. and Ba, J. (2014). Adam: A method for stochastic optimization. *CoRR*, abs/1412.6980.

Kingma, D. P. and Welling, M. (2014). Auto-encoding variational Bayes. In *Proc. ICLR*, Vancouver, Canada.

Koehn, P. (2005). Europarl: A Parallel Corpus for Statistical Machine Translation. In *Proc. MT-Summit X*, Phuket, Thailand.

Koehn, P. (2010). *Statistical Machine Translation*. Cambridge University Press, New York, NY, USA, 1st edition.

Koehn, P., Axelrod, A., Mayne, A. B., Callison-Burch, C., Osborne, M., and Talbot, D. (2005). Edinburgh system description for the 2005 IWSLT speech translation evaluation. In *Proc. IWSLT*, Pittsburgh, PA.

Koehn, P. and Knowles, R. (2017). Six challenges for neural machine translation. In *Proc. NMT workshop*, Vancouver, Canada.

Kudo, T. and Richardson, J. (2018). SentencePiece: A simple and language independent sub-word tokenizer and detokenizer for neural text processing. In *Proc. EMNLP: System Demonstrations*, Brussels, Belgium.

Lample, G., L.D, and M.A.R (2017). Unsupervised machine translation using monolingual corpora only. *CoRR*, abs/1711.00043.

Legrand, J., Auli, M., and Collobert, R. (2016). Neural network-based word alignment through score aggregation. In *Proc. WMT*, pages 66–73, Berlin, Germany.

Liang, P., Taskar, B., and Klein, D. (2006). Alignment by agreement. In *Proc. NAACL*, pages 104–111, New York, NY.

Liu, C., Liu, Y., Sun, M., Luan, H., and Yu, H. (2015). Generalized agreement for bidirectional word alignment. In *Proc. EMNLP*, EMNLP 15, pages 1828–1836, Lisbon, Portugal.

Luong, T., Pham, H., and Manning, C. D. (2015). Effective approaches to attention-based neural machine translation. In *Proc. EMNLP*, pages 1412–1421, Lisbon, Portugal.

Martin, J., Mihalcea, R., and Pedersen, T. (2005). Word alignment for languages with scarce resources. In *Proc. ACL*, pages 65–74, Ann Arbor, Michigan.

McCoy, R. T. and Frank, R. (2018). Phonologically informed edit distance algorithms for word alignment with low-resource languages. In *Proceedings of SCiL 2018*, pages 102–112.

Mihalcea, R. and Pedersen, T. (2003). An evaluation exercise for word alignment. In *Proc.HLT-NAACL-PARALLEL workshop*, Canada.

Ngo-Ho, A.-K. and Yvon, F. (2019). Neural Baselines for Word Alignments. In *Proc. IWSLT*, Hong-Kong, China.

Och, F. J. (2003). Minimum error rate training in statistical machine translation. In *Proc. ACL*, pages 160–167, Sapporo, Japan.

Och, F. J. and Ney, H. (2003). A systematic comparison of various statistical alignment models. *Comput. Linguist.*, 29(1):19–51.

Peters, B., Niculae, V., and Martins, A. F. T. (2019). Sparse sequence-to-sequence models. In *Proc. ACL*, pages 1504–1519, Florence, Italy.

Pham, M. Q., Crego, J., Senellart, J., and Yvon, F. (2018). Fixing translation divergences in parallel corpora for neural MT. In *Proc. EMNLP*, pages 2967–2973, Brussels, Belgium.

Rezende, D. J., Mohamed, S., and Wierstra, D. (2014). Stochastic backpropagation and variational inference in deep latent gaussian models. In *Proc. ICML*, volume 2.

Rios, M., Aziz, W., and Simaan, K. (2018). Deep generative model for joint alignment and word representation. In *Proc. NAACL*, pages 1011–1023, New Orleans, Louisiana.

Sabet, M. J., Dufter, P., and Schtze, H. (2020). Simalign: High quality word alignments without parallel training data using static and contextualized embeddings. *ArXiv e-prints*.

Sennrich, R., Haddow, B., and Birch, A. (2015). Neural machine translation of rare words with subword units. *CoRR*, abs/1508.07909.

Specia, L., Scarton, C., and Paetzold, G. (2017). *Quality estimation for Machine Translation*. Synthesis Lectures on Human Language Technologies. Morgan & Claypool Publishers.

Stahlberg, F., Saunders, D., and Byrne, B. (2018). An operation sequence model for explainable neural machine translation. In *Proc. EMNLP*, pages 10–21, Brussels, Belgium.

Tamura, A., Watanabe, T., and Sumita, E. (2014). Recurrent neural networks for word alignment model. In *Proc. ACL*, pages 1470–1480, Baltimore, MD.

Tiedemann, J. (2011). *Bitext Alignment*. Synthesis Lectures on Human Language Technologies. Morgan & Claypool Publishers.

Vogel, S., Ney, H., and Tillmann, C. (1996). HMM-based word alignment in statistical translation. In *Proc. COLING*, Copenhagen, Denmark.

Wang, W., Alkhouli, T., Zhu, D., and Ney, H. (2017). Hybrid neural network alignment and lexicon model in direct hmm for statistical machine translation. In *Proc. ACL*, pages 125–131, Vancouver, Canada.

Wang, W., Zhu, D., Alkhouli, T., Gan, Z., and Ney, H. (2018). Neural hidden Markov model for machine translation. In *Proc. ACL*, pages 377–382, Melbourne, Australia.

Xiang, B., Deng, Y., and Zhou, B. (2010). Diversify and combine: Improving word alignment for machine translation on low-resource languages. In *Proc. ACL*, pages 22–26, Uppsala, Sweden.

Yang, N., Liu, S., Li, M., Zhou, M., and Yu, N. (2013). Word alignment modeling with context dependent deep neural network. In *Proc. ACL*, pages 166–175, Sofia, Bulgaria.

Yang, Z., Hu, Z., Deng, Y., Dyer, C., and Smola, A. (2017). Neural machine translation with recurrent attention modeling. In *Proc. ACL*, pages 383–387, Valencia, Spain.

Zhang, B., Xiong, D., Su, J., Duan, H., and Zhang, M. (2016). Variational neural machine translation. In *Proc. EMNLP*, pages 521–530, Austin TX.

The Impact of Indirect Machine Translation on Sentiment Classification

Alberto Poncelas alberto.poncelas@adaptcentre.ie
Pintu Lohar pintu.lohar@adaptcentre.ie
Andy Way andy.way@adaptcentre.ie
ADAPT Centre, Dublin City University, Glasnevin, Dublin 9, Ireland

James Hadley hadleyj@tcd.ie
Trinity Centre for Literary and Cultural Translation and ADAPT Centre, Trinity College Dublin, Ireland

Abstract

Sentiment classification has been crucial for many natural language processing (NLP) applications, such as the analysis of movie reviews, tweets, or customer feedback. A sufficiently large amount of data is required to build a robust sentiment classification system. However, such resources are not always available for all domains or for all languages.

In this work, we propose employing a machine translation (MT) system to translate customer feedback into another language to investigate in which cases translated sentences can have a positive or negative impact on an automatic sentiment classifier. Furthermore, as performing a direct translation is not always possible, we explore the performance of automatic classifiers on sentences that have been translated using a pivot MT system.

We conduct several experiments using the above approaches to analyse the performance of our proposed sentiment classification system and discuss the advantages and drawbacks of classifying translated sentences.

1 Introduction

The key factor for building a sentiment classifier is training the model using a dataset of at least two different sentiment classes. This process requires a huge amount of data to build a workable sentiment classification system. However, sometimes it is difficult to find the required resources for the pertinent domain in large enough quantities and in all relevant languages. A typical and efficient approach to solve this problem consists in building the sentiment classification system with a high-resource language such as English and translating the sentences to be classified into this high-resource language.

An example of this is customer feedback classification. Many companies face difficulties analyzing what their clients say about their products and/or services because of the vast amount of feedback. This problem is aggravated for those businesses that have clients from several countries and therefore receive feedback in multiple languages. Although the feedback in multiple languages can be translated into English, the translated sentences may contain errors. Moreover, as the feedback consists of user-generated texts, it tends to be less grammatically strict than texts from literature, which implies that finding an accurate translation becomes more difficult (Lohar et al., 2019).

MT models are built to generate translations that carry the same meaning as the original sentence and are also fluent in the target language. However, in some scenarios, metrics for measuring fluency are less relevant. This is the case in the sentiment analysis of translated sentences, where maintaining the sentiment is the priority, even if the translation is not accurate in terms of *adequacy* and *fluency* (Tebbifakhr et al., 2019). Despite the MT system generating understandable translations, it may not manifest the same sentiment as the original sentence. On top of that, in some cases, it is not possible to perform a direct translation, and so translation is required to be done via a pivot language. This may influence the classifier even more, as the errors produced by MT are propagated.

In this work, we analyze the difference in the performance of a sentiment classifier when using sentences in the original language, and sentences that have been translated (directly and indirectly) using an MT system. We discuss the benefits and disadvantages of using machine-translated sentences for automatic classification.

The remainder of this paper is organised in the following manner. We discuss the related work done in this field in Section 2. In Section 3, we formulate some research questions to be addressed in this area. The experiments are detailed in Section 4. We highlight our results in Section 5. Finally, we conclude our present work in Section 6, followed by some possible future directions in Section 7.

2   Related Work

Several studies have addressed the issue of sentiment classification. The work in Pang et al. (2002) examines the effectiveness of applying machine learning techniques to the sentiment classification of movie reviews. In Li et al. (2010) polarity shifting information is incorporated into a document-level sentiment classification system. First, polarity shifting is detected and then classifier combination methods are applied to perform polarity classification. However, in recent studies, deep learning-based approaches are gaining popularity for sentiment classification (Zhang et al., 2019a,b).

MT plays a significant role in crosslingual sentiment analysis. An approach that is similar to ours is the work of Araujo et al. (2016). Their experiments show that the performance of the English sentiment analysis tools on texts translated into English can be as good as using language-specific tools. Therefore, it may be worth deploying a system following the first approach, assuming some cost on the prediction performance. The work of Barhoumi et al. (2018) shows that the sentiment analysis of Arabic texts translated into English reaches a competitive performance with respect to standard sentiment analysis of Arabic texts. Using a high-quality MT system to translate a text from a specific language into English can eliminate the necessity of developing specific sentiment analysis resources for that language (Shalunts et al., 2016). One of the most recent approaches using MT for sentiment classification is described in Tebbifakhr et al. (2019). Their proposed approach for the sentiment classification of Twitter data in German and Italian shows that feeding an English classifier with machine-oriented translations improves its performance. For low-resource languages, MT-based approaches are considered efficient for analysing the sentiment of texts (Kanayama et al., 2004; Balahur and Turchi, 2012).

Additionally, several approaches aim to influence the MT to favour a sentiment when generating a translation. Lohar et al. (2017) propose training different SMT systems on sentences that have been tagged with a particular sentiment. Similarly, Si et al. (2019) propose methods for generating translations of both positive and negative sentiments from the same sentence in the source language.

In our work, we not only investigate the sentiment classification on direct translation but also on indirect translation. Despite several existing studies on MT translation using a pivot language, both in SMT (Utiyama and Isahara, 2007; Wu and Wang, 2007) and NMT (Cheng et al., 2017; Liu et al., 2018), to the best of our knowledge, this is the first study where indirect translation is explored for automatic sentiment classification.

3   Research Questions

In our experiments, we aim to explore the change in performance of a sentiment classifier when executed on MT-translated sentences. Furthermore, we want to compare the performance when using direct and indirect translation. The research questions (RQs) that we explore in this paper are the following:

RQ1: To what extent do machine-translated sentences impact the performance of a sentiment classifier?

Typically, MT models generate errors when producing translations. In addition, translating user-generated content (UGC) tends to be more difficult as it may contain spelling mistakes, wrong use of uppercase and lowercase letters, etc. Because of this, when customer feedback is translated the MT system may fail to produce a sentence with the same meaning or sentiment as the original sentence. We want to investigate how much MT errors affect the classification and whether they are proportional to the expected translation quality.

RQ2: How much does the indirectly translated sentence impact a sentiment classifier?

In some situations, performing a direct translation into the language of the classifier is not possible. This is the case when language resources are available (e.g. either parallel data, training set for building a classification, etc.). Therefore the translation can be obtained indirectly using a pivot language. We can find many examples of languages that are generally translated via a pivot language. For instance, Irish is often translated via English, Basque and Catalan via Spanish, and Breton via French. The translation quality of a document that is indirectly translated is expected to be lower than a direct translation because the final translation accumulates the errors produced by two MT models.

This may also have a negative impact on the classifier. We want to analyze the performance of the classifier when classifying indirectly-translated sentences.

4   Experiments

4.1   MT settings

We build an NMT system following the transformer approach (Vaswani et al., 2017) using OpenNMT (Klein et al., 2017). The model is trained for a maximum of 400K steps using the recommended parameters,[1] selecting the model that obtains the lowest perplexity on the development set.

A total of six translation models are built for translating French, Spanish and Japanese from/into English (two models for each pair).We use Paracrawl[2] for English-French (51M parallel sentences) and English-Spanish (39M parallel sentences) language pairs, and JParaCrawl (Morishita et al., 2019) dataset (8.7M parallel sentences) for English-Japanese.

All the datsets are tokenized, truecased and then Byte Pair Encoding (BPE) (Sennrich et al., 2016c) is applied with $89, 500$ merge operations.

In order to estimate the performance of the MT models, in Table 1 we present the translation quality when translating a sample of 500 lines from the *news-commentary* dataset. The translations are evaluated using the BLEU (Papineni et al., 2002) metric. For English-French and English-Spanish language pairs the models achieve decent translation quality, but for the English-Japanese pair, BLEU scores are much lower. The reasons for this is that French and

---

[1] https://opennmt.net/OpenNMT-py/FAQ.html
[2] https://www.paracrawl.eu

Language	BLEU
En → Fr	31.77
En → Es	40.13
En → Ja	9.21
Fr → En	32.09
Es → En	40.48
Ja → En	12.85

Table 1: MT performance

Spanish are grammatically and lexically closer to English than Japanese, and in addition, the number of training sentences used to build the MT system is four times smaller.

4.2 Sentiment classifier

In order to build the sentiment analyser, we use the data from the IJCNLP-2017 *Customer Feedback Analysis Task* (Liu et al., 2017b). This dataset consists of a collection of English, French, Spanish and Japanese feedback containing short sentences extracted from reviews of products or services (in the hotel, restaurant or software domain). Each sentence is tagged with one or more categories based on the five-class system proposed by Liu et al. (2017a): comment, complaint, request, bug and meaningless. This is a fine-grained classification where only positive feedback is classified as comments whereas the other classes can be assumed to be different variants of negative feedback: "complaint" is defined as a negative comment and request or bug, which can also be considered negative as the client, or the user, is manifesting something that does not meet the standards of the product or service. In this dataset, the feedback can belong to multiple classes (e.g. a sentence such as *my purchase won't show up.* would be classified as "complaint" and "bug").

Lang	Train		Dev		Test	
	Size	ratio	Size	ratio	Size	ratio
En	3066	53%	500	54%	500	54%
Fr	1961	59%	400	60%	400	60%
Es	1632	61%	300	81%	300	76%
Ja	1527	52%	250	55%	300	56%

Table 2: Statistics of Feedback dataset. *Size* indicates the number of lines, and *ratio* the percentage of positive feedback.

In order to simplify the analysis, we assume that feedback is positive if is classified as a "comment" only, and negative in all other cases. Table 2 describes the dataset. We see that the size of the training data ranges from $1.5K$ to $3K$ lines, depending on the language. In the *ratio* column we indicate the percentage of feedback that is positive (and so $100 - ratio$ would indicate the percentage of negative feedback). We can see that in all datasets positive feedback is predominant, but not enough to consider the dataset unbalanced.

We build the classifier using a bidirectional Gated Recurrent Unit (GRU) (Cho et al., 2014), sigmoid activation function and a batch size of 16. The classification is performed on data with BPE applied.

In Table 3 we present the performance of the classifiers on the original sentences. We present three different metrics: accuracy, precision and recall. As we can see the three metrics have similar values. Therefore in the rest of this paper we will indicate only the accuracy (the

Language	Accuracy	Precision	Recall
En	0.728	0.727	0.729
Fr	0.788	0.779	0.783
Es	0.856	0.798	0.852
Ja	0.816	0.816	0.820

Table 3: Accuracy of the classifier on original sentences.

number of correctly classified feedback over the total amount in the test set).

5 Experiment Results

In our experiments we translate the test set into different languages and compare the performance of the classifier with the sentences classified in the original language (Table 3).

5.1 Direct Translation Results

We classify machine-translated feedback in the first set of experiments. These experiments can be divided into two parts: (i) Feedback translated into English; and (ii) Feedback translated from English.

Language	Accuracy	Accuracy (original language)
En $\rightarrow$ Fr	0.683	0.728
En $\rightarrow$ Es	0.673	0.728
En $\rightarrow$ Ja	0.573	0.728
Fr $\rightarrow$ En	0.754	0.788
Es $\rightarrow$ En	0.805	0.856
Ja $\rightarrow$ En	0.659	0.816

Table 4: Accuracy of the classifier on MT-generated sentences

In Table 4 we present the accuracy of the classifier when used on the translated data. The first column indicates in which direction the test set has been translated. The second column indicates the accuracy of the classifier when translated feedback is used. Therefore, we use the classifier built in the target language. Note that whereas in the first subtable the test set is the same (same English feedback translated into the other languages), in the second subtable each test set is different.

The accuracy of the classifier is lower for machine-translated data when compared to the sentences in the original sentences. In the first subtable the accuracies are lower than the original English classifier (*En* row in Table 3). Similarly, in the second subtable, the accuracies are lower than those of *Fr*, *Es* and *Ja* rows in Table 3.

We observe a relative decrease of between 4% and 6% of performance when using translations from/into French or Spanish. For example, 72.8% of the English feedback is correctly classified by using the English classifier, but when these sentences are translated into French or Spanish and classified with the French and Spanish system, only 68.3% and 67.3% are correct. Similarly, in French and Spanish, 78.8% and 85.6% of the sentences are properly classified, but when translated into English this descend to 75.4% and 80.5%. The worst performance is seen in feedback translated from and into Japanese (around a 20% of decrease). This is probably be related to the estimated translation quality shown in Table 1 where we see that MT models that use Japanese as source or target languages tend to perform worse. Nevertheless, the accuracy of the classifier and translation quality are not completely correlated. For example, when the English feedback is translated into French, classification accuracy decreases to 0.683 (decrease of 6.2%) and when translated into Spanish accuracy decreases more (reaching an accuracy of 0.673 which is a decrease of 7.6%) even though the translation quality should be better (according to Table 1).

In general, we observe that it is preferable to classify the sentences in the original language. Even when translating into a language with higher resources in which a classifier can be trained with more data (as is the case of translating Japanese feedback into English), the accuracy is lower. This may be related to translation quality. However we see that once a threshold of translation quality is achieved, it does not have a big impact on the classifier.

5.2 Indirect Translation Results

In the second set of experiments we analyze the classification of indirectly-translated sentences, using English as a pivot language. We present in Table 5 the accuracy of the system with sentences translated indirectly. The rows indicate the source language and the columns the target language (after being translated from English).

Lang.	Fr	Es	Ja
Fr	0.779	0.725	0.635
Es	0.813	0.852	0.672
Ja	0.667	0.697	0.726

Table 5: Accuracy of classifier when using indirectly-translated sentences. The source language is that indicated in the row and the target language that indicated in the column. In all cases the pivot language is English.

We observe that the highest score in each row is the feedback that was translated back into the original language. In fact, the resulting indirect translation is similar to the original: 53.36 BLEU points for French feedback; 56.63 for Spanish; and 28.17 for Japanese. [3] Although Japanese has a lower BLEU score, we observed that often the differences come from using a different writing system, e.g. both おもう (*omou*) and 思う (*omou*) are the same word (*to think*), but they are written in two different Japanese writing systems.

When comparing the results in Table 5 with those for direct translation (subtable at the bottom of Table 4) we discover that the accuracy is similar. Furthermore, in some cases, indirectly-translated feedback becomes better classified. For example, when the Spanish feedback is translated into English, the accuracy of the classifier is 0.805 whereas translating it further into French results in higher accuracy (0.813). Similarly, when the Japanese feedback is translated into English the accuracy is 0.659 but when translated into French or Spanish the accuracy becomes 0.667 and 0.697, respectively.

As feedback consists of user-generated sentences they are expected to be informal, non-standard and noisy. Therefore, some of the terms may not be recognized by the classifier (which is trained using a small amount of data). However, in our experiments, the MT models are trained with larger amounts of data than the classifier and so they may recognize these terms and produce a less noisy translation.

In addition, we observe that many sentences in French, Spanish and Japanese use terms

---

[3] As BLEU evaluation metric is based on *n*-gram overlaps and Japanese sentences do not have whitespace separations between words, Japanese sentences were evaluated in BPE-split sentences

in English. For example, in Spanish feedback we find *calles de shopping* (meaning *shopping streets*) instead of *calles comerciales*, or in Japanese we find *staff* の接客 (meaning *staff reception*). The classifier in the original language may be unable to identify the words *shopping* or *staff* and this may affect the classification process. When performing translation, even if these OOV terms are copied directly into the target sentence, they will form a well-written sentence. When the feedback is further translated from the English pivot-sentences, the MT model is capable of translating the word.

5.3 Translation Analysis

In Table 6 we present some translation examples that help us illustrate the problems and benefits of using MT-generated sentences in the classification.

Language	Sentence	Sentence (human-translated into English)
Ja	ロケーション	location
Ja → En	location Location Location Location	location location location ...
Ja → En → Ja	場所 場所 場所 場所 場所 場所 場所	location location location ...
Es	seguro volveré	I will come back for sure
Es → En	I will return insurance	I will return insurance
Es → En → Es	voy a devolver el seguro	I will return insurance
Fr	et le quartier pas très sympa.	and the neighborhood is not very nice.
Fr → En	and the neighborhood is not very nice.	and the neighborhood is not very nice.
Fr → En → Fr	et le quartier n'est pas très agréable.	and the neighborhood is not very nice.

Table 6: Translation examples

In the first subtable, we show how the MT engine produces a word-repetition (i.e. *location*) when generating a translation. As the sentence is nonsense, it can be misinterpreted by the classifier. On top of that, the word-repetition problem is further replicated on indirect translation.

One of the problems is that indirect translation may produce errors that are propagated to the following MT system. In Table 6 the Spanish sentence *seguro volveré* is wrongly translated as *I will return insurance* (the word *seguro* can mean either *for sure* or *insurance*). This causes a positive sentence to become negative because of this error, and it is spread to the following translations.

In the second subtable, we show why in some cases using a translation could be beneficial. The original sentence in French *et le quartier pas très sympa.* is not a grammatically-correct sentence as the word *ne* (the negation of a verb in French follows the structure "ne"+VB+"pas") and the verb *est* (*to be*) are omitted which is common in spoken French. The translation into English is accurate in meaning and when the sentence has been translated back to French, the structure of the sentence is correct. Another advantage is that MT-generated texts tend to have a lower lexical diversity (Toral, 2019; Vanmassenhove et al., 2019) which makes the classification easier. This can be seen with the French word *sympa* which is not as frequent as *agréable*. For example, there are $6,065$ occurrences of the word *sympa* in the Paracrawl dataset whereas *agréable* occurs $78,689$ times.

6 Conclusions

In this work we investigated the impact of both direct and indirect translation when evaluated in terms of sentiment preservation (rather than other common criteria such as *adequacy* and *fluency*). We performed translation of customer feedback and categorized it as positive or negative using an automatic classifier. There are several conclusions that we can draw from the experiments carried out.

Sentiment classifiers do not classify translated data as well as original sentences. As expected, the outcome of our experiments shows that it is preferable to use the original feedback rather than a translation for classification. The MT-generated feedback introduces errors (Lohar et al., 2019; Nunez et al., 2019) that causes the classifier to show worse performance.

Translation quality is not completely correlated to the performance of the classifier. Although the automatic sentiment classifier does not perform well on sentences with low-quality translation, after a certain translation-quality threshold the performance of the classifier is not correlated with the translation quality.

There are potential benefits to using MT-translated sentences Although MT models produce errors, they also tend to generate sentences with a lower amount of lexical translation, which facilitates the classification. Moreover, if the feedback, which is UGC, contains terms in the target language it may be easier for the classifier to classify the translated version.

The performance of the classifier on indirectly-translated sentences is similar to that when classifying directly-translated sentences. Despite the decrease in performance when classifying directly-translated feedback, we observe that it is similar to indirectly-translated feedback if the performance of the MT models is good enough. The sentences generated by the first MT system are expected to be of lower lexical diversity as compared to the user-generated sentences. This causes the second MT system in the pipeline to only have to translate simpler sentences.

7 Future Work

One of the limitations of our experiments is that we used an MT model to translate only the test set. An alternative experiment would involve translating the training data instead. The use of synthetic data for building models has been extensively explored in MT-field. Techniques such as back-translation (Sennrich et al., 2016b; Poncelas et al., 2018b), in which synthetic data is created by translating sentences from another language, has proven to be useful for improving MT models. We want to explore whether using machine-generated sentences as training data for the classifier also has an impact on the performance.

In the future, we want to explore other experimental configurations. For example, in this paper we explored a classifier trained with a single language. We want to investigate whether the performance would be similar when using multilingual classifiers (Plank, 2017).

Moreover, in these experiments the MT models were trained on large amounts of data (9M to 51M sentences). Although smaller models are expected to produce lower quality translations, these may be enough for the sentiment classifier to achieve acceptable results. A future extension to this work would involve investigating what is the minimum amount of data necessary for building the MT system to create translations that are good enough for the classifier to perform well. Alternatively, small MT models can be built by selecting a subset of the available data (Silva et al., 2018) that is closer to the user-generated content.

Another configuration would involve adapting the MT models to different categories. Following the approach of (Lohar et al., 2017) we could build different MT models for different classes. Alternatively, models could be adapted to translate feedback of a particular sentiment in a similar way to domain-adaptation. This can be done by fine-tuning with in-domain sets (van der Wees et al., 2017; Poncelas et al., 2018a) or appending a tag with the domain (Sennrich et al., 2016a; Poncelas et al., 2019).

8 Acknowledgements

This research has been supported by the ADAPT Centre for Digital Content Technology which is funded under the SFI Research Centres Programme (Grant 13/RC/2106).

The QuantiQual Project, generously funded by the Irish Research Council's COALESCE scheme (COALESCE/2019/117).

References

Araujo, M., Reis, J., Pereira, A., and Benevenuto, F. (2016). An evaluation of machine translation for multilingual sentence-level sentiment analysis. In *Proceedings of the 31st Annual ACM Symposium on Applied Computing*, pages 1140–1145, Pisa, Italy.

Balahur, A. and Turchi, M. (2012). Multilingual sentiment analysis using machine translation? In *Proceedings of the 3rd Workshop in Computational Approaches to Subjectivity and Sentiment Analysis*, pages 52–60, Jeju, Korea.

Barhoumi, A., Aloulou, C., Camelin, N., Estève, Y., and Belguith, L. (2018). Arabic Sentiment analysis: an empirical study of machine translation's impact. In *Language Processing and Knowledge Management International Conference (LPKM-2018)*, Sfax, Tunisia.

Cheng, Y., Yang, Q., Liu, Y., Sun, M., and Xu, W. (2017). Joint training for pivot-based neural machine translation. In *Proceedings of the Twenty-Sixth International Joint Conference on Artificial Intelligence*, pages 3974–3980, Melbourne, Australia.

Cho, K., van Merriënboer, B., Bahdanau, D., and Bengio, Y. (2014). On the properties of neural machine translation: Encoder–decoder approaches. In *Proceedings of SSST-8, Eighth Workshop on Syntax, Semantics and Structure in Statistical Translation*, pages 103–111, Doha, Qatar.

Kanayama, H., Nasukawa, T., and Watanabe, H. (2004). Deeper sentiment analysis using machine translation technology. In *COLING 2004: Proceedings of the 20th International Conference on Computational Linguistics*, pages 494–500, Geneva, Switzerland.

Klein, G., Kim, Y., Deng, Y., Senellart, J., and Rush, A. M. (2017). Opennmt: Open-source toolkit for neural machine translation. In *Proceedings of the 55th Annual Meeting of the Association for Computational Linguistics-System Demonstrations*, pages 67–72, Vancouver, Canada.

Li, S., Lee, S. Y. M., Chen, Y., Huang, C.-R., and Zhou, G. (2010). Sentiment classification and polarity shifting. In *Proceedings of the 23rd International Conference on Computational Linguistics (Coling 2010)*, pages 635–643, Beijing, China.

Liu, C.-H., Groves, D., Hayakawa, A., Poncelas, A., and Liu, Q. (2017a). Understanding meanings in multilingual customer feedback. In *Proceedings of First Workshop on Social Media and User Generated Content Machine Translation (Social MT 2017)*, Prague, Czech Republic.

Liu, C.-H., Moriya, Y., Poncelas, A., and Groves, D. (2017b). IJCNLP-2017 Task 4: Customer Feedback Analysis. In *Proceedings of the IJCNLP 2017, Shared Tasks*, pages 26–33, Taipei, Taiwan.

Liu, C.-H., Silva, C. C., Wang, L., and Way, A. (2018). Pivot machine translation using chinese as pivot language. In *China Workshop on Machine Translation*, pages 74–85, Wuyishan, China.

Lohar, P., Afli, H., and Way, A. (2017). Maintaining sentiment polarity in translation of user-generated content. *The Prague Bulletin of Mathematical Linguistics*, 108(1):73–84.

Lohar, P., Popović, M., Afli, H., and Way, A. (2019). A systematic comparison between SMT and NMT on translating user-generated content. In *20th International Conference on Computational Linguistics and Intelligent Text Processing*, La Rochelle, France.

Morishita, M., Suzuki, J., and Nagata, M. (2019). JParaCrawl: A large scale web-based Japanese-English parallel corpus. *arXiv preprint arXiv:1911.10668*.

Nunez, J. C. R., Seddah, D., and Wisniewski, G. (2019). Comparison between NMT and PBSMT performance for translating noisy user-generated content. In *Proceedings of the 22nd Nordic Conference on Computational Linguistics (NoDaLiDa)*, pages 2–14, Turku, Finland.

Pang, B., Lee, L., and Vaithyanathan, S. (2002). Thumbs up? sentiment classification using machine learning techniques. In *Proceedings of the 2002 Conference on Empirical Methods in Natural Language Processing (EMNLP 2002)*, pages 79–86, Philadelphia, USA.

Papineni, K., Roukos, S., Ward, T., and Zhu, W.-J. (2002). Bleu: a method for automatic evaluation of machine translation. In *Proceedings of 40th Annual Meeting of the Association for Computational Linguistics*, pages 311–318, Philadelphia, Pennsylvania, USA.

Plank, B. (2017). All-in-1 at ijcnlp-2017 task 4: Short text classification with one model for all languages. In *Proceedings of the IJCNLP 2017, Shared Tasks*, pages 143–148, Taipei, Taiwan.

Poncelas, A., Maillette de Buy Wenniger, G., and Way, A. (2018a). Feature decay algorithms for neural machine translation. In *Proceedings of the 21st Annual Conference of the European Association for Machine Translation*, pages 239–248, Alicante, Spain.

Poncelas, A., Sarasola, K., Dowling, M., Way, A., Labaka, G., and Alegria, I. (2019). Adapting NMT to caption translation in Wikimedia Commons for low-resource languages. *Procesamiento del Lenguaje Natural*, 63:33–40.

Poncelas, A., Shterionov, D., Way, A., de Buy Wenniger, G. M., and Passban, P. (2018b). Investigating backtranslation in neural machine translation. In *21st Annual Conference of the European Association for Machine Translation*, pages 249–258, Alicante, Spain.

Sennrich, R., Haddow, B., and Birch, A. (2016a). Controlling politeness in neural machine translation via side constraints. In *Proceedings of the 2016 Conference of the North American Chapter of the Association for Computational Linguistics: Human Language Technologies*, pages 35–40, San Diego, USA.

Sennrich, R., Haddow, B., and Birch, A. (2016b). Improving neural machine translation models with monolingual data. In *Proceedings of the 54th Annual Meeting of the Association for Computational Linguistics (Volume 1: Long Papers)*, pages 86–96, Berlin, Germany.

Sennrich, R., Haddow, B., and Birch, A. (2016c). Neural machine translation of rare words with subword units. In *Proceedings of the 54th Annual Meeting of the Association for Computational Linguistics (Volume 1: Long Papers)*, volume 1, pages 1715–1725, Berlin, Germany.

Shalunts, G., Backfried, G., and Commeignes, N. (2016). The impact of machine translation on sentiment analysis. In *The Fifth International Conference on Data Analytics*, volume 63, pages 51–56, Venice, Italy.

Si, C., Wu, K., Aw, A., and Kan, M.-Y. (2019). Sentiment aware neural machine translation. In *Proceedings of the 6th Workshop on Asian Translation*, pages 200–206, Hong Kong, China.

Silva, C. C., Liu, C.-H., Poncelas, A., and Way, A. (2018). Extracting in-domain training corpora for neural machine translation using data selection methods. In *Proceedings of the Third Conference on Machine Translation: Research Papers*, pages 224–231, Brussels, Belgium.

Tebbifakhr, A., Bentivogli, L., Negri, M., and Turchi, M. (2019). Machine translation for machines: the sentiment classification use case. In *2019 Conference on Empirical Methods in Natural Language Processing and the 9th International Joint Conference on Natural Language Processing*, pages 1368–1374, Hong Kong, China.

Toral, A. (2019). Post-editese: an exacerbated translationese. In *Proceedings of Machine Translation Summit XVII Volume 1: Research Track*, pages 273–281, Dublin, Ireland.

Utiyama, M. and Isahara, H. (2007). A comparison of pivot methods for phrase-based statistical machine translation. In *Human Language Technologies 2007: The Conference of the North American Chapter of the Association for Computational Linguistics; Proceedings of the Main Conference*, pages 484–491, Rochester, USA.

van der Wees, M., Bisazza, A., and Monz, C. (2017). Dynamic data selection for neural machine translation. In *Proceedings of the 2017 Conference on Empirical Methods in Natural Language Processing*, pages 1400–1410, Copenhagen, Denmark.

Vanmassenhove, E., Shterionov, D., and Way, A. (2019). Lost in translation: Loss and decay of linguistic richness in machine translation. In *Proceedings of Machine Translation Summit XVII Volume 1: Research Track*, pages 222–232, Dublin, Ireland.

Vaswani, A., Shazeer, N., Parmar, N., Uszkoreit, J., Jones, L., Gomez, A. N., Kaiser, Ł., and Polosukhin, I. (2017). Attention is all you need. In *Advances in neural information processing systems*, pages 5998–6008, Long Beach, USA.

Wu, H. and Wang, H. (2007). Pivot language approach for phrase-based statistical machine translation. *Machine Translation*, 21(3):165–181.

Zhang, C., Li, Q., and Song, D. (2019a). Aspect-based sentiment classification with aspect-specific graph convolutional networks. In *Proceedings of the 2019 Conference on Empirical Methods in Natural Language Processing and the 9th International Joint Conference on Natural Language Processing (EMNLP-IJCNLP)*, pages 4568–4578, Hong Kong, China.

Zhang, C., Li, Q., and Song, D. (2019b). Syntax-aware aspect-level sentiment classification with proximity-weighted convolution network. In *Proceedings of the 42nd International ACM SIGIR Conference on Research and Development in Information Retrieval*, SIGIR'19, page 1145–1148, Paris, France.

Towards Handling Compositionality in
Low-Resource Bilingual Word Induction

Viktor Hangya　　　　　　　　　　　　　　hangyav@cis.lmu.de
Alexander Fraser　　　　　　　　　　　　　　fraser@cis.lmu.de
Center for Information and Language Processing, LMU Munich, Munich, Germany

Abstract

Bilingual word embeddings (BWEs) facilitate the translation of single source language words to single target language words. However, often a single source word must be translated using two target words. Previous approaches depend on observing the two target language words as a (frequent) bigram in a corpus. But for many languages only a small amount of written text is available, so that such "atomic" embeddings can only be built for a small number of frequent bigrams. In this paper, we extend atomic embedding based approaches to improve the 1-to-2 word translation of rare words by decomposing the representation of a source word to representations of two target words, allowing to model translations for which the required bigram was not observed in our monolingual corpora. We create a gold standard lexicon for 1-to-2 translation containing source German compounds along with their translations to two English words, and show that our approach improves performance. We also show the importance of bigrams for the downstream task of unsupervised machine translation and show small but significant BLEU score improvements with our approach. Our approach is an important first step in the direction of handling composition in BWEs, beyond simple memorization of seen bigrams.

1   Introduction

Bilingual word embeddings (BWEs) are key components in cross-lingual NLP tasks alleviating data scarcity for many languages. They can be built using source and target language monolingual corpora with either a cheap bilingual signal (Mikolov et al., 2013b; Xing et al., 2015) or no bilingual signal at all (Conneau et al., 2018; Artetxe et al., 2018a). They are applied to many downstream tasks, such as bilingual lexicon induction (BLI) (Vulić and Korhonen, 2016) and cross-lingual transfer learning (Schuster et al., 2019). Unsupervised machine translation (UMT) strongly depends on BWEs. Meaningful translations can be generated without any bilingual signal by using BWEs to translate words 1-to-1.

However, many words in a given language are the composition of multiple smaller lexical units which are expressed individually in other languages, such as the German compound *Waschmaschine → washing machine*. Using the idea of atomic embeddings for frequent bigrams (Mikolov et al., 2013c) previous work proposed 1-to-2 word translations achieving significant improvements in UMT (Lample et al., 2018b; Artetxe et al., 2018b). These approaches start by learning individual vector representations for frequent bigrams using their monolingual contexts, effectively treating them as if they were single words. After the projection of the learned monolingual spaces to BWEs, these special bigrams can also be translated or serve as translation candidates in exactly the same way as unigrams. On the other hand, these approaches need to learn these special atomic embeddings in advance, requiring them to be frequently observed to be learned well. This assumes the availability of large monolingual corpora which are not available for low-resource languages. Relying only on atomic embeddings fails if the target bigrams are out-of-vocabulary or infrequent. For example, if the English bigram in *Cocabauern* → *coca farmers* was not seen in the target corpus, then its embedding will be unknown. Thus it cannot serve as a translation candidate. Furthermore, if it was seen but it is infrequent, its representation will be poor. We therefore have a high chance of translating *Cocabauern* to a similar but more frequent English bigram (e.g. *corn farmers*). This problem was partially addressed in (Del et al., 2018) by generating bigram representations using a linear composition based on the embeddings of the two words in a bigram. This way they are able to generate better embeddings for infrequent bigrams by relying on their frequent unigram components. On the other hand, their approach still suffers from the OOV issue because they are only able to compute a limited number of compositions, which they restrict to observed bigrams.

To overcome these problems we extend atomic embeddings in order to improve translation of rare words by decomposing source language unigrams to two target words. Given the embedding of a unigram (*Cocabauern*) we infer two word vectors which we decode to a bigram (*coca farmers*) by looking for the nearest neighbors of the generated vectors. This way we omit the need for atomic bigram representations on the target side learned in advance and allow the generation of previously unseen bigrams. We employ a multi-layer neural network relying only on unsupervised BWEs and generate cross-lingual training examples using atomic embeddings and back-translation (Sennrich et al., 2016). In addition, we create monolingual examples having a target language bigram as the input and its unigram components as the output, i.e., these examples teach the system to map the atomic embedding of a bigram like "corn_farmers" to the two representations of "corn" and "farmers", which monolingually mimics the cross-lingual translation task. Similarly to auto-encoding based approach, we can generate these monolingual examples easily which are useful for the bilingual task as well since the BWEs on which our system relies represent source and target language words with similar vectors.

We test our system on the new task of bilingual phrase lexicon induction (BPLI), i.e., translating single words to phrases, which we propose here. We use German compound words and their English translations as the test lexicon, since they behave well in 1-to-2 translation, serving as a good starting point for our experiments. We focus on 1-to-2 translation only since they have the highest impact on UMT quality (Lample et al., 2018b). We simulate De-En as low-resource by using a large amount of monolingual data only on the source side (De) while testing various data sizes for the target (En). We show that by combining our proposed approach with atomic embeddings the performance on the BPLI task can be improved. Our analysis shows that mapping a source word to atomically embedded bigrams has high performance when translating frequent source words, while the decomposition of a source word to two target word representations works well when translating infrequent source words. In addition, we show the importance of the system for UMT by including our approach in the pipeline of the UMT system of Artetxe et al. (2018b) and show its positive effects on translation quality.

2   Related Work

Bilingual word embeddings became popular resources for many cross-lingual NLP tasks since they allow the transfer of knowledge from a source language to a target language. Various approaches were proposed. Gouws et al. (2015) rely on parallel corpora, while others create artificial cross-lingual corpora using seed lexicons or document alignments (Vulić and Moens, 2015; Duong et al., 2016). Following Mikolov et al. (2013b), many authors map monolingual word embeddings (MWEs) into shared bilingual spaces (Faruqui and Dyer, 2014; Xing et al., 2015) because only a weak bilingual signal in the form of a seed lexicon is needed. Bilingual Lexicon Induction (BLI) is often used as the intrinsic evaluation of BWE spaces (Mikolov et al., 2013b; Vulić and Korhonen, 2016), where the task is to translate individual source language words to a single target word (1-to-1). Most approaches rely on cosine similarity of word embeddings by predicting the top-1 or top-5 most similar words as translations. In order to evaluate our approach intrinsically, we created a test lexicon as is usually done in BLI, but our test lexicon has single words and their bigram translations.

Recent work showed that building BWEs is possible without any bilingual signal. Adversarial training was used to rotate the source space to match the target in order to extract an initial seed lexicon which is used to fine-tune the projection (Conneau et al., 2018). Others used word neighborhood information to create the initial mapping (Artetxe et al., 2018a; Alvarez-Melis and Jaakkola, 2018). All these works led to the possibility of building MT systems without parallel data which are based on the word translation capabilities of unsupervised BWEs and back-translation of large monolingual data (Sennrich et al., 2016). Systems based on both neural network approaches (Lample et al., 2018a; Artetxe et al., 2018c; Yang et al., 2018) and phrase-based SMT (Lample et al., 2018b; Artetxe et al., 2018b) were proposed. We evaluate our approach on the downstream task of UMT as well by extending the approach of (Artetxe et al., 2018b), showing translation quality improvements.

An important step of statistical UMT systems which gives significant performance improvement is learning atomic representations for bigrams. Statistical UMT allows 1-to-2, 2-to-1 and even 2-to-2 translations. Mikolov et al. (2013c) showed that good quality embeddings can be learned by mining frequent n-grams in monolingual corpora using co-occurrence statistics and learning their representation in the same way as other vocabulary entries. The approach was improved in (Artetxe et al., 2018b) by keeping unigram invariance while learning n-gram embeddings. We give more details about this approach in the following section since we rely on this system in our experiments. On the other hand, the problem of these approaches is that a large amount of monolingual data is required in order to mine frequent bigrams and to learn good quality embeddings for them. Del et al. (2018) alleviated the problem by inferring bigram embeddings by composing the representations of their unigram components. Various composition functions were tested, such as simple addition of vectors or learning a linear projection. Following the work of Yazdani et al. (2015), they use atomic bigram embeddings and the representations of their unigram components as training samples to learn the composition function. However it is not feasible to compose each pair of unigrams in the vocabulary due to their large number, thus the approach considers only those bigram candidates which occur in the input monolingual corpora, typically leading to OOV target bigrams in the case of rare source words. Our approach alleviates these problems by extending previous systems with a decomposition based module for better rare word translation which is able to generate previously unseen bigrams as well.

3   Approach

As mentioned above in the approach of Del et al. (2018) the embeddings of target language bigrams are generated using a composition mechanism which are used as target candidate translations for source words. Since they show that the composition of target language unigrams can be used for 1-to-2 translation, we can assume that source word embeddings encode the meaning of its components. Based on this intuition, we follow a reverse approach where we decompose source word representations into two vectors which we decode into bigrams using the target language vocabulary. The advantage of this approach is that it does not require a predefined list of bigrams. Kumar and Tsvetkov (2019) proposed a supervised MT system which generates word embeddings, instead of word indices, on the output which are then decoded into sentences using beam-search and a word embedding model. Similarly, we generate vectors as an intermediate step instead of word indices directly since our training lexicon covers only a subset of the target language vocabulary (a logit layer would be able to predict only the words in this subset).

We use a two layer feed-forward neural network[1] as the decoder which takes the embedding of the source word as input:

$$[y_{t_1}, y_{t_2}] = W_2 * ReLU(W_1 * drop(x_s)) \tag{1}$$

where x_s is the input while $[y_{t_1}, y_{t_2}]$ is the concatenated output word vectors, W_i are network parameters and $ReLU, drop$ are the non-linearity and dropout functions respectively. As training objective we minimize the mean cosine distance between predicted and gold translations in the training lexicon:

$$\underset{W_1, W_2}{\arg\min} \frac{1}{N} \sum_{i=1}^{N} d([y_{t_1}^i, y_{t_2}^i], [\hat{y}_{t_1}^i, \hat{y}_{t_2}^i]) \tag{2}$$

where $\hat{y}_{t_i}^i$ is the embedding of gold translations and $d(\cdot, \cdot)$ is the cosine distance of the vectors. The probability of a bigram $[w_{t_1}, w_{t_2}]$ is given by:

$$P([w_{t_1}, w_{t_2}] \mid [y_{t_1}, y_{t_2}]) = \frac{s(y_{t_1}, x_{w_{t_1}}) * s(y_{t_2}, x_{w_{t_2}})}{\sum_{w_1, w_2 \in V_t} s(y_{t_1}, x_{w_1}) * s(y_{t_2}, x_{w_2})} \tag{3}$$

where x_{w_i} is the embedding of word w_i, V_t is the target language unigram vocabulary and $s(\cdot, \cdot)$ is the cosine similarity of vectors. Since w_{t_i} can be any unigram in the target vocabulary we only consider the 100 most similar words compared to y_{t_1} and y_{t_2} as possible values for w_{t_1} and w_{t_2} respectively, based on their cosine similarity. By assuming that the rest of the words are irrelevant for the decoding of the output we significantly reduce the search space. In addition, we omit the normalization term during decoding for efficiency.

Atomic Embeddings As the basis of our system we use atomic embeddings of bigrams. We learn BWEs containing such embeddings using the method of (Artetxe et al., 2018b). In the first step the system learns source and target language MWEs containing frequent n-grams based on co-occurrence statistics (Mikolov et al., 2013c). Opposed to previous approaches, which treated n-grams the same way as unigrams, Artetxe et al. (2018b) modified word2vec skip-gram (Mikolov et al., 2013a) in a way that it learns n-gram embeddings keeping unigram invariance, i.e., resulting unigram embeddings are the same as when there are no longer phrases in the vocabulary. This is achieved by only updating n-gram embeddings but not context embeddings when a training example has an n-gram as the center word. The projection of MWEs to a BWE space is done using the unsupervised *VecMap* system (Artetxe et al., 2018a). The method builds an initial mapping relying on intra-lingual similarity distribution of embeddings and iteratively improves the projection through self-learning without any bilingual signal.

Training lexicons Since our aim is to apply our system to setups where no bilingual signal is available, we generate training lexicons automatically, containing source→target translation pairs, relying only on unsupervised BWEs. We build multiple lexicon variations containing either cross-lingual or monolingual training examples. As the quality of atomic embeddings are good in case of frequent bigrams, we use them to learn basic decomposition and to generalize decomposition to rare and OOV bigrams as well. When training our system the source side of each example is represented by a single, while the target by two individual vectors.

---

[1] Simple linear projection resulted in lower performance.

s2t We build a cross-lingual lexicon containing source language unigrams having target language bigram translations, e.g., *Waschmaschine* → *washing machine*. For simplicity, we translate target language bigrams back to the source language using BLI, i.e., by taking to most similar unigram or bigram as the translation based on their vector similarity. We filter pairs which have a bigram on the source side, since we are only interested in unigram→bigram pairs. Finally, we retain only those pairs which have at least 0.2 similarity in order to have a good quality lexicon.

t2t We create a monolingual lexicon as well, containing the same target language bigrams on both source and target sides. We use the atomic bigram embeddings to decompose them to the individual word vectors of their unigram components, e.g., *washing_machine* → *washing machine*, similarity to (Yazdani et al., 2015; Del et al., 2018). Since we rely on BWEs, i.e., words of the two languages are represented in a shared space, this lexicon can be used in the same way as *s2t* by considering the target language bigram vectors on the source side as the noisy representation of the source language bigrams. We take the list of target language bigrams from the BWE vocabulary for this lexicon but clean it by filtering any bigram which has a component that is a stopword, a punctuation mark, a digit, shorter that 4 characters or if its POS sequence[2] is not composed of two nouns, a noun and an adjective or does not start with a verb (gerund, present or past participle) and ends with a noun. We note that the POS patterns reflect German compound composition but they can easily be extended to generalize our approach in future work. In addition, we keep only the most frequent 10K bigrams (or less if 10K is not available). We apply the same filtering to the following two lexicons as well except that we vary the number of the retained entries as described below.

s2t-avg We found that having too many bigrams in the BWE vocabulary when not enough monolingual data is available on the target side leads to bad quality atomic embeddings. This can be alleviated by learning embeddings for frequent bigrams only, but this leads to small *s2t* and *t2t* lexicons. To overcome this problem, we mine additional less frequent bigrams from the target language corpus without learning atomic embeddings for them due to their low frequency. We create a lexicon using these bigrams and by back-translation (Sennrich et al., 2016) applying BLI on their unigram components individually. We then take the average of the two resulting source language unigrams' representations as the source side bigram vector, since atomic embeddings are not available.

t2t-avg We generate a monolingual lexicon in a similar way. We use the target language bigrams from *s2t-avg* and take the average target language representations of the bigrams' components as the source side vector instead of back-translating them. Since learning atomic embeddings is better than averaging, we use only the most frequent 1K bigrams.

Because not all lexicons are equally useful for the training of our system due to their quality, we use them sequentially by performing 10 epochs each on *t2t-avg*, *s2t-avg*, and *t2t* respectively in this order, and then we run 70 epochs on *s2t*. We note that to improve the precision of these lexicons we used CSLS (Conneau et al., 2018) instead of cosine similarity for BLI.

Ensembling In order to improve 1-to-2 translation of rare words we extend atomic embeddings with the decomposition approach by ensembling the outputs of the two modules. We define $T_{w_s}^B$ a set of 100 target language bigrams that are most similar to the input word w_s based on CSLS similarity of embeddings in a given BWE space. Similarly, $T_{w_s}^D$ is a set of most probable 100 translations predicted by our approach. We calculate the ensemble score for each w_s and $t_{w_s} \in T_{w_s}^B \cup T_{w_s}^D$ as:

---

[2]We use *spaCy* for POS tagging `https://spacy.io`

$$S_E(w_s, t_{w_s}) = \sum_{m \in B,D} \lambda_m * S_m(w_s, t_{w_s}), \qquad S_m = \frac{s_m(w_s, t_{w_s})}{\sum_{t \in T^B_{w_s} \cup T^D_{w_s}} s_m(w_s, t)} \qquad (4)$$

where $s_B(\cdot, \cdot)$ is the CSLS similarity between its arguments' representations, $s_D(\cdot, \cdot)$ is the prediction score of the decomposition module and λ_B, λ_D are the weights of the two methods respectively. If a given (w_s, t) is not in $T^m_{w_s}$ we set $s_m(w_s, t)$ to 10^{-6}.

Parameters   The parameters in our experiments are the following: we use 300 dimensional word embeddings, hidden layer of 1000 and dropout probability 0.2 in our decoder, batch size of 32 over 100 training epochs without early stopping. The learning rate of the *Adam* optimizer is 0.001 initially which we multiply by 0.1 in every 10th epoch when using training examples of *s2t* lexicon. We used the development set of the created BPLI lexicon (see below) for tuning the network parameters and the ensemble weights. We implemented our system in PyTorch (Paszke et al., 2019).

We note that previous work learned trigram embeddings as well for UMT systems (Lample et al., 2018b; Artetxe et al., 2018b). We only focus on bigrams since they have the most impact, while higher n-grams have only marginal improvements, as shown by Lample et al. (2018b). However, based on the lexicon generation and equation 1, the extension of our system from bigrams to longer n-grams, which we leave for future work, is technically straight-forward. One needs to generate lexicons for longer n-grams as well, while extending the number of vectors predicted by the decoder. To allow for variable n-gram length the introduction of a *PAD* token is necessary.

4   Evaluation

4.1   Bilingual Phrase Lexicon Induction

We introduce a novel test lexicon containing German compounds and their English translations for the evaluation[3]. We focus on compounds in this work since they behave well in 1-to-2 translations. We will discuss future generalization possibilities of the approach, such as non-compound inputs, at the end of the paper. We take the source compounds from the work of Fritzinger and Fraser (2010) which was created to test German compound splitting accuracy. Since the dataset does not contain English pairs of the words we automatically translated them using Google Translate. Some of the compounds were translated 1-to-1, e.g., $Ackerland \rightarrow farmland$, we filtered them out which resulted in 661 pairs. Besides bigrams on the target side, the lexicon contains 3-grams and 4-grams as well, making up around 10% and 1% of the examples respectively. Since our current system only translates to bigrams, longer phrases count as errors in our evaluation, but we kept these entries in the lexicon to allow future comparison. We use half of the lexicon for parameter tuning and the other half for testing.

As the baseline we learn BWEs containing atomic bigram embeddings using the method of (Artetxe et al., 2018b) described above and perform BLI. For both the baseline (*atomic*) and our system (*ensemble*), we only allow bigram outputs. To build BWEs we use the same monolingual data used in (Artetxe et al., 2018b) which contains German ($89.6M$) and English ($90.2M$) news crawl sentences between 2007 and 2013 released by WMT14. We simulate low-resource settings by decreasing the amount of available sentences on the target side ($all, 1M, 500K$ and $250K$) but keeping the full dataset on the source. Our experiments showed that having too many atomic n-gram embeddings when we have only a low number of sentences results in low quality BWEs which can be improved by decreasing the number of n-gram embeddings. Based

---

[3]The dataset is available at: `https://www.cis.lmu.de/~hangyav/data/BPLI.zip`

on this and the setup of (Artetxe et al., 2018b), we build BWEs containing $200K$ most frequent embeddings for unigrams and $400K$ most frequent bigrams and trigrams on both source and target side, except in the case of $250K$ sentences where we used $10K$. We note that we also tried to experiment with only $100K$ sentences in the monolingual data but even with only unigrams in the vocabulary we couldn't build functional BWEs.

4.2 Unsupervised Machine Translation

We evaluate our system extrinsically as well on the task of unsupervised MT on the WMT news translation shared task test data from 2014 and 2016, similarly to previous work on unsupervised MT (Lample et al., 2018b; Artetxe et al., 2018b). We additionally evaluate on WMT 2019 (Barrault et al., 2019).

To examine the effects of BWEs on MT, we extend the statistical UMT system of (Artetxe et al., 2018b) which strongly relies on BWEs. By default it is comprised of 5 consecutive steps. In step 1 it builds MWEs containing atomic representations for 1-, 2- and 3-grams and projects them to shared BWE spaces in step 2 with the same method as the basis of our system for the BPLI experiments described above. The Moses statistical MT system is used as the translation system (Koehn et al., 2007) which requires two components in this case: a language model and a phrase-table. The former is built with KenLM (Heafield, 2011) while the latter contains phrase translation pairs and their scores for each source word and the 100 most similar target words which are calculated using cosine similarity in step 3. The weights of the two components are tuned in step 4 on a synthetic parallel corpus generated through back-translation and MERT is applied as the tuning algorithm. Finally, in step 5 the system is iteratively refined (for 3 iterations) using back-translation of monolingual data. We use this off-the-shelf system as one of our baselines which we call *atomic* since it uses atomic n-gram embeddings. In addition, we run the same system but without atomic representations for 2- and 3-grams, i.e., with only unigram word embeddings (*unigram*).

Extended UMT   To plug our system into the pipeline we extend the generated phrase-table in step 3 of the atomic baseline to show the additional effects of the bigrams generated by our approach. We filter words from the source language vocabulary which are longer than the average character length in our BPLI test lexicon (13) with the aim to gather compound words automatically. We predict top-100 translations of these words and create a phrase-table using the prediction score of the decomposition module as the translation probability. We then merge it with the baseline phrase-table by taking their union. More precisely, each entry has 5 scores, 4 coming from the baseline and 1 from our extension. In addition, if a source-target pair is missing in one of the tables we set the related values to 10^{-6}. We only extend the De→En phrase-table but as discussed below it also affects the En→De direction as well due to back-translation. We create a secondary phrase-table with the decomposition module instead of generating just one with the extended atomic embeddings because this way the tuning procedure in step 4 is able to tune parameters for the two phrase-tables more precisely. Other steps in the original pipeline are unchanged. We refer to this system as *extended*.

5   Results

5.1   Bilingual Phrase Lexicon Induction

To evaluate BPLI we report top-5 accuracy (acc_5) on lowercased words, as is done in most work on BLI (Mikolov et al., 2013b). Some of the source words in the test lexicon are OOVs, i.e., their embeddings are unknown. We filtered them since no system is able to predict their translations. We show results in Table 1 comparing the baseline *atomic* embeddings and its extension with the decomposition module (*ensemble*). As mentioned earlier we use various target corpora sizes.

	atomic	ensemble	λ_B
250K	12.12	15.06	0.50
500K	34.34	37.35	0.46
1M	43.98	46.99	0.58
all	65.06	65.06	0.70

Table 1: Acc_5 results on the BPLI task in percentage points of the baseline (atomic) and our proposed approach (ensemble). The weight of BWE based similarities are given by λ_B ($\lambda_D = 1.0 - \lambda_B$).

	atomic			decomposition		
	all	≤ 100	≤ 10	all	≤ 100	≤ 10
250K	12.12	2.04	0.00	13.86	8.11	1.15
500K	34.34	27.54	1.52	19.88	15.22	4.55
1M	43.98	31.62	2.13	21.69	14.53	4.26
all	65.06	0.00	0.00	25.90	0.00	0.00

Table 2: Comparison of the two modules on various target language data sizes (1st column) and limited test lexicons containing *all* source words or only those which have a gold translation with frequencies ≤ 100 and ≤ 10 respectively (2nd row).

	all	≤ 100	≤ 10
250K	325	306	235
500K	325	295	200
1M	325	269	162
all	325	69	33

Table 3: Number of test lexicon entries along varying target language corpora sizes (1st column) and bigram frequencies (1nd row).

When only a small amount of target language data is available the quality of atomic embeddings decreases due to a larger number of rare words. By combining the decomposition module with the atomic embeddings the performance increased, especially in case of the low data size setups. As the target language corpus grows there are less rare words that have to be translated 1-to-2, thus the difference between the two systems decreases but even at 1M sentences the difference is significant. No improvements were achieved for *all* in terms of acc_5 since the data size is large ($90.2M$). On the other hand, by looking at acc_1 our system performed 0.6% better. We found ensembling weights to be best when the two models contribute about equally as shown in Table 1.

Atomic vs. Decomposition In Table 2 we compare the two modules of our approach to depict their performance differences. Other than the limited target corpus sizes we create setups where the test BPLI lexicon contains only those compounds which have a gold translation with frequency at most 100 and 10 respectively. Note that the number of entries in these lexicons is changing with the target corpus size which we show in table 3. This is because as the training data size increases the identity of the limited frequency translations changes.

The results show that the decomposition module by itself performs better than atomic embeddings if there is not much data. It works even better in contrast with the atomic system when looking at low frequency bigrams only which clearly shows the advantage of our approach in

	250K	500K	1M	all
s2t	3.61	13.25	15.66	26.51
s2t+t2t	4.82	18.67	15.66	24.70
all 4	13.86	19.88	21.69	25.90
s2t-avg+t2t-avg	9.64	9.04	13.25	14.46

Table 4: Ablation study on the effect of the 4 generated training lexicons on the decomposition module. The 1st column shows the used lexicons. Results are on the full test lexicon with various target language corpora sizes.

	250K	500K	1M	all
s2t	237	949	2,210	14,656
t2t	267	10,000	10,000	10,000
s2t-avg	11,963	23,249	40,818	36,988
t2t-avg	1,000	1,000	1,000	1,000

Table 5: Generated training lexicon sizes in various target language corpora sizes.

low-resource cases. For both $500K$ and $1M$ atomic performs better on the full test lexicon which shows the good quality of atomic embeddings when the data size is large. On the other hand, on frequency ≤ 10 our approach performs better even for $1M$ showing that it can generalize to low-frequency test cases better which explains the good performance of the joint model in Table 1. Furthermore, both systems achieve 0% accuracy on the limited frequency test sets taken from the *all* scenario because these test sets have only a few but very low frequency words which have low quality embeddings, thus making their translation difficult.

Ablation study   We performed an ablation study to analyze the contribution of the generated training lexicons on the decomposition module. We show results using only atomic embeddings on the source side (s2t and s2t+t2t) and no atomic embeddings (s2t-avg+t2t-avg) in Table 4. The former aims at analyzing the effect of having a small number of good quality pairs (training lexicon sizes are shown in Table 5) while the latter gives an intuition of achievable performance when atomic embeddings are unavailable. Results show that the s2t set is the most important, since as its size grows the additional improvements coming from the other sets are decreasing. Note, that in case of using all target language data the best results were achieved when using only s2t. On the other hand, in the lower resource setups the other sets are essential in achieving good performance, especially in case of $250K$ when both s2t and t2t are small due to a small number of frequent bigrams.

5.2   Unsupervised Machine Translation

We compare the performance of using standard BWEs (*unigram*), with the *atomic* approach and our extension of the atomic approach (*extended*) in terms of BLEU in Table 6. We show results of step 4 (parameter tuning) and step 5 (iterative refinement). Our results show that relying on unigram BWEs (as was done for NMT in previous work) performs poorly. Comparing the unigram with the atomic and extended variants it can be seen that using bigram embeddings to perform initial word translation leads to significant improvements in both step 4 and step 5, which is caused by the translation possibility of source words to multiple target words. In addition, we achieved further improvements with the extension of the atomic system with the decomposition module by having better translation entries in the phrase table for rare words. Just as in the BPLI experiments, the combination of atomic and decomposed bigrams has posi-

			wmt14		wmt16		wmt19	
			De-En	En-De	De-En	En-De	De-En	En-De
250K	step4	unigram	3.50	3.30	5.00	4.70	3.50	3.60
		atomic	5.50	4.80	6.70	6.60	4.80	5.80
		extended	5.60	4.90	6.80	6.60	4.90	5.90
	step5	unigram	8.70	7.00	11.60	9.70	10.00	9.20
		atomic	9.90	8.20	13.00	10.90	10.60	10.70
		extended	10.10	8.30	13.40	11.30	11.10	10.80
500K	step4	unigram	5.60	3.80	7.80	5.40	5.80	4.70
		atomic	7.10	5.80	8.50	7.40	6.30	6.30
		extended	7.40	5.90	9.00	7.60	6.80	6.40
	step5	unigram	9.90	8.40	13.50	11.90	11.30	11.20
		atomic	11.80	9.60	15.30	13.10	11.90	12.20
		extended	12.00	9.50	15.40	13.10	12.60	11.70
1M	step4	unigram	7.90	5.30	10.20	7.30	7.60	6.60
		atomic	10.20	7.80	12.70	10.00	9.80	8.60
		extended	10.20	8.00	12.80	10.30	9.90	8.80
	step5	unigram	11.00	9.20	14.40	12.60	11.90	12.00
		atomic	12.70	10.70	16.50	14.10	12.90	12.80
		extended	12.80	10.30	16.50	14.10	13.00	12.60
all	step4	unigram	9.20	5.50	11.70	7.40	8.40	6.40
		atomic	14.93	10.71	18.34	13.46	13.01	11.90
		extended	15.00	11.00	18.60	13.70	13.20	12.40
	step5	unigram	12.70	10.60	17.40	14.40	12.20	13.50
		atomic	17.04	13.39	22.28	17.43	15.70	14.80
		extended	17.40	13.70	22.40	17.70	16.60	15.30

Table 6: BLEU scores comparing the two baseline (with and without n-gram embeddings) and the extended UMT systems. The first column shows the number of sentences in the target language monolingual data used to build BWEs. Step 4 and 5 are the parameter tuning and iterative refinement steps in the UMT training pipeline.

tive effects not only in the low-resource but higher resource cases as well and also when using the full target language dataset. This shows that our system generates useful bigrams, other than those in the BWE vocabulary, which are getting picked by the language model. Improvements can be seen in case of both steps 4 and 5 meaning that the parameter tuning can decide how to trade off the weighting of the atomic embeddings based phrase-table and the decomposition based phrase-tables and there are positive effects during the refinement steps as well. In addition, improvements can be seen in case of the En-De translation direction even though we only extend the De-En phrase table. Since the initial De-En model in step 4 is improved by the extension, it affects the opposite direction as well due to the use of the initial De-En model during back-translation.

6 Conclusion

Unigram BWEs do not model important 1-to-2 word translations. We show the gain for using atomic embeddings for bigrams in order to perform 1-to-2 word translation but this approach can only be applied when there is a large amount of monolingual data available. Our new decomposition based approach for modeling 1-to-2 translation of rare words directly translates source unigram embeddings to target language bigrams allowing us to predict both rare and

OOV bigrams. We proposed a system combining the advantages of atomic embeddings and decomposition which we tested intrinsically on 1-to-2 BLI of German compounds for which we created a new test set. We release our BPLI dataset for further development. We showed improved performance compared to just using atomic embeddings even in less resource-poor setups. Furthermore, our analysis showed that on rare words the decomposition based translation alone outperforms atomic embeddings, further motivating their joint use. We also showed that bigrams are important for statistical UMT systems and that by plugging our system into an UMT pipeline we achieved better performance compared to an off-the-shelf system on this extrinsic task as well.

In this paper we presented first steps towards handling compositionality in BLI and UMT. To be able to extend UMT systems by our approach in general, not only for compound translations as we have done in our preliminary UMT experiment here, the length of the output translations has to be decided dynamically. The proposed architecture is compatible with such a setup with the introduction of a padding token and training lexicon containing unigrams as well but further experimentation is required. The translation of non-compound words, such as when target language functional words are expressed with pre-, in- or suffixes in the source (e.g. $kedd + \underline{en} \rightarrow on\ Tuesday$ in Hungarian or $ver + \underline{me} + mek \rightarrow not\ to\_give$ in Turkish), should be investigated in future work as well.

Acknowledgments

We would like to thank Leonie Weißweiler for her contribution to the construction of the BPLI lexicon and the anonymous reviewers for their valuable input. This project has received funding from the European Research Council (ERC) under the European Union's Horizon 2020 research and innovation programme (grant agreement № 640550).

References

Alvarez-Melis, D. and Jaakkola, T. (2018). Gromov-Wasserstein Alignment of Word Embedding Spaces. In *Proc. EMNLP*, pages 1881–1890.

Artetxe, M., Labaka, G., and Agirre, E. (2018a). A robust self-learning method for fully unsupervised cross-lingual mappings of word embeddings. In *Proc. ACL*, pages 789–798.

Artetxe, M., Labaka, G., and Agirre, E. (2018b). Unsupervised Statistical Machine Translation. In *Proc. EMNLP*, pages 3632–3642.

Artetxe, M., Labaka, G., Agirre, E., and Cho, K. (2018c). Unsupervised Neural Machine Translation. In *Proc. ICLR*.

Barrault, L., Bojar, O., Costa-jussà, M. R., Federmann, C., Fishel, M., Graham, Y., Haddow, B., Huck, M., Koehn, P., Malmasi, S., Monz, C., Müller, M., Pal, S., Post, M., and Zampieri, M. (2019). Findings of the 2019 Conference on Machine Translation (WMT19). In *Proc. WMT*, pages 1–61.

Conneau, A., Lample, G., Ranzato, M., Denoyer, L., and Jégou, H. (2018). Word Translation Without Parallel Data. In *Proc. ICLR*, pages 1–14.

Del, M., Tättar, A., and Fishel, M. (2018). Phrase-based Unsupervised Machine Translation with Compositional Phrase Embeddings. In *Proc. WMT*, pages 361–367.

Duong, L., Kanayama, H., Ma, T., Bird, S., and Cohn, T. (2016). Learning crosslingual word embeddings without bilingual corpora. In *Proc. EMNLP*, pages 1285–1295.

Faruqui, M. and Dyer, C. (2014). Improving vector space word representations using multilingual correlation. In *Proc. EACL*, pages 462–471.

Fritzinger, F. and Fraser, A. (2010). How to Avoid Burning Ducks: Combining Linguistic Analysis and Corpus Statistics for German Compound Processing. In *Proc. WMT*, pages 224–234.

Gouws, S., Bengio, Y., and Corrado, G. (2015). Bilbowa: Fast bilingual distributed representations without word alignments. In *Proc. ICML*.

Heafield, K. (2011). KenLM: Faster and Smaller Language Model Queries. In *Proc. EMNLP*, pages 187–197.

Koehn, P., Hoang, H., Birch, A., Callison-Burch, C., Federico, M., Bertoldi, N., Cowan, B., Shen, W., Moran, C., Zens, R., Dyer, C., Bojar, O., Constantin, A., and Herbst, E. (2007). Moses: Open source toolkit for statistical machine translation. In *Proc. ACL*, pages 177–180.

Kumar, S. and Tsvetkov, Y. (2019). Von Mises-Fisher Loss for Training Sequence to Sequence Models with Continuous Outputs. In *Proc. ICLR*.

Lample, G., Denoyer, L., and Ranzato, M. (2018a). Unsupervised Machine Translation Using Monolingual Corpora Only. In *Proc. ICLR*.

Lample, G., Ott, M., Conneau, A., Denoyer, L., and Ranzato, M. (2018b). Phrase-Based & Neural Unsupervised Machine Translation. In *Proc. EMNLP*, pages 5039–5049.

Mikolov, T., Chen, K., Corrado, G., and Dean, J. (2013a). Efficient estimation of word representations in vector space. In *Proc. ICLR*.

Mikolov, T., Le, Q. V., and Sutskever, I. (2013b). Exploiting Similarities among Languages for Machine Translation. *CoRR*, abs/1309.4.

Mikolov, T., Sutskever, I., Chen, K., Corrado, G. S., and Dean, J. (2013c). Distributed Representations of Words and Phrases and their Compositionality. In *Proc. NIPS*, pages 3111–3119.

Paszke, A., Gross, S., Massa, F., Lerer, A., Bradbury, J., Chanan, G., Killeen, T., Lin, Z., Gimelshein, N., Antiga, L., Desmaison, A., Kopf, A., Yang, E., DeVito, Z., Raison, M., Tejani, A., Chilamkurthy, S., Steiner, B., Fang, L., Bai, J., and Chintala, S. (2019). PyTorch: An Imperative Style, High-Performance Deep Learning Library. In *Proc. NeurIPS*, pages 8024–8035.

Schuster, T., Ram, O., Barzilay, R., and Globerson, A. (2019). Cross-Lingual Alignment of Contextual Word Embeddings, with Applications to Zero-shot Dependency Parsing. In *Proc. NAACL-HLT*, pages 1599–1613.

Sennrich, R., Haddow, B., and Birch, A. (2016). Improving Neural Machine Translation Models with Monolingual Data. In *Proc. ACL*, pages 86–96.

Vulić, I. and Korhonen, A. (2016). On the Role of Seed Lexicons in Learning Bilingual Word Embeddings. In *Proc. ACL*, pages 247–257.

Vulić, I. and Moens, M. (2015). Bilingual word embeddings from non-parallel document-aligned data applied to bilingual lexicon induction. In *Proc. ACL*, pages 719–725.

Xing, C., Wang, D., Liu, C., and Lin, Y. (2015). Normalized Word Embedding and Orthogonal Transform for Bilingual Word Translation. In *Proc. NAACL-HLT*, pages 1006–1011.

Yang, Z., Chen, W., Wang, F., and Xu, B. (2018). Unsupervised Neural Machine Translation with Weight Sharing. In *Proc. ACL*, pages 46–55.

Yazdani, M., Farahmand, M., and Henderson, J. (2015). Learning Semantic Composition to Detect Non-compositionality of Multiword Expressions. In *Proc. EMNLP*, pages 1733–1742.

The OpenNMT Neural Machine Translation Toolkit: 2020 Edition

Guillaume Klein   guillaume.klein@systrangroup.com
François Hernandez   fhernandez@ubiqus.com
Vincent Nguyen   vnguyen@ubiqus.com
Jean Senellart   jean.senellart@systrangroup.com

Abstract

OpenNMT is a multi-year open-source ecosystem for neural machine translation (NMT) and natural language generation (NLG). The toolkit consists of multiple projects to cover the complete machine learning workflow: from data preparation to inference acceleration. The systems prioritize efficiency, modularity, and extensibility with the goal of supporting research into model architectures, feature representations, and source modalities, while maintaining API stability and competitive performance for production usages. OpenNMT has been used in several production MT systems and cited in more than 700 research papers.

1   Introduction

Neural machine translation (NMT) is a recent approach for machine translation that has led to remarkable improvements, particularly in terms of human evaluation, compared to rule-based and statistical machine translation (SMT) systems (Wu et al., 2016). From the initial work on recurrent sequence-to-sequence models (Sutskever et al., 2014) to recent advances on self-attentional models (Vaswani et al., 2017), a significant amount of contributions explored various model architectures, hyper-parameter settings, and data preparation techniques. This exploration is often constrained by engineering issues related to computation efficiency, code design, and model deployment.

In this context, we introduced OpenNMT [1] in late 2016, the first large audience open-source toolkit to design, train, and deploy neural machine translation models. The OpenNMT initiative consists of several projects to assist researchers and developers in their NMT journey, from data preparation to inference acceleration. It supports a wide range of model architectures and training procedures for neural machine translation as well as related tasks such as natural language generation and language modeling.

The open source community around neural machine translation is very active and includes several other projects that have similar goals and capabilities such as Fairseq (Ott et al., 2019), Sockeye (Hieber et al., 2017), or Marian (Junczys-Dowmunt et al., 2018). In the ongoing development of OpenNMT, we aim to build upon the strengths of those systems, while providing unique features and technology support.

In this paper, we briefly give an overview of the OpenNMT project and its history. We then present the key features that make OpenNMT particularly suited for research and production. Finally, we share some benchmarks for comparison and current work directions.

---

[1] `https://opennmt.net`

2   Project overview

OpenNMT is a collection of projects supporting easy adoption of neural machine translation and related tasks. The project has two actively maintained implementations:

- **OpenNMT-py**: A user-friendly and multimodal implementation benefiting from PyTorch ease of use and versatility.

- **OpenNMT-tf**: A modular and stable implementation powered by the TensorFlow 2 ecosystem.

These implementations provide command line utilities and a Python library to configure, train, and run models. Each implementation has its own design and set of features, but both share the goals that started the OpenNMT initiative: ease of use, efficiency, modularity, extensibility, and production readiness. The supported features are compared in Table 1.

Training	py	tf
Automatic evaluation	✓	✓
Checkpoint averaging	✓	✓
Contrastive learning		✓
Early stopping	✓	✓
Gradient accumulation	✓	✓
Supervised alignment	✓	✓
Mixed precision	✓	✓
Moving average	✓	✓
Multi-GPU	✓	✓
Multi-node	✓	✓
Online tokenization		✓
Pretrained embeddings	✓	✓
Scheduled sampling		✓
Vocabulary update		✓
Weighted dataset	✓	✓

Tasks	py	tf
Image/Video to text	✓	
Language modeling		✓
Sequence classification		✓
Sequence tagging		✓
Sequence to sequence	✓	✓
Speech to text	✓	✓
Summarization	✓	

Models	py	tf
ConvS2S	✓	
DeepSpeech2	✓	
GPT-2		✓
Im2Text	✓	
Listen, Attend and Spell		✓
RNMT+		✓
RNN with attention	✓	✓
Transformer	✓	✓

Decoding	py	tf
Beam search	✓	✓
Coverage penalty	✓	✓
CTranslate2 compatibility	✓	✓
Ensemble	✓	
Length penalty	✓	✓
N-best rescoring	✓	✓
N-gram blocking	✓	
Phrase table	✓	
Random noise	✓	✓
Random sampling	✓	✓
Replace unknown	✓	✓

Model configuration	py	tf
Copy attention	✓	
Coverage attention	✓	
Hybrid models		✓
Multi source		✓
Multiple input features	✓	✓
Relative position	✓	✓
Tied embeddings	✓	✓

Table 1: Features implemented by OpenNMT-py (column **py**) and OpenNMT-tf (column **tf**).

The ecosystem is completed by tools that are used in both OpenNMT-py and OpenNMT-tf:

- **Tokenizer**: A fast and customizable text tokenization library that includes Unicode-based segmentation, subword training and encoding (BPE and SentencePiece), protected sequences, and case annotation.

- **CTranslate2**: An optimized inference engine for Transformer models which comes with a custom C++ implementation supporting fast CPU and GPU execution, quantization, parallel translations, and interactive decoding.

Finally, these different projects are integrated in **nmt-wizard-docker** which proposes a way to containerize NMT frameworks and provide a unique command line interface for training, translating, and serving models.

All projects are released on GitHub[2] under the MIT license.

---

[2] https://github.com/OpenNMT

2.1 History

OpenNMT was first released in late 2016 as a Torch7 implementation. This version was the result of a collaboration between Harvard NLP and SYSTRAN and was based on seq2seq-attn, an open-source project developed by Harvard student Yoon Kim. The original demonstration paper (Klein et al., 2017) was awarded "Best Demonstration Paper Runner-Up" at ACL 2017.

After the release of PyTorch (Paszke et al., 2019), the Facebook A.I. Research team shared a complete rewrite of the project that later became OpenNMT-py and initiated the sunsetting of the Torch7 version of OpenNMT. The ecosystem was then extended with OpenNMT-tf which prioritized production, while OpenNMT-py had a focus on research at this time.

After more than 3 years of active development, OpenNMT projects have been starred by over 7,400 users. A community forum[3] is also home of 970 users and more than 9,800 posts about NMT research and how to use OpenNMT effectively.

2.2 Adoption

Cited in over 700 scientific publications as of May 2020, OpenNMT has also been directly used in numerous research papers. The system is employed both to conduct new experiments and as a baseline for sequence-to-sequence approaches. OpenNMT was used for other tasks related to neural machine translation such as summarization (Gehrmann et al., 2018), data-to-text (Wiseman et al., 2017), image-to-text (Deng et al., 2017), automatic speech recognition (Ericson, 2019) and semantic parsing (van Noord and Bos, 2017).

OpenNMT also proved to be widespread in industry. Companies such as SYSTRAN (Crego et al., 2016), Booking.com (Levin et al., 2017), or Ubiqus[4] are known to deploy Open-NMT models in production. We note that a number of industrial entities published scientific papers showing their internal experiments using the framework such as SwissPost (Girletti et al., 2019) and BNP Paribas (Mghabbar and Ratnamogan, 2020), while NVIDIA used OpenNMT as a benchmark for the release of TensorRT 6[5].

3 Key features

3.1 Model architectures catalog

While OpenNMT initially focused on sequence-to-sequence models applied to translation, it has been extended to support additional architectures and model components (see Table 1).

Multiple architectures. The toolkits implement the most used architectures for neural machine translation: recurrent with attention (Bahdanau et al., 2015; Luong et al., 2015), self-attentional (Vaswani et al., 2017), and convolutional (Gehring et al., 2017). The project also includes components for other tasks such as encoders for non-text inputs, decoders for generative languages models, and copy attention mechanisms (See et al., 2017) for summarization.

Modular design. We focus on modularity to allow ideas from one paper to be reused in another context. OpenNMT-tf pushes this mindset to the extreme by requiring users to configure their model via Python code. This enables a high level of modelling freedom to support custom architectures such as hybrid sequence-to-sequence models (Chen et al., 2018), multi-source Transformer models (Libovický et al., 2018), and nested input features.

---

[3]`https://forum.opennmt.net/`
[4]`https://slator.com/features/how-ubiqus-deploys-neural-machine-translation-in-language-operations/`
[5]`https://news.developer.nvidia.com/tensorrt6-breaks-bert-record`

	Model size	CPU	GTX1080	GTX1080Ti	RTX2080Ti	BLEU
OpenNMT-tf	367MB	217.6	1659.2	1762.8	1628.3	26.9
OpenNMT-py	542MB	179.1	1510.0	1709.3	1406.2	26.7
CTranslate2	374MB	389.4	3081.3	3388.0	4196.2	26.7
+ int16	197MB	413.6	3055.7	3380.4	4202.9	26.7
+ int8	110MB	508.3	2654.8	2734.6	3143.4	26.8
+ vmap	121MB	646.2	2921.5	2992.1	3312.9	26.6

Table 2: This table compares model size and translation speed (target tokens per second) for a base English-German Transformer. The BLEU scores are computed on an undisclosed test set and are reported to show that quality is comparable. All runs use a batch size of 32 and a beam size of 4. The CTranslate2 models are generated from the OpenNMT-py model weights. There is a noticeable drop in performance on RTX for both -tf and -py for an unknown reason at the time of this publication.

3.2   Scalable training

As GPU performance has been drastically improving in the last few years, it has been important for software to take it into account not to introduce unnecessary bottlenecks. Both OpenNMT-py and OpenNMT-tf have been constantly optimized to keep up with the available computing power and its intricacies, as well as most mainstream training methods.

Optimized and parallel training.   Training efficiency was an early focus of OpenNMT. It can run the training on multiple GPUs and machines using data parallelism. OpenNMT implementations are also compatible with mixed precision training to make use of NVIDIA's Tensor Cores, and when possible, they employ graph execution.

Optimizations for low-resource hardware.   We also strive to make NMT training possible on low memory systems. OpenNMT supports gradient accumulation which is a way to simulate larger batch sizes that do not fit on the available GPU memory. OpenNMT-py is also able to shard the loss computation to reduce memory usage.

Efficient data pipeline.   Both OpenNMT implementations make use of a producer-consumer design to feed examples to the training. This effectively reduces the data pipeline latency as well as the overall memory usage.

3.3   Optimized and interactive inference engine

CTranslate2 is a unique project that accelerates the execution of Transformer variants trained with OpenNMT-py and OpenNMT-tf. It is a custom C++ implementation with no runtime dependency on PyTorch or TensorFlow. The engine can run on CPU and GPU and is up to 4 times faster than a baseline PyTorch execution as shown in Table 2.

Specialized engine.   As the engine focuses on executing specific model architectures, it implements graph-level optimizations such as layer fusion, memory reusing, and caching.

Fast backend.   On CPU, most of the heavy lifting is done by Intel MKL which is a reference library when it comes to high performance matrix operations. On GPU, the implementation uses several libraries provided by NVIDIA: Thrust, cuBLAS, and TensorRT.

Model quantization.   Quantization support in deep learning frameworks is often incomplete, especially for sequence models. However, CTranslate2 fully supports 16-bit and 8-bit GEneral Matrix Multiplication (GEMM) to reduce the memory and computation requirements.

Multi-level parallelism.   The parallelism can be configured at the batch and file levels. The first level refers to the number of OpenMP threads used to execute a batch while the second corresponds to the number of batches that are executed in parallel. This multi-level approach allows to trade-off latency and throughput.

Decoding optimizations. Multiple decoding tricks can be combined to accelerate speed, for instance restricting target vocabulary using a pretrained mapping, removing finished translations from the batch, sorting sentences by length, or skipping last Softmax in greedy decoding.

Interactive decoding. CTranslate2 also supports interactive decoding features such as auto-completing partial translations and returning alternatives at a specific position in the translation.

3.4 Efficient and customizable tokenization

Tokenizer is a standalone project that provides practical C++ and Python APIs for text tokenization. It focuses on efficiency and includes features that we found useful for training high-quality translation models.

Configurable reversibility. The tokenization can be made reversible by marking either joints or spaces. These markers can be attached to the input tokens or injected as separate tokens.

Advanced text segmentation. Several flags can finely control where to segment: on digits, on alphabet change, on case change, etc. Additionally, we introduced special control characters to prevent segmentation in delimited sequences.

Subword training and encoding. The project can train and apply SentencePiece (Kudo and Richardson, 2018) and BPE (Sennrich et al., 2016) models, while making them compatible with all features listed above.

3.5 Model serving

OpenNMT also provides components to serve translation models. OpenNMT-py includes a REST server that can manage multiple models and unload those that are not used. The server integrates CTranslate2 for efficient execution and Tokenizer for on-the-fly tokenization.

OpenNMT-tf models are compatible with TensorFlow Serving which is a scalable solution to serve machine learning models. OpenNMT-tf models are also compatible with the OpenNMT-py REST server via the CTranslate2 integration.

4   Benchmarks

OpenNMT, as a comprehensive project geared towards Neural Machine Translation, can be used in a fairly straightforward way to build SOTA systems and experiment on various tasks. Anyone can throw together a competitive system using the right data, processing and training procedures. For instance, the results for English to German translation in Table 3 are obtained with the following configuration:

- **Data**: English to German WMT19 task, with the addition of ParaCrawl v5 instead of v3.
- **Tokenization**: 40,000 BPE merge operations, learned and applied with Tokenizer.
- **Model**: Transformer Medium (12 $heads$, 768 d_{model} size, 3072 d_{ff} size).
- **Training**: Trained with OpenNMT-py on 6 RTX 2080 Ti, using mixed precision. Initial batch size is around 50,000 tokens, final batch size around 200,000 tokens.
- **Inference**: Shown scores are obtained with beam search of size 5 and average length penalty.

This vanilla system is constrained to the WMT rules to facilitate reproducibility. The commercial systems it is compared to are not constrained and we don't know the extent of the additional data that may be used. It is also very likely they use some bigger models, when we restrained this experiment to a Transformer Medium to keep the computation budget reasonable.

System	nt14	nt15	nt16	nt17	nt18	nt19	Wall time	GPU time
@30k steps	30.9	33.1	38.1	31.3	47.2	40.6	8h	48h
@100k steps	32.9	34.5	39.3	32.8	47.7	41.1	54h	324h
Online G	30.9	33.9	38.6	31.6	48.0	43.9	-	
Online M	32.3	34.3	40.5	33.1	48.8	43.8	-	

Table 3: OpenNMT system vs. some commercial systems. (BLEU scores obtained with Sacre-BLEU v1.3.7, online translations performed in April 2020.)

During the WMT19 campaign (Barrault et al., 2019), the best BLEU score for English to German was 44.9 but the best human evaluated system scored only 42.7 with an ensemble of Big Tranformers. It is also important to stress that we found many WMT19 references in the test sets (whether for English to German or some other pairs) were obviously being post edits of commercial systems. A very simple way to outline this phenomenon was to score each document with these commercial systems and show the huge difference in BLEU points for some of them. On the other hand, these systems were not over-performing in the same way for previous years test sets. This has been reported by several papers in the WMT19 campaign.

Extending this to a more complete setup, with internal datasets as well as a bigger architecture, OpenNMT tools allow to reach a superior performance. Some results for an internal English to French setup are presented in Table 4.

System	nt14	finance	legal	general	life sciences
OpenNMT	43.2	46.6	37.2	39.6	55.9
Online G	43.3	43.6	33.9	37.9	50.8
Online M	37.6	36.2	28.2	36.7	46.4

Table 4: OpenNMT English to French model performance on test sets of various domains. (BLEU scores obtained with SacreBLEU v1.3.7, online translations performed in April 2020.)

5 Current work

As OpenNMT aims to provide a state-of-the-art ecosystem for neural machine translation, we are continuously reproducing published papers with the goal of cherry-picking features with significant impact and implementing technologies that are part of the complete translation workflow. For example, we are currently working on combining translation memories with NMT.

We are also interested in further accelerating model inference via the CTranslate2 project. Future works include a better support of reduced precision on GPU and integration of optimized backends for non-Intel CPUs.

Finally, we are planning on massively releasing ready-to-use state-of-the-art models for a collection of language pairs to simplify the adoption of NMT.

6 Summary

We presented OpenNMT, an open-source ecosystem for neural machine translation and natural language generation. The toolkit contains multiple projects and features to cover the complete model production workflow. The main implementations, OpenNMT-py and OpenNMT-tf, support many configurable models and efficient training procedures to produce high-quality models. We also published CTranslate2, an optimized inference engine which to our knowledge is one of the fastest decoder of Transformer models. All projects are available on GitHub at
`https://github.com/OpenNMT`.

References

Bahdanau, D., Cho, K., and Bengio, Y. (2015). Neural machine translation by jointly learning to align and translate. In Bengio, Y. and LeCun, Y., editors, *3rd International Conference on Learning Representations, ICLR 2015, San Diego, CA, USA, May 7-9, 2015, Conference Track Proceedings*.

Barrault, L., Bojar, O., Costa-jussÃ, M. R., Federmann, C., Fishel, M., Graham, Y., Haddow, B., Huck, M., Koehn, P., Malmasi, S., Monz, C., MÃller, M., Pal, S., Post, M., and Zampieri, M. (2019). Findings of the 2019 conference on machine translation (wmt19). In *Proceedings of the Fourth Conference on Machine Translation (Volume 2: Shared Task Papers, Day 1)*, pages 1–61, Florence, Italy. Association for Computational Linguistics.

Chen, M. X., Firat, O., Bapna, A., Johnson, M., Macherey, W., Foster, G. F., Jones, L., Parmar, N., Schuster, M., Chen, Z., Wu, Y., and Hughes, M. (2018). The best of both worlds: Combining recent advances in neural machine translation. *CoRR*, abs/1804.09849.

Crego, J., Kim, J., Klein, G., Rebollo, A., Yang, K., Senellart, J., Akhanov, E., Brunelle, P., Coquard, A., Deng, Y., Enoue, S., Geiss, C., Johanson, J., Khalsa, A., Khiari, R., Ko, B., Kobus, C., Lorieux, J., Martins, L., Nguyen, D.-C., Priori, A., Riccardi, T., Segal, N., Servan, C., Tiquet, C., Wang, B., Yang, J., Zhang, D., Zhou, J., and Zoldan, P. (2016). Systran's pure neural machine translation systems.

Deng, Y., Kanervisto, A., Ling, J., and Rush, A. M. (2017). Image-to-markup generation with coarse-to-fine attention. In Precup, D. and Teh, Y. W., editors, *Proceedings of the 34th International Conference on Machine Learning, ICML 2017, Sydney, NSW, Australia, 6-11 August 2017*, volume 70 of *Proceedings of Machine Learning Research*, pages 980–989. PMLR.

Ericson, L. (2019). Opensat19 pashto sad/asr/kws using opennmt and pyaudioanalysis.

Gehring, J., Auli, M., Grangier, D., Yarats, D., and Dauphin, Y. N. (2017). Convolutional sequence to sequence learning. *CoRR*, abs/1705.03122.

Gehrmann, S., Deng, Y., and Rush, A. (2018). Bottom-up abstractive summarization. In *Proceedings of the 2018 Conference on Empirical Methods in Natural Language Processing*, pages 4098–4109, Brussels, Belgium. Association for Computational Linguistics.

Girletti, S., Bouillon, P., Bellodi, M., and Ursprung, P. (2019). Preferences of end-users for raw and post-edited nmt in a business environment. In *Proceedings of the 41st Conference Translating and the Computer*, pages 47–59.

Hieber, F., Domhan, T., Denkowski, M., Vilar, D., Sokolov, A., Clifton, A., and Post, M. (2017). Sockeye: A toolkit for neural machine translation. *CoRR*, abs/1712.05690.

Junczys-Dowmunt, M., Grundkiewicz, R., Dwojak, T., Hoang, H., Heafield, K., Neckermann, T., Seide, F., Germann, U., Fikri Aji, A., Bogoychev, N., Martins, A. F. T., and Birch, A. (2018). Marian: Fast neural machine translation in C++. In *Proceedings of ACL 2018, System Demonstrations*, pages 116–121, Melbourne, Australia. Association for Computational Linguistics.

Klein, G., Kim, Y., Deng, Y., Senellart, J., and Rush, A. (2017). OpenNMT: Open-source toolkit for neural machine translation. In *Proceedings of ACL 2017, System Demonstrations*, pages 67–72, Vancouver, Canada. Association for Computational Linguistics.

Kudo, T. and Richardson, J. (2018). SentencePiece: A simple and language independent subword tokenizer and detokenizer for neural text processing. In *Proceedings of the 2018 Conference on Empirical Methods in Natural Language Processing: System Demonstrations*, pages 66–71, Brussels, Belgium. Association for Computational Linguistics.

Levin, P., Dhanuka, N., and Khalilov, M. (2017). Machine translation at booking.com: Journey and lessons learned.

Libovický, J., Helcl, J., and Mareček, D. (2018). Input combination strategies for multi-source transformer decoder. In *Proceedings of the Third Conference on Machine Translation: Research Papers*, pages 253–260, Brussels, Belgium. Association for Computational Linguistics.

Luong, T., Pham, H., and Manning, C. D. (2015). Effective approaches to attention-based neural machine translation. In *Proceedings of the 2015 Conference on Empirical Methods in Natural Language Processing*, pages 1412–1421, Lisbon, Portugal. Association for Computational Linguistics.

Mghabbar, I. and Ratnamogan, P. (2020). Building a multi-domain neural machine translation model using knowledge distillation.

Ott, M., Edunov, S., Baevski, A., Fan, A., Gross, S., Ng, N., Grangier, D., and Auli, M. (2019). fairseq: A fast, extensible toolkit for sequence modeling. In *Proceedings of NAACL-HLT 2019: Demonstrations*.

Paszke, A., Gross, S., Massa, F., Lerer, A., Bradbury, J., Chanan, G., Killeen, T., Lin, Z., Gimelshein, N., Antiga, L., Desmaison, A., Kopf, A., Yang, E., DeVito, Z., Raison, M., Tejani, A., Chilamkurthy, S., Steiner, B., Fang, L., Bai, J., and Chintala, S. (2019). Pytorch: An imperative style, high-performance deep learning library. In Wallach, H., Larochelle, H., Beygelzimer, A., dAlché-Buc, F., Fox, E., and Garnett, R., editors, *Advances in Neural Information Processing Systems 32*, pages 8024–8035. Curran Associates, Inc.

See, A., Liu, P. J., and Manning, C. D. (2017). Get to the point: Summarization with pointer-generator networks. In *Proceedings of the 55th Annual Meeting of the Association for Computational Linguistics (Volume 1: Long Papers)*, pages 1073–1083, Vancouver, Canada. Association for Computational Linguistics.

Sennrich, R., Haddow, B., and Birch, A. (2016). Neural machine translation of rare words with subword units. In *Proceedings of the 54th Annual Meeting of the Association for Computational Linguistics (Volume 1: Long Papers)*, pages 1715–1725, Berlin, Germany. Association for Computational Linguistics.

Sutskever, I., Vinyals, O., and Le, Q. V. (2014). Sequence to sequence learning with neural networks. In Ghahramani, Z., Welling, M., Cortes, C., Lawrence, N. D., and Weinberger, K. Q., editors, *Advances in Neural Information Processing Systems 27*, pages 3104–3112. Curran Associates, Inc.

van Noord, R. and Bos, J. (2017). Neural semantic parsing by character-based translation: Experiments with abstract meaning representations. *CoRR*, abs/1705.09980.

Vaswani, A., Shazeer, N., Parmar, N., Uszkoreit, J., Jones, L., Gomez, A. N., Kaiser, L. u., and Polosukhin, I. (2017). Attention is all you need. In Guyon, I., Luxburg, U. V., Bengio, S., Wallach, H., Fergus, R., Vishwanathan, S., and Garnett, R., editors, *Advances in Neural Information Processing Systems 30*, pages 5998–6008. Curran Associates, Inc.

Wiseman, S., Shieber, S., and Rush, A. (2017). Challenges in data-to-document generation. In *Proceedings of the 2017 Conference on Empirical Methods in Natural Language Processing*, pages 2253–2263, Copenhagen, Denmark. Association for Computational Linguistics.

Wu, Y., Schuster, M., Chen, Z., Le, Q. V., Norouzi, M., Macherey, W., Krikun, M., Cao, Y., Gao, Q., Macherey, K., Klingner, J., Shah, A., Johnson, M., Liu, X., Łukasz Kaiser, Gouws, S., Kato, Y., Kudo, T., Kazawa, H., Stevens, K., Kurian, G., Patil, N., Wang, W., Young, C., Smith, J., Riesa, J., Rudnick, A., Vinyals, O., Corrado, G., Hughes, M., and Dean, J. (2016). Google's neural machine translation system: Bridging the gap between human and machine translation. *CoRR*, abs/1609.08144.

The Sockeye 2 Neural Machine Translation Toolkit at AMTA 2020

Tobias Domhan domhant@amazon.com
Michael Denkowski mdenkows@amazon.com
David Vilar dvilar@amazon.com
Xing Niu xingniu@amazon.com
Felix Hieber fhieber@amazon.com
Amazon
Kenneth Heafield[*] translate@kheafield.com
Efficient Translation Limited

Abstract

We present Sockeye 2, a modernized and streamlined version of the Sockeye neural machine translation (NMT) toolkit. New features include a simplified code base through the use of MXNet's Gluon API, a focus on state of the art model architectures, distributed mixed precision training, and efficient CPU decoding with 8-bit quantization. These improvements result in faster training and inference, higher automatic metric scores, and a shorter path from research to production.

1 Introduction

Sockeye (Hieber et al., 2017) is a versatile toolkit for research in the fast-moving field of NMT. Since the initial release, it has been used in at least 25 scientific publications, including winning submissions to WMT evaluations (Schamper et al., 2018). Sockeye also powers Amazon Translate, showing industrial-strength performance in addition to the flexibility needed in academic environments. Moreover, we are excited to see that hardware manufacturers are contributing to optimizing MXNet (Chen et al., 2015) and Sockeye for speed. Intel has demonstrated large performance gains for Sockeye inference on Intel Skylake processors.[1] NVIDIA is working on significant performance improvements for Sockeye's Transformer (Vaswani et al., 2017) implementation through fused operators and an optimized beam search. This paper discusses Sockeye 2's streamlined Gluon implementation (§2), support for state of the art architectures and efficient decoding (§3), and improved model training (§4).

2 Gluon Implementation

Sockeye 2 is implemented using Gluon,[2] MXNet's latest and preferred API that combines the strengths of imperative and graph-based programming. Gluon provides a simple Python interface and uses eager execution by default, allowing developers to quickly prototype deep learning models and debug issues step by step. At runtime, Gluon can automatically "hybridize" models

---

[*]Work was done in an external advisory capacity.

[1]https://www.intel.ai/amazing-inference-performance-with-intel-xeon-scalable-processors/#gs.wrgsji

[2]https://mxnet.apache.org/versions/1.6/api/python/docs/api/gluon/index.html

	DE–EN		EN–DE		FI–EN		EN–FI	
Layers	BLEU	Latency	BLEU	Latency	BLEU	Latency	BLEU	Latency
6:6	35.5	602	37.9	791	22.2	575	20.5	808
10:10	35.4	970	37.8	1238	22.3	863	20.8	1258
20:2	34.8	293	37.6	357	23.2	257	20.9	368

Table 1: SacreBLEU scores (Post, 2018) and single-sentence latency in milliseconds on new-stest2019 for models trained on WMT19 constrained data with varying numbers of encoder and decoder layers. Latency values are the 90th percentile of translation time when translating each sentence individually (no batching). We measure single sentence decoding latency on an EC2 c5.2xlarge instance with 4 CPU cores. We report the average over three independent training runs.

by converting them into computation graphs for maximum performance. Adopting this programming model significantly simplifies Sockeye 2's training and inference code, reducing the overall Python line count by 25%. Sockeye 2's hybridized transformer also improves training speed by 14% compared to Sockeye.

3 Focus on State of the Art Models

Due to the success of self-attentional models, we concentrate development of Sockeye 2 on the Transformer architecture (Vaswani et al., 2017). Our starting point is the "base" transformer with 6 encoder and decoder layers, model dimensionality of 512, and feed-forward layer size of 2048. An exploration of different encoder and decoder depths shows that deep encoders with shallow decoders are competitive in BLEU and significantly faster for decoding. Table 1 shows results with different numbers of encoder and decoder layers, denoted by $x{:}y$ where x is the number of encoder layers and y the number of decoder layers. For WMT19 FI-EN and EN-FI benchmarks (Barrault et al., 2019), the 20:2 model outperforms both the 6:6 model and the 10:10 model in terms of BLEU. The 20:2 model also has roughly half the decoding latency of the 6:6 model and roughly one third the latency of the 10:10 model. The relative efficiency of encoder versus decoder layers can be attributed to (1) the ability to parallelize across input tokens, (2) attention to only input tokens, and (3) not needing to run beam search on the source side.

3.1 Source Factors

Sockeye supports source factors in the spirit of Sennrich and Haddow (2016), additional representations that are combined with word embeddings prior to the first encoder layer. In Sockeye 2, we improve source factor support by allowing different types of embedding combinations (concatenation, summation, or average), as well as weight sharing between source factor and word embeddings.

As an example application, we use source factors to represent input case. Variations in case pose a challenge for machine translation systems as different orthographic variations are considered to be independent by the translation model (e.g., "case" is different from "Case" and both are different from "CASE"). We address these variations by lowercasing the input and encoding the original case information as a source factor ("lowercase", "capitalized", "all uppercase" or "mixed"). We refer to this method as "SF-case". An alternative is to lowercase and include the original cased word itself as a source factor, which we refer to as "SF-word". As the original and lowercased versions of many words will be the same, it is useful to share the embeddings, a variant we refer to as "SF-word-share".

	DE – EN				EN – FI			
	Ori	lower	Cap	UPP	Ori	lower	Cap	UPP
Baseline (cased)	36.7	33.0	22.9	9.1	20.7	16.4	3.4	1.1
SF-case (concat)	36.8	34.7	24.2	26.6	20.7	18.2	9.3	7.0
SF-case (sum)	36.8	34.8	23.0	28.4	21.4	18.3	7.7	7.2
SF-word	36.5	33.6	23.1	9.2	20.9	17.0	4.4	1.4
SF-word-share	36.8	33.8	21.9	9.3	21.4	17.2	4.0	1.3

Table 2: Robustness results for several variants of representing case with source factors. Models are evaluated on transformed versions of newstest2019: **Ori**ginal case, **lower**cased, **Cap**italization of the first character of each word, and **UPP**ERCASED. Scores are case-insensitive SacreBLEU (Post, 2018).

To evaluate the robustness of these strategies, we modify test sets by either entirely lowercasing, entirely uppercasing, or capitalizing the first character of each word. We compare a baseline model that was trained on cased input (no source factors) against all "SF-*" methods. The factored models also use BPE type factors as introduced by Sennrich and Haddow (2016). Models use the 20:2 transformer architecture and training settings described in §3. Shown in Table 2, encoding case information with source factors is an effective way to improve robustness against case variation with the two versions of "SF-case" performing best.

3.2 Quantization for Inference

Sockeye 2 now supports 8-bit quantized matrix multiplication (Quinn and Ballesteros, 2018) on CPUs based on the `intgemm` library.[3] By scaling values such that 127 corresponds to the maximum absolute value found in a tensor, matrix multiplication can be conducted with 8-bit integer representations in place of the default 32-bit floating-point representations without significant degradation of overall model accuracy. Parameters can either be quantized offline and stored in a smaller model file or quantized on the fly at loading time. Activations are quantized on the fly while other operators that consume far less runtime remain as 32-bit floats.

Latency-sensitive applications typically run with batch size 1 and small beam sizes, leaving little opportunity for batch parallelism. Instead, matrix multiplication parallelizes over outputs of a layer. To reduce latency, matrix multiplication and quantization are both parallelized with OpenMP.[4] Layer outputs can be computed independently and the layer size is typically much larger than the batch size. Parallelizing over layer inputs would require summing across threads.

Shown in Table 3, quantization significantly reduces non-batched decoding times with minimal effect on BLEU scores. Improvement is most pronounced when running on a single CPU core while models using up to 4 cores still see a significant benefit.[5]

4   Training Improvements

Sockeye 2 significantly accelerates training with Horovod[6] integration (Sergeev and Balso, 2018) and MXNet's automatic mixed precision (AMP). Horovod extends synchronous training to any number of GPUs (including across nodes) while AMP automatically detects and converts parts of the model that can run in FP16 mode without loss of quality. These methods

---

[3] https://github.com/kpu/intgemm

[4] https://www.openmprtl.org

[5] For 1 and 2 cores, we set the number of OpenMP threads to 1 and 2 respectively. For 4 cores, we set the number of OpenMP threads to 3 for best interaction with MXNet's own parallelization over operators.

[6] https://github.com/horovod/horovod

	CPUs	6:6 Layers			20:2 Layers		
		Time (s)	Tok/Sec	BLEU	Time (s)	Tok/Sec	BLEU
Baseline (fp32)	1	1260.8	33.3	22.1	585.0	71.8	23.0
	2	841.6	49.9	22.1	404.7	103.8	23.0
	4	575.8	73.0	22.1	283.2	148.3	23.0
Quantized (int8)	1	511.6	82.1	22.0	285.7	147.0	22.8
	2	435.9	96.4	22.0	242.3	173.4	22.8
	4	334.3	125.7	22.0	173.0	242.9	22.8

Table 3: CPU decoding times and SacreBLEU (Post, 2018) scores for FI-EN newstest2019 with and without 8-bit quantization for both standard (6:6 layer) and deep encoder (20:2 layer) transformer models as described in §3. Models use a vocabulary selection shortlist of 200 items (Devlin, 2017) and translate one sentence at a time (batch size of 1). Benchmarks are run on an EC2 c5.12xlarge instance (Cascade Lake processor) and limited to using 1, 2, or 4 CPU cores.

	DE–EN		EN–FI	
	BLEU	Time	BLEU	Time
Ott et al. (2018)	34.7	30h	20.1	14h
Plateau-Reduce	**34.9**	**28h**	**20.7**	**12h**

Table 4: SacreBLEU (Post, 2018) scores (newstest2019) and training times (8 NVIDIA V100 GPUs) for a 20 encoder 2 decoder layer transformer using the training setup described by Ott et al. (2018) and plateau-reduce, both implemented in Sockeye 2.

also require additional computation per update (synchronizing data across distributed GPUs and checking reduced precision operations for overflow). This overhead can be amortized by significantly increasing the effective batch size; gradients are aggregated per-GPU for several batches, then combined and checked for overflow for a single parameter update. In practice, scaling the effective batch size by N, the learning rate by $\sqrt{N}$ (Krizhevsky, 2014), and leaving other hyper parameters unchanged works well for batches of up to 260K tokens.

Sockeye also provides a data-driven alternative to the popular "inverse square root" learning schedule used by Vaswani et al. (2017) and Ott et al. (2018). Termed "plateau-reduce", this scheduler keeps the same learning rate until validation perplexity does not increase for several checkpoints, at which time it reduces the learning rate and rewinds all model and optimizer parameters to the best previous point. Training concludes when validation perplexity reaches an extended plateau. In a WMT19 benchmark (Barrault et al., 2019), plateau-reduce training produces stronger models in slightly less time than the setup described by Ott et al. (2018). The results are presented in Table 4 where all values are averages over 3 independent training runs with different random initializations and all models train until validation perplexity reaches a plateau.

The relevant hyper parameters for Sockeye 2's large batch training are an effective batch size of 262,144 tokens, a learning rate of 0.00113 with 2000 warmup steps and a reduce rate of 0.9, a checkpoint interval of 125 steps, and learning rate reduction after 8 checkpoints without improvement. After an extended plateau of 60 checkpoints, the 8 checkpoints with the lowest validation perplexity are averaged to produce the final model parameters. While Horovod enables scaling to any number of GPUs, we find that training on 8 GPUs on a single node still delivers the best value when considering both speed and cost.

5   Licensing and availability

Sockeye 2 is available[7] under the Apache 2.0 license. It includes Docker builds to easily run training or inference with all of the latest features on any supported platform.

6   Conclusion

Sockeye 2 provides out-of-the-box support for quickly training strong Transformer models for research or production. Extensive configuration options and the simplified Gluon code base enable rapid development and experimentation. As an open source project, we invite the community to contribute their ideas to Sockeye 2 and hope that the new programming model and various performance improvements enable others to conduct effective and successful research.

References

Barrault, L., Bojar, O., Costa-jussà, M. R., Federmann, C., Fishel, M., Graham, Y., Haddow, B., Huck, M., Koehn, P., Malmasi, S., Monz, C., Müller, M., Pal, S., Post, M., and Zampieri, M. (2019). Findings of the 2019 conference on machine translation (WMT19). In *Procs. of the Fourth Conference on Machine Translation (Vol. 2: Shared Task Papers)*, pages 1–61, Florence, Italy.

Chen, T., Li, M., Li, Y., Lin, M., Wang, N., Wang, M., Xiao, T., Xu, B., Zhang, C., and Zhang, Z. (2015). Mxnet: A flexible and efficient machine learning library for heterogeneous distributed systems. *arXiv preprint arXiv:1512.01274*.

Devlin, J. (2017). Sharp models on dull hardware: Fast and accurate neural machine translation decoding on the cpu. *ArXiv e-prints*, abs/1705.01991.

Hieber, F., Domhan, T., Denkowski, M., Vilar, D., Sokolov, A., Clifton, A., and Post, M. (2017). Sockeye: A toolkit for neural machine translation. *ArXiv e-prints*, abs/1712.05690.

Krizhevsky, A. (2014). One weird trick for parallelizing convolutional neural networks. *arXiv preprint arXiv:1404.5997*.

Ott, M., Edunov, S., Grangier, D., and Auli, M. (2018). Scaling neural machine translation. In *Procs. of the Third Conference on Machine Translation, Vol. 1: Research Papers*, pages 1–9, Belgium, Brussels.

Post, M. (2018). A call for clarity in reporting bleu scores. In *Procs. of the Third Conference on Machine Translation, Vol. 1: Research Papers*, pages 186–191, Belgium, Brussels.

Quinn, J. and Ballesteros, M. (2018). Pieces of eight: 8-bit neural machine translation. In *Proceedings of the 2018 Conference of the North American Chapter of the Association for Computational Linguistics: Human Language Technologies, Volume 3 (Industry Papers)*, pages 114–120, New Orleans - Louisiana. Association for Computational Linguistics.

Schamper, J., Rosendahl, J., Bahar, P., Kim, Y., Nix, A., and Ney, H. (2018). The RWTH Aachen University supervised machine translation systems for WMT 2018. In *Procs. of the Third Conference on Machine Translation, Vol. 2: Shared Task Papers*, pages 500–507, Belgium, Brussels.

Sennrich, R. and Haddow, B. (2016). Linguistic input features improve neural machine translation. In *Proceedings of the First Conference on Machine Translation: Volume 1, Research Papers*, pages 83–91, Berlin, Germany. Association for Computational Linguistics.

Sergeev, A. and Balso, M. D. (2018). Horovod: fast and easy distributed deep learning in tensorflow. *CoRR*, abs/1802.05799.

---

[7]https://github.com/awslabs/sockeye

Vaswani, A., Shazeer, N., Parmar, N., Uszkoreit, J., Jones, L., Gomez, A. N., Kaiser, Ł., and Polosukhin, I. (2017). Attention is all you need. In *Advances in neural information processing systems*, pages 5998–6008.

THUMT: An Open-Source Toolkit for Neural Machine Translation

Zhixing Tan[†], **Jiacheng Zhang**[†], **Xuancheng Huang**[†], **Gang Chen**[†], **Shuo Wang**[†],
Maosong Sun[†‡], **Huanbo Luan**[†], and **Yang Liu**[†‡] [*]
[†]Institute for Artificial Intelligence
Department of Computer Science and Technology, Tsinghua University
Beijing National Research Center for Information Science and Technology
[‡]Beijing Academy of Artificial Intelligence

Abstract

THUMT is an open-source toolkit for neural machine translation (NMT) developed by the Natural Language Processing Group at Tsinghua University. The toolkit is easy to use, modify and extend while provides the latest advances in NMT research and production. THUMT implements several standard NMT models and supports distributed training across multiple machines, fast inference, and model visualization. Experiments on English-German and Chinese-English datasets show that THUMT can obtain results that are comparable to state-of-the-art NMT systems.

1 Introduction

Machine translation (MT), which investigates the use of computers to translate human languages automatically, is an important task in natural language processing and artificial intelligence communities. With the availability of bilingual machine-readable texts, data-driven approaches to machine translation have gained wide popularity since the 1990s (Hutchins and Lovtskii, 2000). Recent several years have witnessed the rapid development of end-to-end neural machine translation (NMT) (Sutskever et al., 2014; Bahdanau et al., 2014; Vaswani et al., 2017). Capable of learning representations from data, NMT has quickly replaced conventional statistical machine translation (SMT) (Brown et al., 1993; Koehn et al., 2003; Chiang, 2005) to become the new *de facto* method in practical MT systems (Wu et al., 2016).

This paper introduces THUMT, an open-source NMT toolkit targeting both academia and industry. THUMT originally developed with Theano (Theano Development Team, 2016) and begins its launch in June 2017. With the emerging of new deep learning frameworks, THUMT added TensorFlow (Abadi et al., 2016) implementation in October 2017 and PyTorch (Paszke et al., 2019) implementation in August 2019. The current status of the three implementations are as follows:

- THUMT-Theano (Zhang et al., 2017): the original project developed with Theano, which is no longer updated because MLA put an end to Theano. It implemented the standard attention-based model (RNNsearch) (Bahdanau et al., 2014), minimum risk training (MRT) (Shen et al., 2015) for optimizing model parameters with respect to evaluation metrics, semi-supervised training (SST) (Cheng et al., 2016) for exploiting monolingual

---

[*]Corresponding author.

Features	Theano	TensorFlow	PyTorch
Models	RNNsearch	Seq2Seq, RNNsearch, Transformer	Transformer
Criterions	MLE, MRT, SST	MLE	MLE
Optimizers	SGD, Adadelta, Adam	Adam	SGD, Adadelta, Adam
LRP	Yes	Yes	No
Gradient Aggregation	No	Yes	Yes
Distributed Training	No	Yes	Yes
Mixed-Precision	No	Yes	Yes
TensorBoard	No	Yes	Yes

Table 1: Available features in different implementations.

corpora to learn bi-directional translation models, and layer-wise relevance propagation (LRP) (Ding et al., 2017) for visualizing and analyzing RNNsearch.

- THUMT-TensorFlow: an implementation focuses on performance. It implemented the sequence-to-sequence model (Seq2Seq) (Sutskever et al., 2014), the standard attention-based model (RNNsearch) (Bahdanau et al., 2014), the Transformer model (Transformer) (Vaswani et al., 2017), and LRP visualization for RNNsearch and Transformer. It also added new features such as multi-GPU training, distributed training, ensemble inference, and TensorBoard visualization.

- THUMT-PyTorch: a new implementation developed with PyTorch, which is more flexible and easier to use by the virtue of dynamic eager execution. It implemented the Transformer model and also supports multi-GPU training, distributed training, ensemble inference, and TensorBoard visualization.

THUMT is developed by the Tsinghua Natural Language Processing Group. The latest source code is available at GitHub [1] and is dual licensed. Open-source licensing is under the BSD-3-Clause, which allows free use for research purposes. THUMT has been used in many researches as well as several production MT systems.

2   Features

The primary goal of THUMT is to provide a toolkit that is easy to run and modify while featuring the latest deep learning techniques. The design of THUMT is highly modular. It is easy to add new models, optimizers, and learning rate schedules to THUMT. The toolkit provides command-line interface to train and infer from an NMT model, and also supports multi-GPU training, distributed training as well as mixed-precision training to make full use of the modern hardware features. Table 1 lists available features in different implementations. We will give a brief introduction to the components and features provided by the toolkit.

2.1   Models

THUMT implemented three mainstream NMT models: Seq2Seq (Sutskever et al., 2014), RNNsearch (Bahdanau et al., 2014), and Transformer (Vaswani et al., 2017). Seq2Seq uses a recurrent neural network (RNN) to encode the input sentence into a fixed-size hidden representation and uses another RNN to generate translation conditioned on the representation. RNNsearch exploits variable representation with attention mechanism and achieves significant improvements over Seq2Seq model. Transformer uses deep self-attention layers instead of RNN layers in both encoder and decoder. It achieves the best performance among the three models.

---

[1] https://github.com/THUNLP-MT/THUMT

THUMT also implemented relative position embedding (Shaw et al., 2018) in its Transformer implementation. Instead of adding absolute positions to its input, this approach considers relative positions in the self-attention mechanism. We offer two options in our Tensorflow implementation, one can turn on or off the relative position embedding and set the desired maximum relative distance. Note that we only implement relative position embedding in self-attention but not in encoder-decoder attention.

2.2 Training

THUMT supports both single machine multi-GPU training and multi-machine distributed training. THUMT-TensorFlow uses the Horovod (Sergeev and Del Balso, 2018) toolkit for distributed training while THUMT-PyTorch adopts `torch.distributed` module to achieve the same functionality.

Modern NMT models (e.g. Transformer) usually require using large batch sizes during training. However, it is normally impractical to fit a large batch into a single GPU device. To alleviate this problem, we allow THUMT to split the batch into several smaller batches and collect the gradient on each batch independently. Then we aggregate the gradients and perform optimization. Gradient aggregation simulates large batch size training with multiple small batch training, which significantly reduce the memory requirement for training NMT models.

The latest GPU (e.g. Nvidia V100) supports half-precision computation which significantly improve the training speed and reduce the memory requirement. However, training with half-precision is less stable than single-precision because of the reduced precision. To address this problem, THUMT implemented mixed-precision training which uses half-precision in the forward pass while switches to single-precision in the backward pass to maintain numerical stability. Furthermore, THUMT also apply dynamic loss scaling during the forward pass to increase the numerical precision.

THUMT provides different optimizers, learning rate schedules, and validation functionality for users to control the training process. These options can be easily changed through the command-line interface. New optimizers and learning rate schedules can be easily integrated into THUMT with minor modifications.

2.3 Inference

THUMT supports beam-search and random sampling during inference. The user can specify the batch size, beam size, and length penalty before decoding. Apart from beam-search, the user can also choose to employ random sampling, which samples a word from multinomial distribution at each step. THUMT also supports decoding with half-precision to speed up the inference stage.

Model averaging is beneficial to the performance of neural machine translation models. THUMT provides an additional script to carry out model averaging. The users can either average the lastest n checkpoints or the top-n best checkpoints sorted by validation scores into a single checkpoint.

Model ensemble is another way to improve the performance of neural machine translation. THUMT can ensemble multiple NMT models regardless of their architecture, provided all models share the same vocabulary. When performing inference, if the number of checkpoints assigned by the users is more than one, THUMT will perform model ensemble automatically by calculating an arithmetic mean of the log-probabilities provided by all checkpoints. Normally, model ensemble can achieve significant improvements. However, it requires more memory and computations.

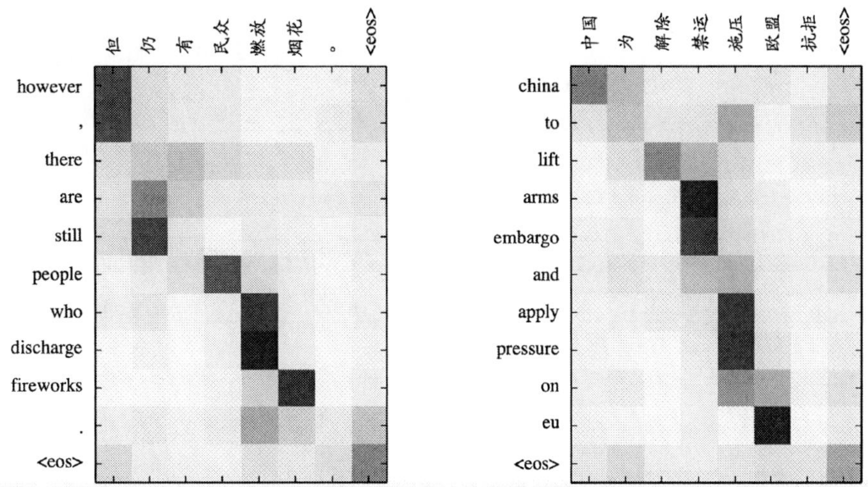

Figure 1: Visualization with LRP for the Transformer Model.

2.4 Visualization

Although NMT achieves state-of-the-art translation performance, it is hard to understand how it works because all internal information is represented as real-valued vectors or matrices. To address this problem, THUMT features a visualization tool to use layer-wise relevance propagation (LRP) (Bach et al., 2015) to visualize and interpret neural machine translation models (Ding et al., 2017).

Figure 1 shows an example of visualizing the Transformer model. Although the transformer model uses attention mechanisms extensively, it is hard to determine the most representative head. For LRP, it is possible to calculate the global relevance between source words and target words, which helps analyze the internal workings of NMT. Please refer to Ding et al. (2017) for more details.

3 Experiments

3.1 Setup

We evaluate THUMT on English-German and Chinese-English translation tasks. The evaluation metric is case-sensitive BLEU (Papineni et al., 2002). Following Vaswani et al. (2017), translations are generated via beam-search with a beam size of 4 and a length penalty of 0.6.

For English-German, we use the WMT14 training corpus which contains 4.5M sentence pairs with 103M English words and 96M German words. We also use a shared source-target vocabulary of about 37000 tokens encoded by BPE (Sennrich et al., 2016). We use `newstest2014` as the test set.

For Chinese-English translation, we use the training corpus provided by WMT18 [2]. The corpus consists of 24M sentence pairs with 509M Chinese words and 576M English words. We use 32K BPE operations to build vocabularies. The test set is `newstest2017`.

We train the Transformer model on the two datasets. Unless otherwise noted, the setting is the same as Vaswani et al. (2017). All models are trained on 4 machines interconnected with InfiniBand, and each machine has 8 GTX 2080Ti GPUs.

---

[2]`http://data.statmt.org/wmt18/translation-task/preprocessed/zh-en`

Model	Size	Speed (tokens/sec)	
		Training	*Inference*
Transformer	Base	60K	620
Transformer	Big	35K	550

Table 2: Speed of THUMT, evaluated on WMT14 English-German (En-De). Speed of training is reported with a 8-GPU setting and speed of inference is reported with a single GPU setting.

Direction	Model	Size	Steps	GPUs	BS/GPU	Precision	BLEU
En → De	Transformer (Vaswani et al., 2017)	Base	100K	8	-	FP32	27.30
		Big	300K	8	-	FP32	28.40
Zh → En	Transformer (Hassan et al., 2018)	Big	-	-	-	FP32	24.20
En → De	Transformer	Base	100K	4	2×4096	FP16	26.85
		Base	100K	8	4096	FP16	26.76
		Base	100K	4	2×4096	FP32	26.91
		Base	100K	8	4096	FP32	26.95
		Base	85K	8	2×4096	FP16	27.40
		Big	300K	8	4096	FP16	28.71
		Big	20K	16	8×4096	FP16	28.68
		Big	25K	32	8×2048	FP16	28.51
Zh → En	Transformer	Big	300K	8	2×4096	FP16	24.07

Table 3: Benchmarks on WMT14 English-German (En-De) and WMT18 Chinese-English (Zh-En) datasets. We use "2×4096" to denote aggregating gradients for 2 steps with 4096 batch size per step. "FP32" and "FP16" denote training with single-precision and mixed-precision, respectively. We use distributed settings enable training with more than 8 GPUs.

3.2 Results

Table 2 shows the speed of THUMT. The speed of training is reported with a 8-GPU setting and the speed of inference is reported with a single GPU setting. The training speed of Transformer model is around 35K to 60K tokens per second, depending on the model size. It takes about 1 day to train a Transformer big model with 32 GPUs. The inference speed is about 620 tokens per second for the base Transformer model and 550 tokens per second for the big model. Currently, THUMT does not support inference with CPUs, and we plan to add this functionality in the future.

Table 3 shows the results on English-German and Chinese-English translation. For English-German, we trained Transformer base/big models with several different settings by varying model sizes, training steps, and number of GPUs. All Transformer big models performed better than Transformer base models. When we trained the Transformer base model using mixed-precision (FP16) instead of single-precision (FP32), the performance only drops slightly. As the number of tokens in each mini-batch increases from 32,768 to 65,536, the performance improves from 26.95 to 27.40 even though the training steps reduce from 100K to 85K. For Chinese-English, we trained a Transformer big model using mixed-precision in 300K steps, and the number of tokens in mini-batch is 65,536. The BLEU score on the test dataset is 24.07. The models trained using THUMT are comparable to those reported by Vaswani et al. (2017) and Hassan et al. (2018) in terms of BLEU score.

4 Conclusion and Future works

We have introduced a new open-source toolkit for NMT that supports mainstream models, distributed training, and fast inference. The toolkit also features a visualization tool for analyzing the translation process of THUMT. The toolkit is freely available at `http://thumt.thunlp.org`.

Currently, the users still rely on external tools to prepare the training corpus. We plan to add preprocessing functionality to make THUMT self-contained. We will continually add new features to THUMT to make it a better toolkit for both research and production.

Acknowledgements

This work was supported by the National Key R&D Program of China (No. 2017YFB0202204), National Natural Science Foundation of China (No. 61925601, No. 61761166008, No. 61772302), Beijing Academy of Artificial Intelligence, and the NExT++ project supported by the National Research Foundation, Prime Ministers Office, Singapore under its IRC@Singapore Funding Initiative.

References

Abadi, M., Barham, P., Chen, J., Chen, Z., Davis, A., Dean, J., Devin, M., Ghemawat, S., Irving, G., Isard, M., et al. (2016). Tensorflow: A system for large-scale machine learning. In *Proceedings of OSDI*.

Bach, S., Binder, A., Montavon, G., Klauschen, F., Müller, K.-R., and Samek, W. (2015). On pixel-wise explanations for non-linear classifier decisions by layer-wise relevance propagation. *PloS one*.

Bahdanau, D., Cho, K., and Bengio, Y. (2014). Neural machine translation by jointly learning to align and translate. *arXiv preprint arXiv:1409.0473*.

Brown, P. F., Pietra, V. J. D., Pietra, S. A. D., and Mercer, R. L. (1993). The mathematics of statistical machine translation: Parameter estimation. *Computational linguistics*.

Cheng, Y., Xu, W., He, Z., He, W., Wu, H., Sun, M., and Liu, Y. (2016). Semi-supervised learning for neural machine translation. *arXiv preprint arXiv:1606.04596*.

Chiang, D. (2005). A hierarchical phrase-based model for statistical machine translation. In *Proceedings of ACL*.

Ding, Y., Liu, Y., Luan, H., and Sun, M. (2017). Visualizing and understanding neural machine translation. In *Proceedings of ACL*.

Hassan, H., Aue, A., Chen, C., Chowdhary, V., Clark, J., Federmann, C., Huang, X., Junczys-Dowmunt, M., Lewis, W., Li, M., et al. (2018). Achieving human parity on automatic chinese to english news translation. *arXiv preprint arXiv:1803.05567*.

Hutchins, J. and Lovtskii, E. (2000). Petr petrovich troyanskii (1894–1950): A forgotten pioneer of mechanical translation. *Machine translation*, 15(3):187–221.

Koehn, P., Och, F. J., and Marcu, D. (2003). Statistical phrase-based translation. In *Proceedings of NAACL*.

Papineni, K., Roukos, S., Ward, T., and Zhu, W. (2002). Bleu: A method for automatic evaluation of machine translation. In *Proceedings of ACL*.

Paszke, A., Gross, S., Massa, F., Lerer, A., Bradbury, J., Chanan, G., Killeen, T., Lin, Z., Gimelshein, N., Antiga, L., et al. (2019). Pytorch: An imperative style, high-performance deep learning library. In *Proceedings of NIPS*.

Sennrich, R., Haddow, B., and Birch, A. (2016). Neural machine translation of rare words with subword units. In *Proceedings of ACL*.

Sergeev, A. and Del Balso, M. (2018). Horovod: fast and easy distributed deep learning in tensorflow. *arXiv preprint arXiv:1802.05799*.

Shaw, P., Uszkoreit, J., and Vaswani, A. (2018). Self-attention with relative position representations. In *Proceedings of NAACL-HLT*.

Shen, S., Cheng, Y., He, Z., He, W., Wu, H., Sun, M., and Liu, Y. (2015). Minimum risk training for neural machine translation. *arXiv preprint arXiv:1512.02433*.

Sutskever, I., Vinyals, O., and Le, Q. V. (2014). Sequence to sequence learning with neural networks. In *Proceedings of NIPS*.

Theano Development Team (2016). Theano: A Python framework for fast computation of mathematical expressions. *arXiv e-prints*.

Vaswani, A., Shazeer, N., Parmar, N., Uszkoreit, J., Jones, L., Gomez, A. N., Kaiser, Ł., and Polosukhin, I. (2017). Attention is all you need. In *Proceedings of NIPS*.

Wu, Y., Schuster, M., Chen, Z., Le, Q. V., et al. (2016). Google's neural machine translation system: Bridging the gap between human and machine translation. *arXiv preprint arXiv:1609.08144*.

Zhang, J., Ding, Y., Shen, S., Cheng, Y., Sun, M., Luan, H., and Liu, Y. (2017). Thumt: An open source toolkit for neural machine translation. *arXiv preprint arXiv:1706.06415*.

Dynamic Masking for Improved Stability in Online Spoken Language Translation

Yuekun Yao ykyao.cs@gmail.com
Barry Haddow bhaddow@staffmail.ed.ac.uk
School of Informatics, University of Edinburgh, 10 Crichton Street, Edinburgh, Scotland

Abstract

For spoken language translation (SLT) in live scenarios such as conferences, lectures and meetings, it is desirable to show the translation to the user as quickly as possible, avoiding an annoying lag between speaker and translated captions. In other words, we would like low-latency, online SLT. If we assume a pipeline of automatic speech recognition (ASR) and machine translation (MT) then a simple but effective approach to online SLT is to pair an online ASR system, with a *retranslation strategy*, where the MT system retranslates every update received from ASR. However this can result in annoying "flicker" as the MT system updates its translation. A possible solution is to add a fixed delay, or "mask" to the the output of the MT system, but a fixed global mask re-introduces undesirable latency to the output. We introduce a method for dynamically determining the mask length, which provides a better latency–flicker trade-off curve than a fixed mask, without affecting translation quality.

1 Introduction

A common approach to Spoken Language Translation (SLT) is to use a cascade (or pipeline) consisting of automatic speech recognition (ASR) and machine translation (MT). In a live translation setting, such as a lecture or conference, we would like the transcriptions or translations to appear as quickly as possible, so that they do not "lag" noticeably behind the speaker. In other words, we wish to minimise the latency of the system. Many popular ASR toolkits can operate in an *online* mode, where the transcription is produced incrementally, instead of waiting for the speaker to finish their utterance. However online MT is less well supported, and is complicated by the reordering which is often necessary in translation, and by the use of encoder-decoder models which assume sight of the whole source sentence.

Some systems for online SLT rely on the *streaming* approach to translation, perhaps inspired by human interpreters. In this approach, the MT system is modified to translate incrementally, and on each update from ASR it will decide whether to update its translation, or wait for further ASR output (Cho and Esipova, 2016; Ma et al., 2019; Zheng et al., 2019a,b; Arivazhagan et al., 2019).

The difficulty with the streaming approach is that the system has to choose between committing to a particular choice of translation output, or waiting for further updates from ASR, and does not have the option to revise an incorrect choice. Furthermore, all the streaming approaches referenced above require specialised training of the MT system, and modified inference algorithms.

To address the issues above, we construct our online SLT system using the *retranslation* approach (Niehues et al., 2018; Arivazhagan et al., 2020a), which is less studied but more straightforward. It can be implemented using any standard MT toolkit (such as Marian (Junczys-Dowmunt et al., 2018) which is highly optimised for speed) and using the latest advances in text-to-text translation. The idea of retranslation is that we produce a new translation of the current sentence every time a partial sentence is received from the ASR system. Thus, the translation of each sentence prefix is independent and can be directly handled by a standard MT system. Arivazhagan et al. (2020b) directly compared the retranslation and streaming approaches and found the former to have a better latency–quality trade-off curve.

When using a completely unadapted MT system with the retranslation approach, however, there are at least two problems we need to consider:

1. MT training data generally consists of full sentences, and systems may perform poorly on partial sentences

2. When MT systems are asked to translate progressively longer segments of the conversation, they may introduce radical changes in the translation as the prefixes are extended. If these updates are displayed to the user, they will introduce an annoying "flicker" in the output, making it hard to read.

We illustrate these points using the small example in Figure 1. When the MT system receives the first prefix ("Several") it attempts to make a longer translation, due to its bias towards producing sentences. When the prefix is extended (to "Several years ago"), the MT system completely revises its original translation hypothesis. This is caused by the differing word order between German and English.

Several $\longrightarrow$ Mehrere Male
Several times

Several years ago $\longrightarrow$ Vor einigen Jahre
Several years ago

Figure 1: Sample translation with standard en→de MT system. We show the translation output, and its back-translation into English.

The first problem above could be addressed by simply adding sentence prefixes to the training data of the MT system. In our experiments we found that using prefixes in training could improve translation of partial sentences, but required careful mixing of data, and even then performance of the model trained on truncated sentences was often worse on full sentences.

A way to address both problems above is with an appropriate retranslation strategy. In other words, when the MT system receives a new prefix, it should decide whether to transmit its translation in full, partially, or wait for further input, and the system can take into account translations it previously produced. A good retranslation strategy will address the second problem above (too much flickering as translations are revised) and in so doing so address the first (over-eagerness to produce full sentences).

In this paper, we focus on the retranslation methods introduced by Arivazhagan et al. (2020a) – mask-k and biased beam search. The former is a delayed output strategy which does not affect overall quality, reduces flicker, but can significantly increase the latency of the translation system. The latter alters the beam search to take into account the translation of the previous prefix, and is used to reduce flicker without influencing latency much, but can also damage translation quality.

Our contribution in this paper is to show that by using a straightforward method to predict how much to mask (i.e. the value of k in the mask-k strategy) we obtain a more optimal trade-off of flicker and latency than is possible with a fixed mask. We show that for many prefixes the mask can be safely reduced. We achieve this by having the system make probes of possible extensions to the source prefix, and observing how stable the translation of these probes is – instability in the translation requires a larger mask. Our method requires no modifications to the underlying MT system, and has no effect on translation quality.

2   Related Work

Early work on incremental MT used prosody (Bangalore et al., 2012) or lexical cues (Rangarajan Sridhar et al., 2013) to make the translate-or-wait decision. The first work on incremental neural MT used confidence to decide whether to wait or translate (Cho and Esipova, 2016), whilst in (Gu et al., 2017) they learn the translation schedule with reinforcement learning. In Ma et al. (2019), they address simultaneous translation using a transformer (Vaswani et al., 2017) model with a modified attention mechanism, which is trained on prefixes. They introduce the idea of wait-k, where the translation does not consider the final k words of the input. This work was extended by Zheng et al. (2019b,a), where a "delay" token is added to the target vocabulary so the model can learn when to wait, through being trained by imitation learning. The MILk attention (Arivazhagan et al., 2019) also provides a way of learning the translation schedule along with the MT model, and is able to directly optimise the latency metric.

In contrast with these recent approaches, retranslation strategies (Niehues et al., 2018) allow the use of a standard MT toolkit, with little modification, and so are able to leverage all the performance and quality optimisations in that toolkit. Arivazhagan et al. (2020a) pioneered the retranslation system by combining a strong MT system with two simple yet effective strategies: biased beam search and mask-k. Their experiments show that the system can achieve low flicker and latency without losing much performance. In an even more recent paper, Arivazhagan et al. (2020b) further combine their retranslation system with prefix training and make comparison with current best streaming models (e.g. MILk and wait-k models), showing that such a retranslation system is a strong option for online SLT.

3   Retranslation Strategies

Before introducing our approach, we describe the two retranslation strategies introduced in Arivazhagan et al. (2020a): mask-k and biased beam search.

The idea of mask-k is simply that the MT system does not transmit the last k tokens of its output – in other words it masks them. Once the system receives a full sentence, it transmits the translation in full, without masking. The value of k is set globally and can be tuned to reduce the amount of flicker, at the cost of increasing latency. Arivazhagan et al. (2020a) showed good results for a mask of 10, but of course for short sentences a system with such a large mask would not produce any output until the end of the sentence.

In biased beam search, a small modification is made to the translation algorithm, changing the search objective. The technique aims to reduce flicker by ensuring that the translation produced by the MT system stays closer to the translation of the previous (shorter) prefix. Suppose that S is a source prefix, S' is the extension of that source prefix provided by the ASR, and T is the translation of S produced by the system (after masking). Then to create the translation T' of S', biased beam search substitutes the model probability $p(t'_i|t'_{<i}, S')$ with the following expression:

$$p^B(t'_i|t'_{<i}, S') = (1 - \beta) \cdot p(t'_i|t'_{<i}, S') + \beta \cdot \delta(t'_i, t_i)$$

where t'_i is the ith token of the translation hypothesis T', and β is a weighting which we set to 0 when $t_{<i} \neq t'_{<i}$. In other words, we interpolate the translation model with a function that keeps it close to the previous translation, but stop applying the biasing once the new translation diverges from the previous one.

As we noted earlier, biased beam search can degrade the quality of the translation, and we show experiments to illustrate this in Section 6.1. We also note that biased beam search assumes that the ASR simply extends its output each time it updates, when in fact ASR systems may rewrite their output. Furthermore, biased beam search requires modification of the underlying inference algorithm (which in the case of Marian is written in highly optimised, hand-crafted GPU code), removing one of the advantages of the retranslation approach (that it can be easily applied to standard MT systems).

4 Dynamic Masking

In this section we introduce our improvement to the mask-k approach, which uses a variable mask, that is set at runtime. The problem with using a fixed mask, is that there are many time-steps where the system is unlikely to introduce radical changes to the translation as more source is revealed, and on these occasions we would like to use a small mask to reduce latency. However the one-size-fits-all mask-k strategy does not allow this variability.

The main idea of dynamic masking is to *predict* what the next source word will be, and check what effect this would have on the translation. If this changes the translation, then we mask, if not we output the full translation.

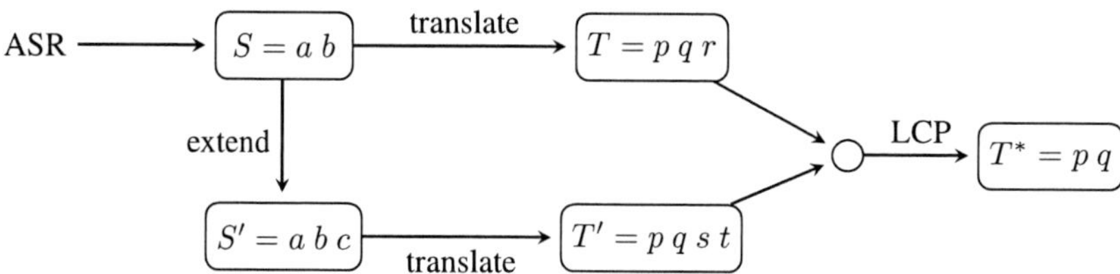

Figure 2: The source prediction process. The string $a\,b$ is provided by the ASR system. The MT system then produces translations of the string and its extension, compares them, and outputs the longest common prefix (LCP)

More formally, we suppose that we have a source prefix $S = s_1 \ldots s_p$, a source-to-target translation system, and a function $pred_k$, which can predict the next k tokens following S. We translate S using the translation system to give a translation hypothesis $T = t_1 \ldots t_q$. We then use $pred_k$ to predict the tokens following s_p in the source sentence to give an extended source prefix $S' = s_1 \ldots s_p s_{p+1} \ldots s_{p+k}$, and translate this to give another translation hypothesis T'. Comparing T and T', we select the longest common prefix T^*, and output this as the translation, thus masking the final $|T| - |T^*|$ tokens of the translation. If S is a complete sentence, then we do not mask any of the output, as in the mask-k strategy. The overall procedure is illustrated in Figure 2.

In fact, after initial experiments, we found it was more effective to refine our strategy, and not mask at all if the translation after dynamic mask is a prefix of the previous translation. In this case we directly output the last translation. In other words, we do not mask if $is\_prefix(T_i^*, T_{i-1}^*)$ but instead output T_{i-1}^* again, where T_i^* denotes the masked translation for the ith ASR input. We also notice that this refinement does not give any benefit to the mask-k strategy in our experiments. The reason that this refinement is effective is that the translation of the extended prefix can sometimes exhibit instabilities early in the sentence (which then disappear in a subsequent prefix). Applying a large mask in response to such instabilities increases latency, so we effectively "freeze" the output of the translation system until the instability is resolved. An example to illustrate this refinement can be found in Figure 10.

To predict the source extensions (i.e. to define the $pred_k$ function above), we first tried using a language model trained on the source text. This worked well, but we decided to add two simple strategies in order to see how important it was to have good prediction. The extension strategies we include are:

lm-sample We sample the next token from a language model (LSTM) trained on the source-side of the parallel training data. We can choose n possible extensions by choosing n distinct samples.

lm-greedy This also uses an LM, but chooses the most probable token at each step.

unknown We extend the source sentence using the UNK token from the vocabulary.

random We extend by sampling randomly from the vocabulary, under a uniform distribution. As with lm-sample, we can generalise this strategy by choosing n different samples.

5 Evaluation of Retranslation Strategies

Different approaches have been proposed to evaluate online SLT, so we explain and justify our approach here. We follow previous work on retranslation (Niehues et al., 2018; Arivazhagan et al., 2020a,b) and consider that the performance of online SLT should be assessed according to three different aspects – quality, latency and flicker. All of these aspects are important to users of online SLT, but improving on one can have an adverse effect on other aspects. For example outputting translations as early as possible will reduce latency, but if these early outputs are incorrect then either they can be corrected (increasing flicker) or retained as part of the later translation (reducing quality). In this section we will define precisely how we measure these system aspects. We assume that selecting the optimal trade-off between quality, latency and flicker is a question for the system deployer, that can only be settled by user testing.

Latency The latency of the MT system should provide a measure of the time between the MT system receiving input from the ASR, and it producing output that can be potentially be sent to the user. A standard (text-to-text) MT system would have to wait until it has received a full sentence before it produces any output, which exhibits high latency.

We follow Ma et al. (2019) by using a latency metric called average lag (AL), which measures the degree to which the output lags behind the input. This is done by averaging the difference between the number of words the system has output, and the number of words expected, given the length of the source prefix received, and the ratio between source and target length. Formally, AL for source and target sentences S and T is defined as:

$$\mathrm{AL}(S,T) = \frac{1}{\tau} \sum_{t=1}^{\tau} g(t) - \frac{(t-1)|S|}{|T|}$$

where τ is the number of target words generated by the time the whole source sentence is received, $g(t)$ is the number of source words processed when the target hypothesis first reaches a length of t tokens. In our implementation, we calculate the AL at token (not subword) level with the standard tokenizer in sacreBLEU (Post, 2018), meaning that for Chinese output we calculate AL on characters.

This metric differs from the one used in Arivazhagan et al. (2020a)[1], where latency is defined as the mean time between a source word being received and the translation of that source word being finalised. We argue against this definition, because it conflates latency and

---

[1] In the presentation of this paper at ICASSP, the authors used a latency metric similar to the one used here, and different to the one they used in the paper

flicker, since outputting a translation and then updating is penalised for both aspects. The update is penalised for flicker since the translation is updated (see below) and it is penalised for latency, since the timestamp of the initial output is ignored in the latency calculation.

Flicker The idea of flicker is to obtain a measure of the potentially distracting changes that are made to the MT output, as its ASR-supplied source sentence is extended. We assume that straightforward extensions of the MT output are fine, but changes which require re-writing of part of the MT output should result in a higher (i.e. worse) flicker score. Following Arivazhagan et al. (2020a), we measure flicker using the normalised erasure (NE), which is defined as the minimum number of tokens that must be erased from each translation hypothesis when outputting the subsequent hypothesis, normalised across the sentence. As with AL, we also calculate the NE at token level for German, and at character level for Chinese.

Quality As in previous work Arivazhagan et al. (2020a), quality is assessed by comparing the full sentence output of the system against a reference, using a sentence similarity measure such as BLEU. We do not evaluate quality on prefixes, mainly because of the need for a heuristic to determine partial references. Further, quality evaluation on prefixes will conflate with evaluation of latency and flicker and thus we simply assume that if the partial sentences are of poor quality, that this will be reflected in the other two metrics (flicker and latency). Note that our proposed dynamic mask strategy is only concerned with improving the flicker–latency trade-off curve and has no effect on full-sentence quality, so MT quality measurement is not the focus of this paper. Where we do require a measure of quality (in the assessment of biased beam search, which does change the full-sentence translation) we use BLEU as implemented by sacreBLEU (Post, 2018).

6 Experiments

6.1 Biased Beam Search and Mask-k

We first assess the effectiveness of biased beam search and mask-k (with a fixed k), providing a more complete experimental picture than in Arivazhagan et al. (2020a), and demonstrating the adverse effect of biased beam search on quality. For these experiments we use data released for the IWSLT MT task (Cettolo et al., 2017), in both English→German and English→Chinese. We consider a simulated ASR system, which supplies the gold transcripts to the MT system one token at a time[2].

For training we use the TED talk data, with dev2010 as heldout and tst2010 as test set. The raw data set sizes are 206112 sentences (en-de) and 231266 sentences (en-zh). We preprocess using the Moses (Koehn et al., 2007) tokenizer and truecaser (for English and German) and jieba[3] for Chinese. We apply BPE (Sennrich et al., 2016) jointly with 90k merge operations. For our MT system, we use the transformer-base architecture (Vaswani et al., 2017) as implemented by Nematus (Sennrich et al., 2017). We use 256 sentence mini-batches, and a 4000 iteration warm-up in training.

As we mentioned in the introduction, we did experiment with prefix training (using both alignment-based and length-based truncation) and found that this improved the translation of prefixes, but generally degraded translation for full sentences. Since prefix translation can also be improved using the masking and biasing techniques, and the former does not degrade full sentence translation, we only include experimental results when training on full sentences.

---

[2]A real online ASR system typically increments its hypothesis by adding a variable number of tokens in each increment, and may revise its hypothesis. Also, ASR does not normally supply sentence boundaries, or punctuation, and these must be added by an intermediate component. Sentence boundaries may change as the ASR hypothesis changes. In this work we make simplifying assumptions about the nature of the ASR, in order to focus on retranslation strategies, leaving the question of dealing with real online ASR to future work.

[3]https://github.com/fxsjy/jieba

In Figure 3 we show the effect of varying β and k on our three evaluation measures, for English→German.

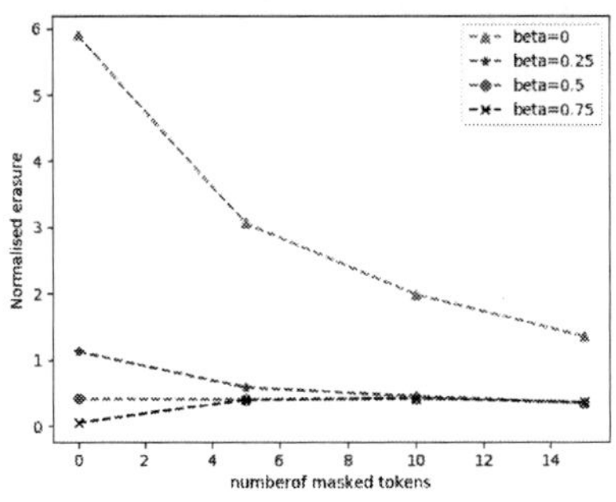

(a) Masking versus flicker (measued by erasure)

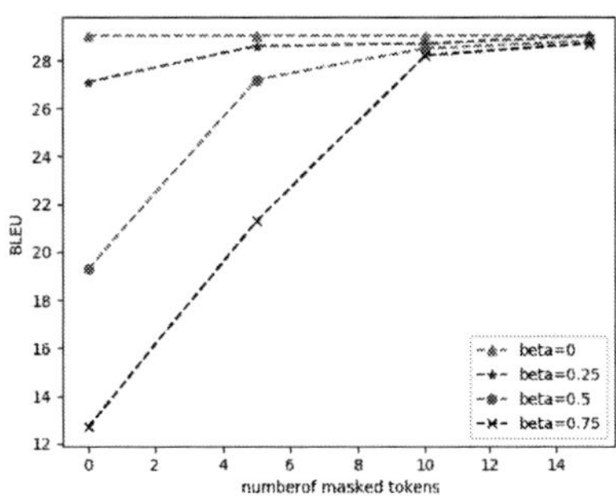

(b) Masking versus quality (measured by BLEU).

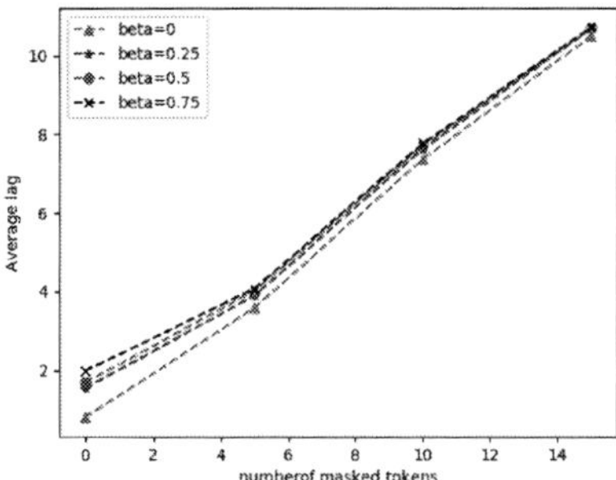

(c) Masking versus latency (measured by average lagging).

Figure 3: Effect of varying mask-k, at different values of the biased beam search interpolation parameter, on the three measures proposed in Section 5.

Looking at Figure 3(a) we notice that biased beam search has a strong impact in reducing flicker (erasure) at all values of β. However the problem with this approach is clear in Figure 3(b), where we can see the reduction in BLEU caused by this biasing. This can be offset by increasing masking, also noted by Arivazhagan et al. (2020a), but as we show in Figure 3(c) this comes at the cost of an increase in latency.

Our experiments with en→zh show a roughly similar pattern, as shown in Figure 4. We find that lower levels of masking are required to reduce the detrimental effect on BLEU of the biasing, but latency increases more rapidly with masking.

6.2 Dynamic Masking

We now turn our attention to the dynamic masking technique introduced in Section 4. We use the same data sets and MT systems as in the previous section. To train the LM, we use the source side of the parallel training data, and train an LSTM-based LM.

To assess the performance of dynamic masking, we measure latency and flicker as we vary the length of the source extension (k) and the number of source extensions (n). We consider the 4 different extension strategies described at the end of Section 4. We do not show translation

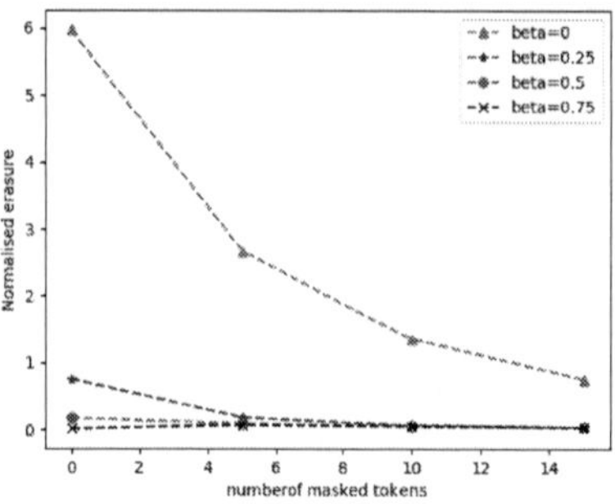
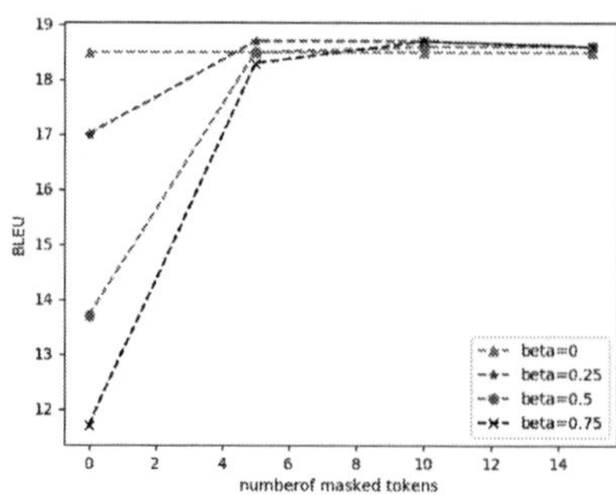

(a) Masking versus flicker (measured by erasure) (b) Masking versus quality (measured by BLEU).

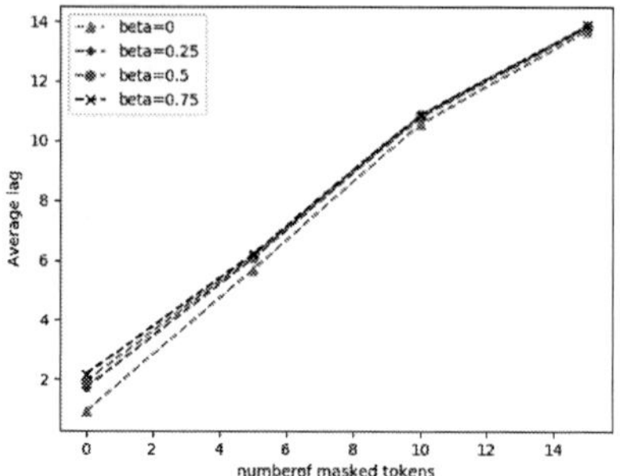

(c) Masking versus latency (measured by average lagging).

Figure 4: Effect of varying mask-k, at different values of the biased beam search interpolation parameter, on English-to-Chinese corpus

quality since the translation of the complete sentence is unaffected by the dynamic masking strategy. The results for both en→de and en→zh are shown in Figure 5, where we compare to the strategy of using a fixed mask-k. The oracle data point is where we use the full-sentence translations to set the mask so as to completely avoid flicker.

We observe from Figure 5 that our dynamic mask mechanism improves over the fixed mask in all cases, Pareto-dominating it on latency and flicker. Varying the source prediction strategy and parameters appears to preserve the same inverse relation between latency and flicker, although offering a different trade-off. Using several random source predictions (the green curve in both plots) offers the lowest flicker, at the expense of high latency, whilst the shorter LM-based predictions show the lowest latency, but higher flicker. We hypothesise that this happens because extending the source randomly along several directions, then comparing the translations is most likely to expose any instabilities in the translation and so lead to a more conservative masking strategy (i.e. longer masks). In contrast, using a single LM-based predictions gives more plausible extensions to the source, making the MT system more likely to agree on its translations of the prefix and its extension, and so less likely to mask. Using several LM-based samples (the black curve) adds diversity and gives similar results to random (except that random is quicker to execute). The pattern across the two language pairs is similar, although we observe a more dispersed picture for the en→zh results.

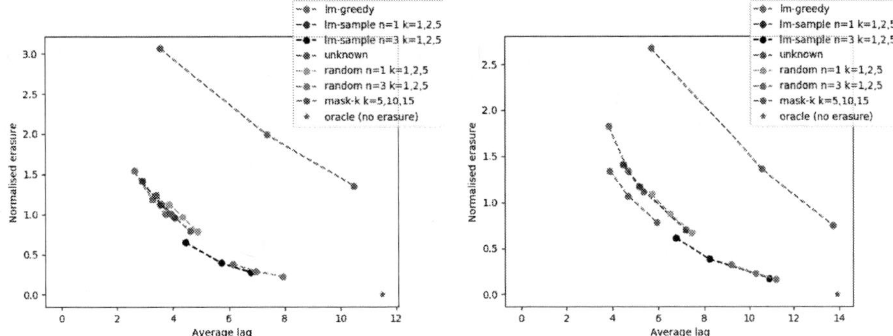

(a) Dynamic Masking for en→de MT system trained on full sentences (measured by AL and NE)

(b) Dynamic Masking for en→zh MT system trained on full sentences (measured by AL and NE)

Figure 5: Effect of dynamic mask with different source prediction strategies. The strategies are explained in Section 3, and the oracle means that we use the full-sentence translation to set the mask.

We note that, whilst Figure 5 shows that our dynamic mask approach Pareto-dominates the mask-k, it does not tell the full story since it averages both the AL and NE across the whole corpus. To give more detail on the distribution of predicted masks, we show histograms of all masks on all prefixes for two of the source prediction strategies in Figure 6. We select the source extension strategies at opposite ends of the curve, i.e. the highest AL / lowest NE strategy and the lowest AL / highest NE strategy, and show results from en→de. We can see from the graphs in Figure 6 that the distribution across masks is highly skewed, with majority of prefixes having low masks, below the mean. This is in contrast with the mask-k strategy where the mask has a fixed value, except at the end of a sentence where there is no mask. Our strategy is able to predict, with a reasonable degree of success, when it is safe to reduce the mask.

In order to provide further experimental verification of our retranslation model, we apply the strategy to a larger-scale English→Chinese system. Specifically, we use a model that was trained on the entire parallel training data for the WMT20 en-zh task[4], in addition to the TED corpus used above. For the larger model we prepared as before, except with 30k BPE merges separately on each language, and then we train a transformer-regular using Marian. By using this, we show that our strategy is able to be easily slotted in a different model from a different translation toolkit. The results are shown in Figure 7. We can verify that the pattern is unchanged in this setting.

We illustrate the improved stability preovided by our masking strategy, by drawing three examples from the English→German system's translation of our test set, in Figures 8–10. In each example we show the source prefix (as provided by the ASR), its translation, its extension (in these examples, provided by the *lm-greedy* strategy with $n = 1, k = 1$), the translation of its extension, and the output after applying the dynamic mask.

In the first example (Figure 8) the MT system produces quite unstable translations of short prefixes, but the dynamic masking algorithm detects this instability and applies short masks to cover it up. Since the translation of the prefix and the translation of its extension differ, a short mask is applied and the resulting translation avoids erasure.

In the second example in Figure 9, there is genuine uncertainty in the translation because

---

[4] `www.statmt.org/wmt20/translation-task.html`

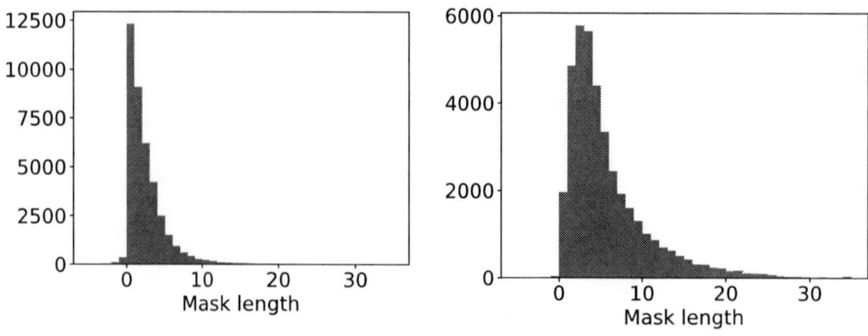

(a) Masks for *lm-greedy* strategy, $n = 1, k = 1$.   (b) Masks for *random* strategy, $n = 3, k = 5$.

Figure 6: Histograms of mask lengths over all prefixes for $en - de$ test set. The strategy on the left has low latency but higher erasure (AL=1.54, NE=3.83) whereas the one on the right has low erasure but higher latency (AL=11.2, NE=0.22). In both cases we see that the vast majority of prefixes have low masks; in other words the skewed distribution means most are below the mean.

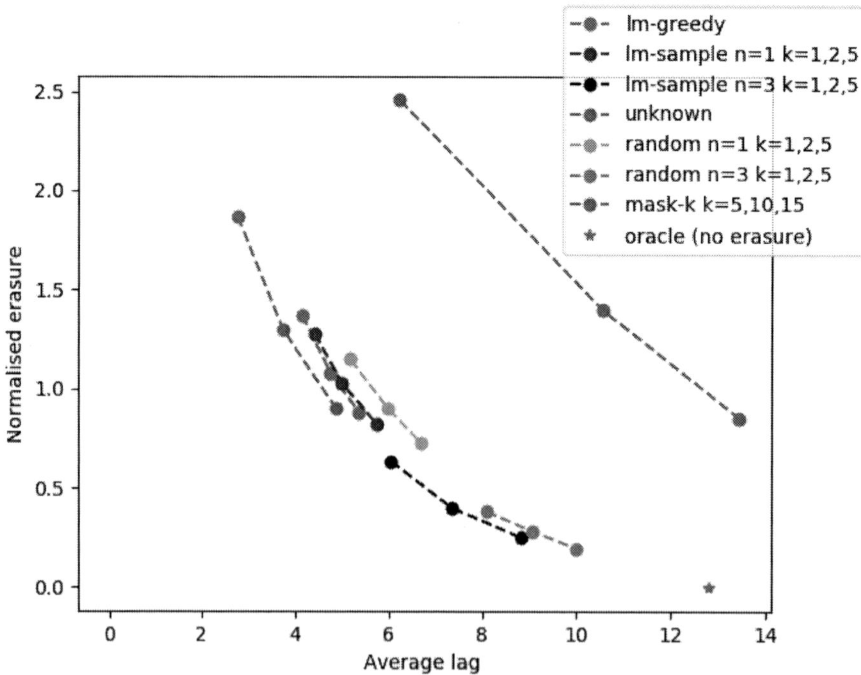

Figure 7: Effect of dynamic mask with different strategies, applied to a larger-scale en→zh system.

	Source	Translation	Output
prefix	Here	Hier sehen sie es	
extension	Here's	Hier ist es	Hier
prefix	Here are	Hier sind sie	
extension	Here are some	Hier sind einige davon	Hier sind
prefix	Here are two	Hier sind zwei davon	
extension	Here are two things	Hier sind zwei Dinge	Hier sind zwei
prefix	Here are two patients	Hier sind zwei Patienten	
extension	Here are two patients.	Hier sind zwei Patienten.	Hier sind zwei Patienten

Figure 8: In this example, the dynamic mask covers up the fact that the MT system is unstable on short prefixes. Using the translation of the LM's predicted extension of the source, the system can see that the translation is uncertain, and so applies a mask.

	Source	Translation	Output
prefix	But you know	Aber Sie wissen es	
extension	But you know,	Aber wissen Sie, sie wissen schon	Aber
prefix	But you know what?	Aber wissen Sie was?	Aber wissen Sie was?

Figure 9: Here the dynamic masking is able to address the initial uncertainty between a question and statement, which can have different word orders in German. The translation of the initial prefix and its extension produce different word orders, so the system conservatively outputs "Aber", until it receivers further input.

	Source	Translation	Output
prefix	to paraphrase : it's not the strongest of	Um zu Paraphrasen: Es ist nicht die Stärke der Dinge	
extension	to paraphrase : it's not the strongest of the	Um zu paraphrasen: Es ist nicht die Stärke der Dinge	Um zu paraphrasen: Es ist nicht die Stärke der Dinge
prefix	to paraphrase : it's not the strongest of the	Um zu Paraphrasen: Es ist nicht die Stärke der Dinge	
extension	to paraphrase : it's not the strongest of the world	Zum paraphrasen: Es ist nicht die stärksten der Welt	Um zu paraphrasen: Es ist nicht die Stärke der Dinge

Figure 10: In this example we illustrate the refinement to the dynamic masking method, that is used typically when there are small uncertainties early in the sentence. For the second prefix, its translation and the translation of its extension differ at the beginning ("um zu" vs "zum"). Applying the LCP rule would result in a large mask, but instead we output the translation of the previous prefix

the fragment "But you know" can be translated both as subject-verb and verb-subject in German, depending on whether its continuation is a statement or a question. The extension predicted by the LM is just a comma, but it is enough to reveal the uncertainty in the translation and mean that the algorithm applies a mask.

The last example (Figure 10) shows the effect of our refinement to the dynamic masking method, in reducing spurious masking. For the second prefix, the translations of the prefix and its extension differ at the start, between "Um zu" and "Zum". Instead of masking to the LCP (which would mask the whole sentence in this case) the dynamic mask algorithm just sticks with the output from the previous prefix.

7 Conclusion

We propose a dynamic mask strategy to improve the stability for the retranslation method in online SLT. We have shown that combining biased beam search with mask-k works well in retranslation systems, but biased beam search requires a modified inference algorithm and hurts the quality and additional mask-k used to reduce this effect gives a high latency. Instead, the dynamic mask strategy maintains the translation quality but gives a much better latency–flicker trade-off curve than mask-k. Our experiments also show that the effect of this strategy depends on both the length and number of predicted extensions, but the quality of predicted extensions is less important.

For future research, we would like to combine biased beam search with dynamic mask to see if it can give a better trade-off between quality and latency than (Arivazhagan et al., 2020a) when the flicker is small enough. We would also like to experiment our dynamic masking strategy on prefixes provided by a real ASR system.

Acknowledgements

 This work has received funding from the European Union's Horizon 2020 Research and Innovation Programme under Grant Agreement No 825460 (Elitr).

References

Arivazhagan, N., Cherry, C., I, T., Macherey, W., Baljekar, P., and Foster, G. (2020a). Re-Translation Strategies For Long Form, Simultaneous, Spoken Language Translation. In *ICASSP 2020 - 2020 IEEE International Conference on Acoustics, Speech and Signal Processing (ICASSP)*.

Arivazhagan, N., Cherry, C., Macherey, W., Chiu, C.-C., Yavuz, S., Pang, R., Li, W., and Raffel, C. (2019). Monotonic Infinite Lookback Attention for Simultaneous Machine Translation. In *Proceedings of the 57th Annual Meeting of the Association for Computational Linguistics*, pages 1313–1323, Florence, Italy. Association for Computational Linguistics.

Arivazhagan, N., Cherry, C., Macherey, W., and Foster, G. (2020b). Re-translation versus Streaming for Simultaneous Translation. *arXiv e-prints*, page arXiv:2004.03643.

Bangalore, S., Rangarajan Sridhar, V. K., Kolan, P., Golipour, L., and Jimenez, A. (2012). Real-time incremental speech-to-speech translation of dialogs. In *Proceedings of the 2012 Conference of the North American Chapter of the Association for Computational Linguistics: Human Language Technologies*, pages 437–445, Montréal, Canada. Association for Computational Linguistics.

Cettolo, M., Federico, M., Bentivogli, L., Niehues, J., Stüker, S., Sudoh, K., Yoshino, K., and Federmann, C. (2017). Overview of the IWSLT 2017 Evaluation Campaign. In *Proceedings of IWSLT*.

Cho, K. and Esipova, M. (2016). Can neural machine translation do simultaneous translation? *CoRR*, abs/1606.02012.

Gu, J., Neubig, G., Cho, K., and Li, V. O. (2017). Learning to translate in real-time with neural machine translation. In *Proceedings of the 15th Conference of the European Chapter of the Association for Computational Linguistics: Volume 1, Long Papers*, pages 1053–1062, Valencia, Spain. Association for Computational Linguistics.

Junczys-Dowmunt, M., Grundkiewicz, R., Dwojak, T., Hoang, H., Heafield, K., Neckermann, T., Seide, F., Germann, U., Fikri Aji, A., Bogoychev, N., Martins, A. F. T., and Birch, A. (2018). Marian: Fast neural machine translation in C++. In *Proceedings of ACL 2018, System Demonstrations*, pages 116–121, Melbourne, Australia. Association for Computational Linguistics.

Koehn, P., Hoang, H., Birch, A., Callison-Burch, C., Federico, M., Bertoldi, N., Cowan, B., Shen, W., Moran, C., Zens, R., Dyer, C., Bojar, O., Constantin, A., and Herbst, E. (2007). Moses: Open source toolkit for statistical machine translation. In *Proceedings of the 45th Annual Meeting of the Association for Computational Linguistics Companion Volume Proceedings of the Demo and Poster Sessions*, pages 177–180, Prague, Czech Republic. Association for Computational Linguistics.

Ma, M., Huang, L., Xiong, H., Zheng, R., Liu, K., Zheng, B., Zhang, C., He, Z., Liu, H., Li, X., Wu, H., and Wang, H. (2019). STACL: Simultaneous translation with implicit anticipation and controllable latency using prefix-to-prefix framework. In *Proceedings of the 57th Annual Meeting of the Association for Computational Linguistics*, pages 3025–3036, Florence, Italy. Association for Computational Linguistics.

Niehues, J., Pham, N.-Q., Ha, T.-L., Sperber, M., and Waibel, A. (2018). Low-latency neural speech translation. In *Proceedings of Interspeech*.

Post, M. (2018). A call for clarity in reporting BLEU scores. In *Proceedings of the Third Conference on Machine Translation: Research Papers*, pages 186–191, Brussels, Belgium. Association for Computational Linguistics.

Rangarajan Sridhar, V. K., Chen, J., Bangalore, S., Ljolje, A., and Chengalvarayan, R. (2013). Segmentation strategies for streaming speech translation. In *Proceedings of the 2013 Conference of the North American Chapter of the Association for Computational Linguistics: Human Language Technologies*, pages 230–238, Atlanta, Georgia. Association for Computational Linguistics.

Sennrich, R., Firat, O., Cho, K., Birch, A., Haddow, B., Hitschler, J., Junczys-Dowmunt, M., Läubli, S., Miceli Barone, A. V., Mokry, J., and Nădejde, M. (2017). Nematus: a toolkit for neural machine translation. In *Proceedings of the Software Demonstrations of the 15th Conference of the European Chapter of the Association for Computational Linguistics*, pages 65–68, Valencia, Spain. Association for Computational Linguistics.

Sennrich, R., Haddow, B., and Birch, A. (2016). Neural machine translation of rare words with subword units. In *Proceedings of the 54th Annual Meeting of the Association for Computational Linguistics (Volume 1: Long Papers)*, pages 1715–1725, Berlin, Germany. Association for Computational Linguistics.

Vaswani, A., Shazeer, N., Parmar, N., Uszkoreit, J., Jones, L., Gomez, A. N., Kaiser, Ł., and Polosukhin, I. (2017). Attention is all you need. In *Advances in neural information processing systems*, pages 5998–6008.

Zheng, B., Zheng, R., Ma, M., and Huang, L. (2019a). Simpler and faster learning of adaptive policies for simultaneous translation. In *Proceedings of the 2019 Conference on Empirical Methods in Natural Language Processing and the 9th International Joint Conference on Natural Language Processing (EMNLP-IJCNLP)*, pages 1349–1354, Hong Kong, China. Association for Computational Linguistics.

Zheng, B., Zheng, R., Ma, M., and Huang, L. (2019b). Simultaneous translation with flexible policy via restricted imitation learning. In *Proceedings of the 57th Annual Meeting of the Association for Computational Linguistics*, pages 5816–5822, Florence, Italy. Association for Computational Linguistics.

On Target Segmentation for
Direct Speech Translation

Mattia A. Di Gangi[*]   mdigangi@apptek.com
AppTek GmbH, 52062 Aachen, Germany

Marco Gaido   mgaido@fbk.eu
Matteo Negri   negri@fbk.eu
Marco Turchi   turchi@fbk.eu
Fondazione Bruno Kessler, Trento, Italy

Abstract

Recent studies on direct speech translation show continuous improvements by means of data augmentation techniques and bigger deep learning models. While these methods are helping to close the gap between this new approach and the more traditional cascaded one, there are many incongruities among different studies that make it difficult to assess the state of the art. Surprisingly, one point of discussion is the segmentation of the target text. Character-level segmentation has been initially proposed to obtain an open vocabulary, but it results on long sequences and long training time. Then, subword-level segmentation became the state of the art in neural machine translation as it produces shorter sequences that reduce the training time, while being superior to word-level models. As such, recent works on speech translation started using target subwords despite the initial use of characters and some recent claims of better results at the character level. In this work, we perform an extensive comparison of the two methods on three benchmarks covering 8 language directions and multilingual training. Subword-level segmentation compares favorably in all settings, outperforming its character-level counterpart in a range of 1 to 3 BLEU points.

1   Introduction

The recent surge in direct (or end-to-end) speech translation (ST) research (Bérard et al., 2016; Weiss et al., 2017) has favored a blooming of models and data augmentation techniques that contributed to increase the translation quality scores. However, despite the evidence of a general improving field, the state of the art is still not clearly defined and some contrasting claims are present in literature. One aspect that still needs clarification is the segmentation of the words in the target sentences. Some studies followed the setting of Listen, Attend and Spell (Chan et al., 2016) for automatic speech recognition (ASR) and segmented the target text at character level (Weiss et al., 2017; Bérard et al., 2018; Di Gangi et al., 2019b). Other studies followed Jia et al. (2019) in using subword-level segmentation (Pino et al., 2019; Bahar et al., 2019a; Liu et al., 2019), motivated by the impractical training time when using a character-level segmentation on large datasets due to the increased sequence length.

A research strand in neural machine translation (NMT) (Cherry et al., 2018; Kreutzer and Sokolov, 2018; Ataman et al., 2019), based on recurrent models, showed that character-level

---

The first author performed this work while he was a Ph.D. student at FBK.

models can outperform subword-level models, but need architectural changes to make the computation more efficient and increase the capacity of the models. Indeed, while the subword-level models can store, to some extent, syntactic and semantic information of words in their embedding layers, character embeddings cannot do the same as the function of a word is not obtained by character composition.

The idea of the superiority of the subword level is suggested for speech translation by Bahar et al. (2019b), who claim that their baseline is stronger than the ones used in previous studies because of their use of BPE-segmented words (Sennrich et al., 2016) on the target side instead of characters. In contrast, two recent works in multilingual speech translation claim better results when using characters, and consequently do not show the weaker results when using BPE (Di Gangi et al., 2019c; Inaguma et al., 2019). To the best of our knowledge, the only previous study that uses both segmentation strategies was proposed by Indurthi et al. (2019). However, the systems built for the two settings are not directly comparable with each other as they use different data and training scheme. In particular, they use data augmentation for subword-level models but not for character-level models. By itself, data augmentation can be sufficient to explain the higher scores in the former case, hiding the contribution of the different segmentation method. In this paper, we aim to assess the effect of target-side segmentation by directly comparing character- and subword-level models on some of the most popular ST benchmarks. In particular we use: Augmented Librispeech (Kocabiyikoglu et al., 2018), the most used benchmark so far; MuST-C (Di Gangi et al., 2019a), which represents the largest training set for 8 language directions; How2 (Sanabria et al., 2018), which is a quite large dataset and has been used in a recent IWSLT shared task (Niehues et al., 2019). In order to shed light over this contrasting claims we perform our experiments both in a classical one-to-one translation and in a one-to-many multilingual translation settings. Our results show that the subword-level segmentation, in our setting, is always preferable and it outperforms the character-level segmentation by up to 3 BLEU points (Papineni et al., 2002). The gap is confirmed in the multilingual setup. A final analysis shows that subword-level models are superior independently from the sequence length, and their increased capacity allows them to choose among more options in the generation phase.

2 Direct Speech Translation

Spoken language translation (hereby speech translation) has been traditionally performed using a cascade of statistical models involving at least ASR and MT (Casacuberta et al., 2008), which benefits from the possibility of using state-of-the-art models for all the components, but the translations may be negatively impacted by early wrong decisions (error propagation). Direct speech translation aims to solve the error propagation problem by removing all the intermediate steps. A single sequence-to-sequence model is trained to output the translation of the given audio input and all its parameters are optimized jointly for the translation task by minimizing the cross-entropy loss. Besides the goal of outperforming the cascaded approach, direct ST can provide additional benefits such as lower latency and computational cost, and a reduced memory footprint.

Model. We use the S-Transformer architecture (Di Gangi et al., 2019b), an adaptation of Transformer (Vaswani et al., 2017) to the ST task. S-Transformer takes as input a spectrogram to which it applies two successive strided 2D convolutional neural networks (CNNs, (LeCun et al., 1998)), each followed by batch normalization (Ioffe and Szegedy, 2015) and ReLU non-linearities. The output of the second CNN block, whose size is one fourth of the original size in both dimensions, is then processed by two successive 2D self-attention layers (Dong et al., 2018). The output is projected to the Transformer encoder layer size and summed with the positional encoding before being passed to the self-attention layers. The Transformer encoder and decoder are equal to the original Transformer, except for a logarithmic distance penalty used in the encoder multi-head attention layers to focus the attention on a local context.

3 Target-side segmentation

Character and subword segmentation are two different approaches to achieve an open vocabulary in NLP models. However, their differences directly impact the number of model parameters, the sequence lengths and the re-use of a model.

Characters. Early work in direct ST splits target text into characters (Weiss et al., 2017; Bérard et al., 2018), following Chan et al. (2016) that presents the first promising sequence-to-sequence models for ASR. Character-level segmentation is appealing because it produces a small dictionary that directly results in a small number of embedding parameters. Also, it removes preprocessing steps and additional hyperparameters that contribute to the *pipeline jungle* that accounts for technical debt in deployed systems (Sculley et al., 2015). On the other side, character-level segmentation results in very long sequences that affect negatively the training time, while the dependency range between words becomes longer, hence more difficult to learn.

Subwords. Subword-level segmentation uses algorithms that split all the words of a language in subwords according to rules that are motivated linguistically or statistically. The most popular segmentation algorithm in MT is the byte-pair encoding (BPE, (Sennrich et al., 2016)), which learns N rules for creating tokens in an iterative fashion. The initial set of tokens is given by the characters in the vocabulary. Then, for N iterations, the most frequent two-token sequence is merged in a new token that is added to the current set, and a new rule is created to generate the new token from the constituents. N is a hyperparameter of the model, and all the data processed by the model have to be segmented using the same learnt rules. Subword-level segmentation allows to find a trade-off between sequence length and dictionary size and reduce the token sparseness. With small data, a linguistically-motivated segmentation provides a strong inductive bias (Ataman et al., 2017) that prevents the emerging of implausible subwords.

Comparison. In MT, despite some early attempts to use character-level NMT (Lee et al., 2017), it soon became clear that this type of models requires some additional precautions to be competitive with BPE-based models (Cherry et al., 2018; Kreutzer and Sokolov, 2018; Ataman et al., 2019). The internal sequence representation should be compressed horizontally in order to reduce both the dependency range and the computational burden. However, this can be done on the encoder side and not in the decoder side, where the compression cannot happen until the new tokens have been generated. At the same time, Cherry et al. (2018) suggest that the embedding layer for characters cannot store useful information, as characters do not have a semantic or syntactical use, and thus more layers and more capacity is required for the whole model. Indeed, the model should learn basic character sequences that form words and how they interact. This process requires a large capacity to memorize sequences. In the rest of this paper, we compare models trained using the two types of target segmentation in a hyperparameter setting that we found good for the character-level models. Our experimental results show a consistent higher quality for subword-level models, and a following analysis will provide insights about the differences in the two systems.

4 Experimental setting

4.1 Model and training settings.

We use the S-Transformer BIG+LOG (Di Gangi et al., 2019b) setting, which uses convolutions with stride (2, 2), 16 output channels in each convolution, Transformer layers of size 512 and hidden feed forward layer size of $1,024$. All our models are trained with the adam optimizer

(Kingma and Ba, 2015) using the policy proposed in (Vaswani et al., 2017) and dropout 0.1. We always use 4,000 warm-up training steps, and final learning rate of $5e^{-3}$. The loss to optimize is cross entropy with label smoothing (Szegedy et al., 2016) set to 0.1. The maximum batch size, where not otherwise reported, is given by the minimum of 768,000 audio frames or 512 segment pairs, achieved using delayed updates (Saunders et al., 2018). Sequences longer than $2,000$ audio frames (20 seconds) are discarded from the training set to prevent memory errors. Decoding is performed with beam search of size 5. All trainings are performed on two GPUs Nvidia K80 with 12G of RAM. The systems are implemented using the codebase in urlhttps://github.com/mattiadg/FBK-Fairseq-ST, which is based on Fairseq (Gehring et al., 2017) and hence PyTorch (Paszke et al., 2017).

For all settings, we first train an ASR model on the (*audio, transcript*) portion of the dataset, and then use its encoder weights to initialize the encoder of our ST models.

4.2 Datasets

Dataset	Hours	# Pairs	# Char	# BPE
Librispeech	200	94.5K	132	8154
How2	300	185k	124	8196
MuST-C				
En-De	408	234k	188	7436
En-Es	504	270k	348	7828
En-Fr	492	280k	212	7268
En-It	465	258k	180	7500
En-Nl	442	253k	180	7444
En-Pt	385	211k	180	7532
En-Ro	432	240k	204	7676
En-Ru	489	270k	244	7468

Table 1: Statistics of all the corpora. BPE vocabulary is computed with 8,000 merge rules.

We use three speech translation datasets: Augmented Librispeech (Kocabiyikoglu et al., 2018), How2 (Sanabria et al., 2018) and MuST-C (Di Gangi et al., 2019a). They vary in terms of size, language and domain, allowing us to experiment in different conditions. Their statistics are summarized in Table 1.

Augmented Librispeech is a small English→French dataset that has been widely used in previous studies. It is built starting from the English audiobooks of Librispeech (Panayotov et al., 2015), whose texts have been aligned with the French translations of their books. The result is a corpus of 100 hours of speech and 47k segments, which has been doubled by translating all the source segments with Google Translate.

How2 is an English→Portuguese corpus for multimedia translation. It has been built from video-tutorials downloaded from Youtube with their transcripts and then translated into Portuguese. Its size is 50% larger than Augmented Librispeech.

MuST-C is a one-to-many multilingual corpus for English→German, Spanish, French, Italian, Dutch, Portuguese, Romanian, Russian. It has been built from TED talks, using transcripts and translations provided by `www.ted.com` after some steps of filtering. Every portion of MuST-C is currently the largest ST corpus available for the corresponding language pair.

4.3 Data processing and evaluation

For all audio sequences, we compute their spectrograms using 40 Mel-filterbanks. The audio frames are extracted with windows of 25 milliseconds and steps of 10 milliseconds. Only for

Librispeech, an additional energy feature is extracted, as described in (Bérard et al., 2018).

The target texts are tokenized (and special characters deescaped) using the Moses toolkit (Koehn et al., 2007) tokenizer. Text between parentheses is removed from the training data and from the references in order to remove non-speech audio effects.[1] Finally, the resulting texts are split either into characters as in (Di Gangi et al., 2019b) or with BPE Sennrich et al. (2016)[2]. The unidirectional translation experiments use $8,000$ merge rules[3], while the multilingual experiments compute $20,000$ merge rules among all the target languages. English texts, used for training the ASR models, are lower-cased and their punctuation is removed before word segmentation.

All results are computed using case-sensitive BLEU score on word-level text tokenized with the Moses toolkit and evaluated with `multi-bleu.pl`, unless otherwise specified.

5 Experiments and Results

In this section we report on two blocks of experiments. In the first block, we train separate unidirectional ST models on Librispeech, each language portion of MuST-C, and How2, analysing how the two segmentation methods affect the final results. In the second block of experiments, we run one-to-many-multilingual training on MuST-C using two different approaches, again with both segmentation techniques. For all experiments, we use the same set of hyperparameters described in §4.1.

Work	Notes	BLEU
(Bérard et al., 2018)	Multitask	13.4
(Di Gangi et al., 2019b)		13.5
(Liu et al., 2019)	PT	14.3
(Inaguma et al., 2019)	BIG + SP	15.7
(Pino et al., 2019)	PT + TTS PT	16.4
(Liu et al., 2019)	KD	17.0
(Bahar et al., 2019b)	BIG + PT + SA	17.0
(Pino et al., 2019)	BIG + MT	21.7
This work Char	PT	16.2 (16.5)
This work BPE	PT	17.1 (17.2)

Table 2: Results on Librispeech. Notes: Multitask = Multitask training with ASR; PT = pretraining; SP = speed perturbation; TTS PT = pretraining on synthetic data generated with TTS; KD = knowledge distillation; SA = SpecAugment; BIG = large model.

5.1 Unidirectional direct ST

Librispeech. Table 2 shows the results for Librispeech and compares them with previous studies. Our character-level model outperforms the one in (Di Gangi et al., 2019b) by +2.7 BLEU points, probably due to the different learning policy with a higher learning rate,[4] and achieves a score of 16.2. The BPE-level model further improves this score by additional 0.9 points, reaching the score of 17.1. Among the other results, we are able to compare only with the work by Bahar and colleagues, who used `mteval-v13.pl` for their evaluation. Our results computed with the same script are reported in parentheses. We find remarkable that our

---

[1]MuST-C contains annotations like (Applause), (Laughter), (Music), and others.

[2]We used the implementation provided in https://github.com/rsennrich/subword-nmt

[3]It performed better than alternatives in preliminary experiments, but we observed little variability in results.

[4]The work by Di Gangi and colleagues used Adam with a fixed learning rate of $1e^{-4}$ for Librispeech.

Model	De	Es	Fr	It	Nl	Pt	Ro	Ru
(Indurthi et al., 2019)								
Metalearning Char	17.2	-	29.2	-	-	-	-	-
Cascade BPE	20.9	-	33.7	-	-	-	-	-
Metalearning BPE	22.1	-	34.1	-	-	-	-	-
(Pino et al., 2019)								
Cascade	-	-	-	-	-	-	21.0	-
Direct	-	-	-	-	-	-	17.3	-
(Nguyen et al., 2019)								
MuST-C only	-	-	-	-	-	23.6	-	-
+ How2	-	-	-	-	-	26.9	-	-
(Di Gangi et al., 2020)								
MuST-C only	17.0	21.5	27.0	17.5	21.8	21.5	16.4	12.2
This work								
Char	17.6	21.6	26.5	18.0	21.5	21.6	16.9	11.6
BPE	**19.1**	**23.7**	**30.3**	**20.1**	**23.1**	**23.7**	**19.5**	**12.8**

Table 3: Results on MuST-C test sets.

BPE model obtains the same score as the one reported in Bahar et al. (2019b), which has been trained with SpecAugment (Park et al., 2019). The other results have been added, despite not being comparable, to show the range of the published scores. Notice that, in (Pino et al., 2019), the authors achieve only 16.4 BLEU when augmenting the dataset with synthetic audio and encoder pre-training. To improve this score up to 21.7, the same authors used a big Transformer model trained on synthetic parallel data generated from the ASR Librispeech dataset translated with an NMT system. Table 2 also lists the augmentation methods used by the other studies. These results highlight the importance of the training hyper-parameters. In particular, our model has about 35M parameters, and its results are comparable with the models used in most of the other studies that have almost 300M parameters, and are probably overfitting the training data.

MuST-C. The results on all the languages of MuST-C are presented in Table 3. Our character-level results are similar but not identical to the ones presented in (Di Gangi et al., 2020). Our BPE-level results outperform the ones at character level by at least 1.2 BLEU point on En-Ru and up to 3.3 points on En-Fr, with improvements of about 2 points in most of the languages. This difference should be taken into account when comparing with results reported in literature, which are obtained with a different segmentation technique.

Also for this benchmark, we report indicative results from previous work but we cannot ensure that they are obtained with the same tokenization. However, the scores of our models are in the same range as in the previous studies, confirming their value as strong baselines.

How2. For this experiment, we trained two models with the two different segmentation techniques, and additionally we trained another BPE-based model concatenating the two training sets of MuST-C and How2. The results are presented in Table 4. The performance of our character-level model is slightly worse but comparable with the results reported in (Di Gangi et al., 2020) and in (Nguyen et al., 2019). Both models are trained with character segmentation, but the second one used a training set augmented with speed perturbation. Our subword-level model outperforms significantly all the character-level models, obtaining a result of 41.2 that is equivalent to the score reported in Di Gangi et al. (2019b) when using also MuST-C En-Pt. If we also add MuST-C to the training set, we get a comparable score to Nguyen et al. (2019) in the same condition (but using only 400 BPE rules, the best number of segmentation rules according

Model	BLEU
(Di Gangi et al., 2020)	39.4
+ MuST-C	41.0
(Nguyen et al., 2019) CHAR	39.9
+ MuST-C BPE	43.8
This work Char	39.1
This work BPE	41.2
+ MuST-C	43.5

Table 4: Comparing our results on How2 with the published results.

	De	Nl	Es	Fr	It	Pt
Char						
Unidirectional	17.6	21.5	21.6	26.5	18.0	21.6
C-Decoder	18.4	21.9	21.1	25.4	17.4	21.5
S-Decoder	18.2	21.7	21.9	26.5	18.5	22.7
BPE						
Unidirectional	19.1	23.1	23.7	30.3	20.1	23.7
C-Decoder	20.7	24.6	22.6	27.6	19.3	23.3
S-Decoder	20.9	25.4	23.5	29.9	20.1	25.1

Table 5: BLEU score results with *concat* (C-*) and *sum* (S-*) *target forcing* on 6 languages. Unidirectional refers to *one-to-one* systems. The other results are computed with one multilingual system for En→De,NL and one for En→Es,Fr,It,Pt.

to their experiments), which additionally used speed perturbation for data augmentation.

5.2 Multilingual direct ST

One-to-many multilingual translation uses a single model to translate one source language (English in this case) into two or more target languages. As there is a single encoder and a single decoder shared among all the language directions, the model requires to be informed about the target language. To this aim, the *target forcing* approach by Johnson et al. (2017) pre-pends to the source sentence a "language token" indicating the target language. In multilingual ST there is no source sentence (the input is indeed a sequence of audio features), so some variations have been proposed to adapt this approach. Inaguma et al. (2019) proposed to prepend the language token to the target sequence, replacing the *start of sentence* token. Di Gangi et al. (2019c) proposed two variants: *concat*, which is analogous to the method proposed by Inaguma and colleagues; and *sum*, which performs an element-wise sum of the language token embedding to all the elements in the target sequence. Here, we run experiments at both character- and BPE-level with the two methods and verify if their claims about the BPE segmentation being less effective holds true in the multilingual case.

We train two groups of systems, one for En→{De,Nl} (Germanic) and one for En→{Es,Fr,It,Pt} (Romance), using both segmentation strategies as well as the two *target forcing* variants in the decoder. The results are presented in Table 5. Our character-level models improve slightly and comparably over the unidirectional systems for the Germanic targets, while for the Romance targets the *sum* approach is better by improving by more than 1 BLEU point for Portuguese and smaller improvements in the other cases. However, the difference between the *concat* and *sum* approaches is more evident in the BPE-level case, where the former is generally worse than the unidirectional systems and the latter is comparable or better. The larger improvements are for German, Dutch and Portuguese with, respectively, +1.8, +2.3 and +1.4. For the Romance languages, the *concat* approach produces in general a score degradation with respect to the unidirectional systems. The *sum* approach, instead, is at least on par with the uni-directional baselines. The only real improvement among Romance languages can be measured for Portuguese, which has about 25% less data than the other languages and can benefit from positive transfer learning. The reason of the different behaviors of multilingual approaches is beyond the scope of this paper and we defer the analysis to other studies. These results indicate that, besides significantly outperforming the character-level models also in the multilingual set-ting (up to 3.7 BLEU points in En-Nl), under some conditions (for the Germanic languages) the BPE-level models can benefit more also from the multilingual training, widening the already large gap between the baselines.

6   Analysis

We are now interested in understanding why the BPE-level models are better performing than their character-level counterparts. To this aim, we analyze the translation quality on sentences with different target lengths and the output distribution peakiness. The goals are: *i)* checking if the differences between the two models depend on the sentence length, and *ii)* verifying the idea that character-level models need to memorize more (see §3).

Length comparison.   The plots in Figures 1 and 2 show the BLEU scores achieved by the systems for groups of different reference length (measured in number of characters) for, re-spectively, En-Fr and En-Ru. Let DELTA be the reference length difference between BPE and character segmentations, we can observe that it has a clear upward trend in En-Fr, while in En-Ru DELTA is larger in the first bin, before increasing again for the longest sentences. The trend for character-level models is to have a larger BLEU score in the second bin than in the first one, then a smooth transition to the third bin, and finally a dramatic degradation in the last two bins. The degradation in the last two bins is less evident for the BPE-level models. Similar patterns are found in the other language directions. This first analysis shows that BPE-level models achieve a higher quality in all length bins and can better manage long translations.

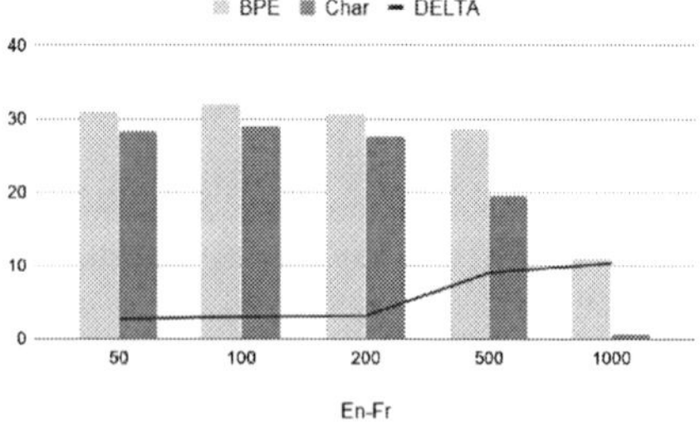

Figure 1: BLEU score by reference length (number of characters) for character- and BPE-level models in English-French.

TER.   The TER (Snover et al., 2006) scores translations at sentence level as a function of er-rors (insertions, deletions, substitutions, shifts) with respect to a reference. We compute TER with a focus on MuST-C French translations to obtain more details about the score difference between the two systems. We use the sentence-level scores to divide the translations in three groups according to the system that produced the best translation (or a tie). We say that the

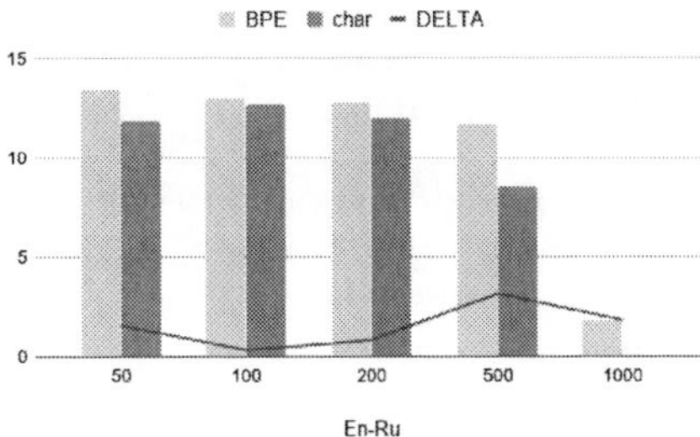

Figure 2: BLEU score by reference length (number of characters) for character- and BPE-level models in English-Russian.

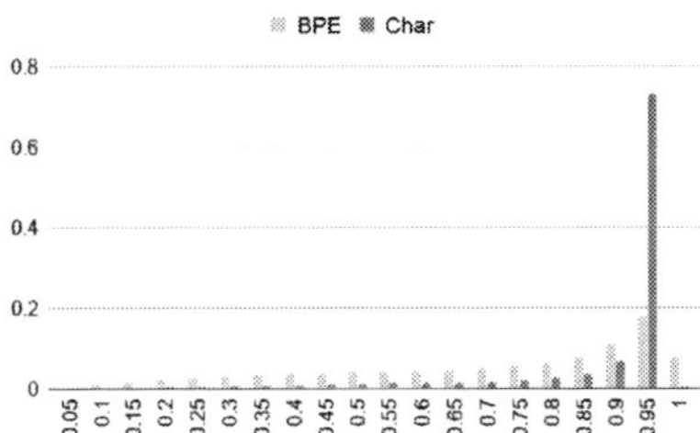

Figure 3: Histograms of the probabilities of the symbols selected by beam search in the test set of MuST-C En-Fr.

system that produces the best translation is the winner for that segment. The results are summarized in Table 6. First, we can observe a big difference on the percentage of wins for the two systems: the BPE-level system wins in 44.6% of the cases, against 30.2% for the Char-level system and only a 25% of ties. When breaking the results according to the segment groups, both systems achieve the lowest average error rate in the Tie group. By a manual inspection, we found that these are not easy or short sentences that are translated equally, but the systems generate different translations often with different errors, which are overall balanced though. Then, it is interesting to understand whether a pattern exists in the Char Winner group. We found that these are mostly hard cases in terms of terminology. Both systems produce poor translations in such cases, but the shorter translations by the Char-level system reduce the TER. For the BPE winner segments, the TER difference can range from small to high values, and it increases with the reference length. To summarize, this inspection found that the BPE-level system is equal to or better than the Char-level system on 70% of the segments, and the superiority is clear on long segments. Also, it suggests that systems trained on such small datasets suffer from significant vocabulary issues and data augmentation methods can be considered as a partial but effective solution to this problem.

Distribution peakiness. The peakiness of the output conditional distribution is an indicator of how the model is confident in its choice. Over-confident distributions are a signal of over-fitting and Meister et al. (2020) showed that models producing higher-entropy distributions provide better translation. Here, we consider the conditional probability of each token selected by beam search in the whole test set, and group them in bins of size 0.05. In the general case, this approach would give little information about the whole distribution, but in this case we find

	Char Winner	BPE Winner	Tie	Total	% Win
Char	51.2	61.4	46.3	57.6	30.2
BPE	66.1	46.4	46.3	53.9	44.6

Table 6: Average TER of the two systems on the groups of sentences where the best translation is produced by Char, BPE, or there is a tie. The best translation is decided according to the TER score for each individual sentence. The last two columns show the TER computed on the whole test set and the percentage of times when one system won.

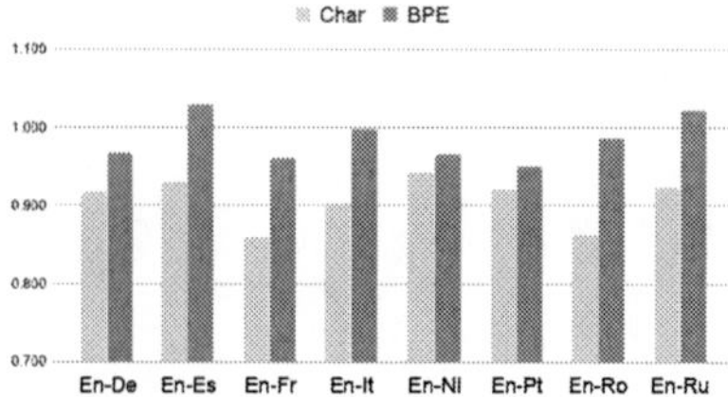

Figure 4: Comparison of the length of the produced output with respect to the reference.

that it is sufficient to discriminate the working of the two types of system. We show only the results with MuST-C En-Fr, but the other models follow a similar behavior. As it is shown in Figure 3, both models have their mode in the bin containing probabilities between 0.9 and 0.95. However, while for the BPE-level model the mode accounts for less than 20% of the cases, for the character-level model it is more than 70%. Additionally, the cumulative probability of the bins from 0.8 to 1.0 is 0.90. This shows that the probability mass is concentrated in one single symbol in the vast majority of cases. A manual inspection revealed that the few occurrences of low probabilities for the first choice occur mostly in two cases: when choosing the first character of a word, mostly for content words, or for choosing the first character of a suffix when it decides a word inflection. The network is thus capable of outputting easily some memorized sequences, and its uncertainty increases only in a few critical points. This model overconfidence may reduce the effectiveness of beam search in evaluating alternative options because of the large score difference.

Discussion. Our analysis revealed that BPE-level models produce, in average, better translations for all reference lengths with a higher difference in the longest sentences. The inability of character-level models to properly translate long sequences is confirmed by their tendency to generate shorter outputs, as shown in Figure 4. Additionally, BPE-level models produce better translations more often than the char-level models do (44% vs 30%, see Table 6). Finally, we found that character-level models generate output conditional distributions that are significantly more peaked, confirming their higher reliance on memorization and overfitting. Cherry et al. (2018) observed for NMT that character-level models require a very large capacity, which can be the topic of future work. Here, we showed that our results hold for a large number of domains and target languages, and with strong baseline models.

7   Related work

Direct ST has been proposed with the idea to skip the transcription phase of a cascaded system to improve translation quality (Bérard et al., 2016). However, the small data condition of this task appeared to be the main obstacle to overcome, which has been tackled with techniques like transfer learning or multitask learning (Weiss et al., 2017; Bérard et al., 2018) in order to leverage knowledge from the tasks of ASR and MT. This techniques resulted to be useful, but the improvements were limited and really effective only in very small data conditions (Anastasopoulos and Chiang, 2018; Bansal et al., 2018). Furthermore, Sperber et al. (2019) argued that current sequence-to-sequence architectures are not effective in leveraging the additional data, and an evolution of the two-stage-decoding model (Kano et al., 2017) is more data-efficient. In an attempt to transfer knowledge from MT to ST, Liu et al. (2019) used knowledge distillation, but the real game-changing approach appeared to be the use of synthetic parallel data generated with TTS and MT systems (Jia et al., 2019). Pino et al. (2019) showed that using data with the target side generated by MT outperforms model pretraining. Separately, Bahar and colleagues studied the contributions of pretraining and of the CTC loss for multitask learning (Bahar et al., 2019a) and the effectiveness of SpecAugment (Bahar et al., 2019b), but without synthetic parallel data. In a different attempt to leverage more data, Di Gangi et al. (2019c) and Inaguma et al. (2019) proposed multilingual ST. Despite showing a general direction of improvement, the results from these studies are not directly comparable for several reasons: *i)* the use of characters or subwords in the target side; *ii)* the use of different model architectures, with sizes ranging from 9M to about 300M parameters; *iii)* the studies experiment only on few datasets, and the results obtained in small datasets are not always portable to larger datasets. We tried to shed light on some of the mentioned problems by 1) proving that the target segmentation is highly relevant for the final result, 2) using a single architecture and model size that can be compared with literature, and 3) setting strong baselines for 10 common benchmarks.

8   Conclusion

The optimal target text segmentation was a source of doubts according to literature on direct speech translation, with studies making strong claims in one sense or another without a clear proof. In this work, we performed a thorough investigation across different ST benchmarks using hyperparameters proposed for the character level, and we found that the BPE segmentation is always preferable both in terms of computational burden and translation quality. Our experimental results define new strong baselines for the chosen benchmarks, often performing similarly to models using data augmentation. In light of our findings, we invite the community to take into account the target segmentation when comparing different systems and to take more care of their baselines to really measure improvements in the field.

References

Anastasopoulos, A. and Chiang, D. (2018). Tied multitask learning for neural speech translation. In *Proceedings of the 2018 Conference of the North American Chapter of the Association for Computational Linguistics: Human Language Technologies, Volume 1 (Long Papers)*, pages 82–91, New Orleans, Louisiana. Association for Computational Linguistics.

Ataman, D., Firat, O., Di Gangi, M. A., Federico, M., and Birch, A. (2019). On the importance of word boundaries in character-level neural machine translation. In *Proceedings of the 3rd Workshop on Neural Generation and Translation*, pages 187–193, Hong Kong. Association for Computational Linguistics.

Ataman, D., Negri, M., Turchi, M., and Federico, M. (2017). Linguistically Motivated Vocabulary Reduction for Neural Machine Translation from Turkish to English. *The Prague Bulletin of Mathematical Linguistics*, 108(1):331–342.

Bahar, P., Bieschke, T., and Ney, H. (2019a). A comparative study on end-to-end speech to text translation. In *2019 IEEE Automatic Speech Recognition and Understanding Workshop (ASRU)*, pages 792–799. IEEE.

Bahar, P., Zeyer, A., Schlüter, R., and Ney, H. (2019b). On Using SpecAugment for End-to-End Speech Translation. In *Proceedings of the 16th International Workshop on Spoken Language Translation 2019*, Hong Kong.

Bansal, S., Kamper, H., Livescu, K., Lopez, A., and Goldwater, S. (2018). Low-Resource Speech-to-Text Translation. *Proceedings of Interspeech 2018*, pages 1298–1302.

Bérard, A., Besacier, L., Kocabiyikoglu, A. C., and Pietquin, O. (2018). End-to-end automatic speech translation of audiobooks. In *2018 IEEE International Conference on Acoustics, Speech and Signal Processing (ICASSP)*, pages 6224–6228. IEEE.

Bérard, A., Pietquin, O., Servan, C., and Besacier, L. (2016). Listen and Translate: A Proof of Concept for End-to-End Speech-to-Text Translation. In *NIPS Workshop on End-to-End Learning for Speech and Audio Processing 2016*.

Casacuberta, F., Federico, M., Ney, H., and Vidal, E. (2008). Recent Efforts in Spoken Language Translation. *IEEE Signal Processing Magazine*, 25(3):80–88.

Chan, W., Jaitly, N., Le, Q., and Vinyals, O. (2016). Listen, attend and spell: A neural network for large vocabulary conversational speech recognition. In *2016 IEEE International Conference on Acoustics, Speech and Signal Processing (ICASSP)*, pages 4960–4964. IEEE.

Cherry, C., Foster, G., Bapna, A., Firat, O., and Macherey, W. (2018). Revisiting Character-Based Neural Machine Translation with Capacity and Compression. In *Proceedings of the 2018 Conference on Empirical Methods in Natural Language Processing*, pages 4295–4305, Brussels, Belgium. Association for Computational Linguistics.

Di Gangi, M. A., Cattoni, R., Bentivogli, L., Negri, M., and Turchi, M. (2019a). MuST-C: a Multilingual Speech Translation Corpus. In *Proceedings of the 2019 Conference of the North American Chapter of the Association for Computational Linguistics: Human Language Technologies, Volume 1 (Long and Short Papers)*, pages 2012–2017, Minneapolis, Minnesota. Association for Computational Linguistics.

Di Gangi, M. A., Negri, M., and Turchi, M. (2019b). Adapting Transformer to End-to-End Spoken Language Translation. In *INTERSPEECH 2019*, pages 1133–1137. International Speech Communication Association (ISCA).

Di Gangi, M. A., Negri, M., and Turchi, M. (2019c). One-to-many multilingual end-to-end speech translation. In *2019 IEEE Automatic Speech Recognition and Understanding Workshop (ASRU)*, pages 585–592. IEEE.

Di Gangi, M. A., Nguyen, V.-N., Negri, M., and Turchi, M. (2020). Instance-based Model Adaptation for Direct Speech Translation. In *ICASSP 2020-2020 IEEE International Conference on Acoustics, Speech and Signal Processing (ICASSP)*, pages 7914–7918. IEEE.

Dong, L., Xu, S., and Xu, B. (2018). Speech-Transformer: a No-Recurrence Sequence-to-Sequence Model for Speech Recognition. In *2018 IEEE International Conference on Acoustics, Speech and Signal Processing (ICASSP)*, pages 5884–5888. IEEE.

Gehring, J., Auli, M., Grangier, D., Yarats, D., and Dauphin, Y. N. (2017). Convolutional Sequence to Sequence Learning. In *Proceedings of the 34th International Conference on Machine Learning-Volume 70*, pages 1243–1252.

Inaguma, H. et al. (2019). ESPnet How2 Speech Translation System for IWSLT 2019: Pre-training, Knowledge Distillation, and Going Deeper. In *Proceedings of IWSLT 2019*.

Indurthi, S. et al. (2019). Data efficient direct speech-to-text translation with modality agnostic meta-learning. In *Proc. of ICASSP 2020*.

Ioffe, S. and Szegedy, C. (2015). Batch Normalization: Accelerating Deep Network Training by Reducing Internal Covariate Shift. In *International Conference on Machine Learning*, pages 448–456.

Jia, Y. et al. (2019). Leveraging Weakly Supervised Data to Improve End-to-End Speech-to-Text Translation. In *ICASSP 2019-2019 IEEE International Conference on Acoustics, Speech and Signal Processing (ICASSP)*, pages 7180–7184. IEEE.

Johnson, M. et al. (2017). Google's Multilingual Neural Machine Translation System: Enabling Zero-Shot Translation. *Transactions of the Association for Computational Linguistics*, 5:339–351.

Kano, T., Sakti, S., and Nakamura, S. (2017). Structured-Based Curriculum Learning for End-to-End English-Japanese Speech Translation. *Proceedings of Interspeech 2017*, pages 2630–2634.

Kingma, D. and Ba, J. (2015). Adam: A method for stochastic optimization. In *Proceedings of the International Conference on Learning Representation 2015*.

Kocabiyikoglu, A. C., Besacier, L., and Kraif, O. (2018). Augmenting Librispeech with French Translations: A Multimodal Corpus for Direct Speech Translation Evaluation. In *Proceedings of LREC 2018*.

Koehn, P. et al. (2007). Moses: Open Source Toolkit for Statistical Machine Translation. In *Proceedings of the 45th Annual Meeting of the Association for Computational Linguistics Companion Volume Proceedings of the Demo and Poster Sessions*, pages 177–180, Prague, Czech Republic. Association for Computational Linguistics.

Kreutzer, J. and Sokolov, A. (2018). Learning to Segment Inputs for NMT Favors Character-Level Processing. In *Proceedings of IWSLT 2018*.

LeCun, Y., Bottou, L., Bengio, Y., and Haffner, P. (1998). Gradient-based Learning Applied to Document Recognition. *Proceedings of the IEEE*, 86(11):2278–2324.

Lee, J., Cho, K., and Hofmann, T. (2017). Fully Character-Level Neural Machine Translation without Explicit Segmentation. *Transactions of the Association for Computational Linguistics*, 5:365–378.

Liu, Y., Xiong, H., He, Z., Zhang, J., Wu, H., Wang, H., and Zong, C. (2019). End-to-End Speech Translation with Knowledge Distillation. In *Proceedings of Interspeech 2019*.

Meister, C., Salesky, E., and Cotterell, R. (2020). Generalized Entropy Regularization or: There's Nothing Special about Label Smoothing. In *Proceedings of the 58th Annual Meeting of the Association for Computational Linguistics*, pages 6870–6886, Online. Association for Computational Linguistics.

Nguyen, M. H. et al. (2019). On-trac consortium end-to-end speech translation systems for the iwslt 2019 shared task. In *16th International Workshop on Spoken Language Translation 2019*.

Niehues, J. et al. (2019). The IWSLT 2019 Evaluation Campaign. In *16th International Workshop on Spoken Language Translation 2019*.

Panayotov, V., Chen, G., Povey, D., and Khudanpur, S. (2015). Librispeech: an ASR Corpus Based on Public Domain Audio Books. In *2015 IEEE International Conference on Acoustics, Speech and Signal Processing (ICASSP)*, pages 5206–5210. IEEE.

Papineni, K., Roukos, S., Ward, T., and Zhu, W.-J. (2002). Bleu: a method for automatic evaluation of machine translation. In *Proceedings of the 40th Annual Meeting of the Association for Computational Linguistics*, pages 311–318, Philadelphia, Pennsylvania, USA. Association for Computational Linguistics.

Park, D. S. et al. (2019). SpecAugment: A Simple Data Augmentation Method for Automatic Speech Recognition. *Proceedings of Interspeech 2019*, pages 2613–2617.

Paszke, A. et al. (2017). Automatic differentiation in pytorch. In *NIPS 2017 Workshop Autodiff*.

Pino, J. et al. (2019). Harnessing indirect training data for end-to-end automatic speech translation: Tricks of the trade. In *Proceedings of the 16th International Workshop on Spoken Language Translation 2019*.

Sanabria, R. et al. (2018). How2: A Large-scale Dataset For Multimodal Language Understanding. In *Proceeding of ViGIL 2018*. NeurIPS.

Saunders, D., Stahlberg, F., de Gispert, A., and Byrne, B. (2018). Multi-representation ensembles and delayed SGD updates improve syntax-based NMT. In *Proceedings of the 56th Annual Meeting of the Association for Computational Linguistics (Volume 2: Short Papers)*, pages 319–325, Melbourne, Australia. Association for Computational Linguistics.

Sculley, D. et al. (2015). Hidden technical debt in machine learning systems. In *Proceedings of the 29th COnference on Neural Information Processing Systems 2015*, Montreal, Canada.

Sennrich, R., Haddow, B., and Birch, A. (2016). Neural Machine Translation of Rare Words with Subword Units. In *Proceedings of the 54th Annual Meeting of the Association for Computational Linguistics (Volume 1: Long Papers)*, pages 1715–1725, Berlin, Germany. Association for Computational Linguistics.

Snover, M., Dorr, B., Schwartz, R., Micciulla, L., and Makhoul, J. (2006). A Study of Translation Edit Rate with Targeted Human Annotation. In *Proceedings of association for machine translation in the Americas.*, volume 200.

Sperber, M., Neubig, G., Niehues, J., and Waibel, A. (2019). Attention-passing models for robust and data-efficient end-to-end speech translation. *Transactions of the Association for Computational Linguistics*, 7:313–325.

Szegedy, C., Vanhoucke, V., Ioffe, S., Shlens, J., and Wojna, Z. (2016). Rethinking the Inception Architecture for Computer Vision. In *Proceedings of the IEEE conference on computer vision and pattern recognition*, pages 2818–2826.

Vaswani, A., Shazeer, N., Parmar, N., Uszkoreit, J., Jones, L., Gomez, A. N., Kaiser, Ł., and Polosukhin, I. (2017). Attention is All You Need. In *Advances in neural information processing systems*, pages 5998–6008.

Weiss, R. J., Chorowski, J., Jaitly, N., Wu, Y., and Chen, Z. (2017). Sequence-to-Sequence Models Can Directly Translate Foreign Speech. *Proceedings of Interspeech 2017*, pages 2625–2629.

Domain Robustness in Neural Machine Translation

Mathias Müller   mmueller@cl.uzh.ch
Annette Rios   rios@cl.uzh.ch
Rico Sennrich   sennrich@cl.uzh.ch
Department of Computational Linguistics, University of Zurich, Switzerland

Abstract

Translating text that diverges from the training domain is a key challenge for machine translation. Domain robustness—the generalization of models to unseen test domains—is low for both statistical (SMT) and neural machine translation (NMT). In this paper, we study the performance of SMT and NMT models on out-of-domain test sets. We find that in unknown domains, SMT and NMT suffer from very different problems: SMT systems are mostly adequate but not fluent, while NMT systems are mostly fluent, but not adequate. For NMT, we identify such hallucinations (translations that are fluent but unrelated to the source) as a key reason for low domain robustness. To mitigate this problem, we empirically compare methods that are reported to improve adequacy or in-domain robustness in terms of their effectiveness at improving domain robustness. In experiments on German→English OPUS data, and German→Romansh (a low-resource setting) we find that several methods improve domain robustness. While those methods do lead to higher BLEU scores overall, they only slightly increase the adequacy of translations compared to SMT.

1 Introduction

Even though neural models have improved the state-of-the-art in machine translation considerably in recent years, they still underperform in specific conditions. One such condition is out-of-domain translation. Koehn and Knowles (2017) found that neural machine translation (NMT) systems perform poorly in such settings and that their poor performance cannot be explained solely by the fact that out-of-domain translation is difficult: non-neural, statistical machine translation (SMT) systems were superior at this task. For this reason, Koehn and Knowles (2017) identified translation of out-of-domain text as a key challenge for NMT.

Catastrophic failure to translate out-of-domain text can be viewed as overfitting to the training domain, i.e. systems learn idiosyncrasies of the domain rather than more general features. Our goal is to learn models that generalize well to unseen data distributions, including data from other domains. We will refer to this property of showing good generalization to unseen domains as **domain robustness**.

We consider domain robustness a desirable property of NLP systems, along with other types of robustness, such as robustness against adversarial examples (Goodfellow et al. 2015) or typos in the input (Belinkov and Bisk, 2018). While domain adaptation with small amounts of parallel or monolingual in-domain data has proven very effective for NMT (e.g. Luong and Manning, 2015; Sennrich et al., 2016a; Kobus et al., 2017; Li et al., 2019), the target domain(s) may be unknown when a system is built, and there are language pairs for which training data is only available for limited domains. Hence, domain robustness of systems without any domain adaptation is not only of theoretical interest, but also relevant in practice.

SRC *Aber geh subtil dabei vor.*

REF *But be subtle about it.*

HYP *Pharmacokinetic parameters are not significantly affected in patients with renal impairment (see section 5.2).*

Figure 1: Example illustrating how a German→English NMT system trained on medical text *hallucinates* the translation of an out-of-domain input sentence.

Model architectures and training techniques have evolved since Koehn and Knowles (2017)'s study, and it is unclear to what extent this problem still persists. We therefore revisit the hypothesis that NMT systems exhibit low domain robustness. In preliminary experiments, we demonstrate that current models still fail at out-of-domain translation: BLEU scores drop drastically for test domains other than the training domain. However, the overall out-of-domain translation quality of NMT systems is now on par with SMT systems.

An analysis of our baseline systems reveals that **hallucinated** content occurs frequently in out-of-domain translations (see Figure 1 for an example). Several authors present anecdotal evidence for NMT systems occasionally falling into a *hallucination* mode where translations are grammatically correct but unrelated to the source sentence (Arthur et al., 2016; Koehn and Knowles, 2017; Nguyen and Chiang, 2018). Our manual evaluation shows that hallucination is more pronounced in out-of-domain translation. We therefore expect methods that alleviate the hallucination problem to indirectly improve domain robustness.

As a means to reduce hallucination, we experiment with several techniques and assess their effectiveness in improving domain robustness: reconstruction (Tu et al., 2017; Niu et al., 2019), subword regularization (Kudo, 2018), neural noisy channel models (Li and Jurafsky, 2016; Yee et al., 2019), and defensive distillation (Papernot et al., 2016), as well as combinations of these techniques. The main contributions of this paper are:

- we perform an analysis of SMT and NMT systems that confirms that while in-domain BLEU increased, domain robustness remains a major problem even with state-of-the-art Transformer architectures. Our comparison of SMT and NMT shows differences in how performance degrades in unseen domains: SMT mostly suffers in terms of fluency, while NMT tends to produce more fluent, but less adequate translations (hallucinations).

- we test several techniques related to adequacy, robustness, or out-of-domain translation in regard to their effectiveness in improving domain robustness in NMT. We find that several techniques are moderately successful, most notably reconstruction, which reduces the average percentage of hallucinations in out-of-domain test sets from 35% to 29%.

- we show that despite moderate improvements, domain robustness remains a challenge in NMT, and provide code and data sets to serve as baselines for future work.

2 Data Sets

We report experiments on two different translation directions: German→English (DE→EN) and German→Romansh (DE→RM).

2.1 German→English

For all DE→EN experiments, we use the same corpora as Koehn and Knowles (2017), available from OPUS (Lison and Tiedemann, 2016).

DE–EN				DE–RM		
domains	corpora		size	domains	corpora	size
medical	EMEA		1.1m	law	Allegra,	
IT	GNOME, KDE, PHP, Ubuntu, OpenOffice		380k		Press Releases	100k
koran	Tanzil		540k	blogs	Convivenza	20k
law	JRC-Acquis		720k			
subtitles	OpenSubtitles2018		22.5m			

Table 1: Data sets common to all of our experiments. Size indicates number of sentence pairs.

We use corpora from OPUS to define five domains: *medical, IT, koran, law* and *subtitles*. See Table 1 for an overview of sizes per domain. The domains are quite distant, and we therefore expect that systems trained on a single domain will have low domain robustness if tested on other domains.

For each domain, we select 2000 consecutive sentence pairs each for development and testing. Our test sets are different from Koehn and Knowles (2017), so results are not directly comparable. In all experiments, the *medical* domain serves as the training domain, while the remaining four domains are used for testing.

2.2 German→Romansh

To complement our DE→EN experiments, we also train systems for DE→RM. Romansh is a Romance language that, with an estimated 40 000 native speakers, is low-resource, but has some parallel resources thanks to its status as an official Swiss language. Domain robustness is of particular relevance in low-resource settings since training data is typically only available for few domains. Our training data consists of 100 000 sentence pairs, specifically the Allegra corpus by Scherrer and Cartoni (2012) which contains mostly law text, and an in-house collection of government press releases. As test domain (unseen during training), we use blog posts from Convivenza[1]. From both data sets we randomly select 2000 consecutive sentence pairs as test sets.

3   State-of-the-art Models Exhibit Low Domain Robustness

In this section, we establish that current NMT systems exhibit low domain robustness by analyzing our baseline systems automatically and manually.

3.1   Experimental Setup for Baseline Models

We use Moses scripts for punctuation normalization and tokenization. We apply truecasing trained on in-domain training data. Similarly, we apply BPE (Sennrich et al., 2016b) with 32k (DE→EN) and 16k (DE→RM) merge operations learned from in-domain data. We train two baselines:

NMT Baseline A standard Transformer base model trained with Sockeye (Vaswani et al., 2017; Hieber et al., 2018).

SMT Baseline A standard, phrase-based statistical model trained with Moses (Koehn et al., 2007), using mtrain (Läubli et al., 2018) as frontend with standard settings.

---

[1]https://www.suedostschweiz.ch/blogs/convivenza

	SMT	NMT
in-domain		
medical	58.4	**61.5**
out-of-domain		
IT	**21.4**	17.1
koran	**1.4**	1.1
law	19.8	**25.3**
subtitles	**4.7**	3.4
average (out-of-domain)	**11.8**	11.7

(a)

	SMT	NMT
in-domain		
law	45.2	**52.5**
out-of-domain		
blogs	15.5	**18.9**

(b)

Table 2: BLEU scores of (a) baseline DE→EN systems trained on *medical* data, (b) baseline DE→RM systems trained on *law* data.

We always test on several domains, including the training domain. We use a beam size of 10 to translate test data. We report case-sensitive BLEU (Papineni et al., 2002) scores on detokenized text, computed with SacreBLEU (Post, 2018)[2].

3.2 Analysis of Baseline Systems

Tables 2a and 2b show automatic evaluation results for all our baseline models. Neural models achieve good performance on the respective in-domain test sets (61.5 BLEU on *medical* for DE→EN; 52.5 BLEU on *law* for DE→RM), but on out-of-domain text, translation quality is clearly diminished, with an average BLEU of roughly 12 (DE→EN) and 19 (DE→RM). The following analysis will focus on our DE→EN baseline systems.

Compared to results reported by Koehn and Knowles (2017), NMT has improved markedly since their study was conducted, and is now on par with SMT in out-of-domain settings (11.8 BLEU versus 11.7). However, on the in-domain test set, our NMT baseline outperforms the SMT baseline by 3 BLEU. This result suggests that higher in-domain performance does not guarantee better out-of-domain translations.

Unknown words constitute one possible reason for failing to translate out-of-domain texts. As shown in Table 3a, the percentage of words that are not seen during training is much higher in all out-of-domain test sets. However, unknown words cannot be the only reason for low translation quality: The test sets with the lowest BLEU scores (*koran* and *subtitles*) actually have an out-of-vocabulary (OOV) rate similar to the *IT* test set, where BLEU scores are much higher for both baseline models.

Additionally, our SMT baseline shows better generalization to some domains unseen at training time, while the average BLEU is comparable to the NMT baseline. In the *IT* domain, the result is most extreme: the SMT system beats the neural system by 4.3 BLEU. This demonstrates that the low domain robustness of NMT is not (only) a data problem, but also due to the model's inductive biases.

As a further control, we train additional baseline systems trained on *all* domains.[3] We use it to test whether the data we have held out for out-of-domain testing is inherently more difficult to translate than the in-domain test set. The results in Table 3b show that this is not the case.

---

[2]SacreBLEU version signature: `BLEU+c.mixed+#.1+s.exp+tok.13a+v.1.4.1`.

[3]The *subtitles* domain (23m sentences) was subsampled to 1m sentence pairs so as not to overwhelm the remaining domains (3m sentences in total). We also removed any overlap between the training and test sets.

	OOV rate
in-domain	
medical	2.42%
out-of-domain	
IT	20.09%
koran	18.63%
law	9.39%
subtitles	18.16%

(a)

	SMT	NMT
in-domain		
medical	53.2	**61.4**
out-of-domain		
IT	31.9	**44.7**
koran	15.2	**15.9**
law	58.3	**62.3**
subtitles	14.9	**18.5**
average (out-of-domain)	30.1	**35.4**

(b)

Table 3: For the language pair DE→EN: (a) Out-of-vocabulary (OOV) rates of in-domain and out-of-domain test sets. (b) BLEU scores of baselines trained on a concatenation of *all* domains.

For the NMT baseline, BLEU ranges between 15.9 and 62.3, with an average out-of-domain BLEU of 35.4.

3.2.1 Hallucination

NMT models can be understood as language models of the target language, conditioned on a representation of a source text. This means that NMT models have no explicit mechanism—as SMT models do—that enforces coverage of the source sentence, and if the representation of an out-of-domain source sentence is outside the training distribution, it can be seemingly ignored. This gives rise to a tendency to *hallucinate* translations, i.e. to produce translations that are fluent, but unrelated to the content of the source sentence (Lee et al., 2018).

We hypothesize that hallucination is more common in out-of-domain settings. A small manual evaluation performed by the main author confirms that this is indeed the case. We evaluate the fluency and adequacy of our baselines (we refer to them as **NMT** and **SMT**). In a blind setup, we annotate a random sample of 100 sentence pairs per domain. As controls, we mix in pairs of `(source, actual reference)`, treating the reference translation as an additional system.

Evaluation of adequacy The annotator is presented with a sentence pair and asked to judge whether the translation is adequate, partially adequate or inadequate.

Evaluation of fluency We use the same data as for the evaluation of adequacy, however, the annotator is shown only the translation, without the corresponding source sentence. The annotator is asked whether the given sentence is fluent, partially fluent or not fluent.

Figure 2 shows the results of the manual evaluation in terms of adequacy and fluency. For visualization, individual fluency values are computed as follows:

$$1.0 * n_f + 0.5 * n_p + 0.0 * n_n$$

Where n_f, n_p and n_n are the number of fluent, partially fluent and non-fluent translations, respectively. Adequacy values are computed in the same way. On the in-domain test set, both baselines achieve high adequacy and fluency, with the NMT baseline effectively matching the adequacy and fluency of the reference translations.

Regarding adequacy, the in-domain samples contain only a small number of translations with content unrelated to the source (1% to 2%). On out-of-domain data, on the other hand, both baselines produce a high number of inadequate translations: 57% (SMT) and 84% (NMT).

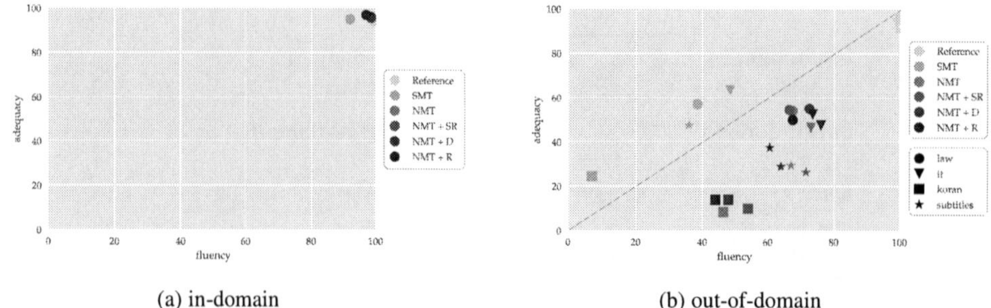

(a) in-domain   (b) out-of-domain

Figure 2: Manual evaluation of adequacy and fluency for DE→EN. Legend: marker colors are different systems, marker types are different domains. SR=Subword Regularization, D=Distillation, R=Reconstruction

	in-domain	OOD average
Reference	2%	2%
NMT	2%	35%
SMT	1%	4%
NMT + Subword Regularization	1%	37%
NMT + Distillation	3%	33%
NMT + Reconstruction	1%	29%

Table 4: Percentage of translations judged to be hallucinations (both **not adequate** and at least **partially fluent**) in the manual evaluation.

These results suggest that the extremely low BLEU scores on these two test sets (see Table 2a) are in large part due to made up content in the translations.

Regarding fluency in out-of-domain settings, SMT and NMT baselines behave very differently: SMT translations are more adequate, while NMT translations are more fluent. This trend is most extreme in the *koran* domain, where only 2% of SMT translations are found to be fluent (compared to 36% for NMT).

Further analysis of both annotations shows that NMT translations found to be inadequate are not necessarily disfluent in out-of-domain settings. Table 4 shows that, on average, on out-of-domain data, 35% of NMT translations are both inadequate and fluent, while the same is only true for 4% of SMT translations. We refer to translations of this kind as **hallucinations**.

To summarize our analysis of baseline models, we find that the domain robustness of current NMT systems is still lacking and that inadequate, but fluent translations are a prominent issue. This motivates our choice of techniques to improve domain robustness.

4 Approaches to Improve Domain Robustness

We discuss approaches that can potentially remedy the problem of low domain robustness, and compare them in subsequent experiments.

4.1 Subword Regularization

Subword regularization (Kudo, 2018) is a form of data augmentation that, instead of applying a fixed subword segmentation like BPE, probabilistically samples a new subword segmentation for each epoch. At test time, the model either uses 1-best segmentation, or translates the k-best segmentations and selects the highest-probability translation.

Kudo (2018) reports large improvements on low-resource and out-of-domain settings. In particular, improvements on in-house patent, web, and query test sets were in the range of 2–10 BLEU. In this work, we evaluate subword regularization on public datasets. We apply sampling at training time and translate 1-best segmented sentences at test time.

4.2 Defensive Distillation

We hypothesize that defensive distillation can be used to improve domain robustness. Defensive distillation exploits *knowledge distillation* to fend off adversarial attacks.

Knowledge distillation is a technique to derive models from existing ones, instead of training from scratch. The idea was introduced for simple image classification models by Ba and Caruana (2014) and Hinton et al. (2015). A first model (called the teacher) is trained in the usual fashion. Then, a second model (called the student) is trained using the predictions of the teacher model instead of the labels in the training data.

Typically, knowledge distillation is used to approach the performance of a complex teacher model (or ensemble of models) with a simpler student model. Another application is *defensive distillation* (e.g. Papernot et al. 2016), where the student shares the network architecture with the teacher, with the purpose not being model compression, but improving the model's generalization to samples outside of its training set, and specifically robustness against adversarial examples (Szegedy et al., 2013; Goodfellow et al., 2014).

Defensive distillation has been shown to be effective at improving robustness to adversarial examples in image recognition. In this work, we apply it to NMT and test its effect on domain robustness, which Papernot et al. (2016) hint at but do not empirically test. As proposed by Kim and Rush (2016), we train the student model on teacher translations produced with beam search, instead of training on soft prediction labels.

4.3 Reconstruction

Reconstruction (Tu et al., 2017) is a change to the model architecture that addresses the problem of adequacy. The authors propose to extend encoder-decoder models with a *reconstructor* component that learns to reconstruct the source sentence from decoder states. The reconstructor has two uses: as a training objective, it forces the decoder representations to retain information that will be useful for reconstruction; during inference, it can provide scores that can be used for reranking.

However, we observed in initial experiments that reconstruction from hidden states can be too easy: the reconstruction loss on training batches diminishes very quickly, to the point of being insignificant. To prevent the model from simply reserving parts of the decoder hidden states to memorize the input sentence, we use reconstruction from actual translations instead of hidden states (Niu et al., 2019). Translations are produced with differentiable sampling via the Straight-Through Gumbel Softmax (Jang et al., 2017), which still allows joint optimization of translation and reconstruction. While Niu et al. (2019) implement reconstruction for recurrent architectures, we apply the technique to Transformers.

In order to avoid introducing any additional parameters for reconstruction, as recommended in Niu et al. (2019), we train a multilingual, bi-directional system with shared parameters as a further baseline. This bi-directional system is used to initialize the fine-tuning of reconstruction models. We empirically test whether our bilingual baseline and this multilingual baseline have comparable performance.

4.4 Neural Noisy Channel Reranking

Even though the methods we presented previously do lead to improved out-of-domain translation quality, the models still suffer from low adequacy. Also, our reconstruction models only perform reconstruction during training, and the reverse translation direction is not exploited, for instance by reranking translations (Tu et al., 2017).

We conjecture that this problem can be addressed with a neural noisy channel model (Li and Jurafsky, 2016). Standard NMT systems only model $p(y|x)$, which can lead to a "failure mode that can occur in conditional models in which inputs are explained away by highly predictive output prefixes" (Yu et al., 2017). Noisy channel models propose to also model $p(x|y)$ and $p(y)$ to alleviate this effect.

In practical terms, noisy channel models are implemented by modifying the core decoding algorithm, or simply as n-best list reranking. We adopt the latter, since n-best list reranking was shown to have equal or better performance than more computationally costly methods that score partial hypotheses during beam search (Yee et al., 2019).

5 Experimental Setup for Proposed Methods

This section describes how we preprocessed data and trained the models described in Section 4. Unless stated otherwise, the data is preprocessed in the same way as for the baselines (see Section 3.1).

Subword Regularization Models We integrate subword regularization in Sockeye, using the Python library provided by Kudo (2018)[4]. The training data is **not** segmented with BPE in this case. Instead, the training tool is given truecased data, and new segmentations are sampled before each training epoch. We use the following hyperparameters: we set the smoothing parameter α to 0.1 and use an n-best size of 64. For the validation and test data we use 1-best segmentation.

Defensive Distillation Models We use our baseline Transformer model as the teacher model. We translate the original training set with beam size 10. The student is trained on the translations of the teacher model using the same hyperparameters and being initialized with the parameters of the teacher model.

Reconstruction Models We implement differentiable sampling reconstruction for Transformer models in Sockeye and release the implementation.[5] We first train a multilingual Transformer model using the approach of Johnson et al. (2017).

After early stopping, we continue training with reconstruction as an additional loss. All hyperparameters remain the same, except for the new loss and a lower initial learning rate. For testing we select the model with the lowest validation perplexity. We use the reconstruction loss only for training, not for reranking.

Noisy Channel Reranking For each hypothesis, we store an n-best list of 50. We produce the following scores: $p(y|x)$ (usual translation score), $p(x|y)$ (translation score in reverse direction) and $p(y)$ (language model score in target language). $p(y|x)$ and $p(x|y)$ are computed with the same model since it is bi-directional.

In order to produce $p(y)$ scores we train a Transformer language model with fairseq (Ott et al., 2019) using standard settings. We impose a large penalty of -100 for hypotheses that contain subwords not found in the target side training data.

The final hypothesis score for reranking is computed as a weighted multiplication:

$$\text{score}(x, y) = p(y|x)^{\lambda_{tf}} * p(x|y)^{\lambda_{tb}} * p(y)^{\lambda_{lm}}$$

---

[4]https://github.com/google/sentencepiece
[5]https://github.com/ZurichNLP/sockeye/tree/domain-robustness

	DE→EN			DE→RM		
	λ_{tf}	λ_{tb}	λ_{lm}	λ_{tf}	λ_{tb}	λ_{lm}
(5) Multilingual	0.7	0.26	0.04	0.9	0.09	0.01
(6) Reconstruction	0.6	0.32	0.08	0.9	0.09	0.01
(7) Multilingual + SR	0.5	0.42	0.08	0.9	0.09	0.01
(8) Reconstruction + SR	0.5	0.46	0.04	0.9	0.09	0.01

Table 5: Best weights for noisy channel reranking found with grid search on in-domain development set. Row numbers correspond to the ones in Table 6. λ_{tf}=forward translation weight, λ_{tb}=backward translation weight, λ_{lm}= language model weight

The best weights are found with simple grid search on the in-domain development set, with $\lambda_{tf} \in [0.0, 0.1, ..., 1.0]$, $\lambda_{lm} \in [0.0, 0.01, ..., 0.1, 0.2, ..., 1.0]$, and $\lambda_{tb} = 1 - \lambda_{tf} - \lambda_{lm}$. The best weight combination is then used to compute scores and perform reranking for the test data of all domains. Table 5 lists optimal weights found for each model individually.

6   Results

We evaluate models in terms of BLEU on different domains (see Section 6.1) and also annotate a subset of translations manually for fluency and adequacy (see Section 6.2).

6.1   Automatic evaluation

Table 6 shows the results of our automatic evaluation. Overall, the proposed methods are able to outperform the SMT and NMT baselines but not in a consistent manner across domains or data conditions: an increase in in-domain BLEU does not always mean a similar increase on out-of-domain data. Similarly, an increase in BLEU in high-resource conditions (DE→EN) does not consistently lead to better results in low-resource conditions (DE→RM).

Subword regularization The results for subword regularization are mixed (see Row 3 in Table 6). For DE→EN, in-domain translation quality is comparable to the NMT baseline, while the average out-of-domain BLEU falls short of the NMT baseline (-0.5 BLEU). However, in the low-resource condition (DE→RM), subword regularization improves both in-domain and out-of-domain translation (+1.2 in both cases).

This result is surprising given the larger gains reported by Kudo (2018). To validate our implementation of subword regularization, we reproduce an experiment from Kudo (2018) with English-Vietnamese data from IWSLT 15 (see Table 7). With subword regularization we observe an improvement of 0.8 BLEU, which is lower than the 2 BLEU improvement reported by Kudo (2018), but we also note that our baseline model is stronger.

If subword regularization is combined with multilingual or reconstruction models (see Rows 7 and 8 in Table 6), we observe no improvements on in-domain test sets, but gains on 3 out of 4 out-of-domain data sets, indicating that subword regularization is in fact helpful for domain robustness.

Defensive Distillation Distilling the training data also leads to improvements in BLEU on out-of-domain text (see Row 4 in Table 6). The average gain is +1.4 for DE→EN, but only +0.4 for DE→RM. In-domain performance is either comparable or slightly worse (-0.4 BLEU for DE→EN) than the NMT baseline. The technique was originally shown to guard against adversarial attacks, where inputs are only infinitesimally different from training examples. Our results indicate that generalization to out-of-domain inputs – that are farther from the training data – is similarly improved.

	DE→EN		DE→RM	
	in-domain	average OOD	in-domain	average OOD
(1) SMT	58.4	11.8	45.2	15.5
(2) NMT	61.5	11.7	52.5	18.9
(3) NMT + SR	61.4	11.2	**53.7**	20.1
(4) NMT + D	61.1	13.1	52.5	19.3
(5) Multilingual	61.4	11.7	52.8	19.6
(6) Reconstruction	61.5	12.5	53.4	21.2
(7) Multilingual + SR	60.3	12.8	52.4	20.1
(8) Reconstruction + SR	60.3	**13.2**	52.4	20.3
(9) Multilingual + NC	62.7	11.8	53.1	21.4
(10) Reconstruction + NC	**62.8**	13.0	53.3	**21.6**
(11) Multilingual + SR + NC	60.7	12.3	53.1	21.4
(12) Reconstruction + SR + NC	60.8	13.1	52.4	20.7

Table 6: BLEU scores (higher is better) of all systems on test data. SR=Subword Regularization, D=Distillation, NC=Noisy Channel Model, average OOD=average BLEU score over out-of-domain test sets.

	Baseline (BPE)	Subword Regularization
Kudo (2018)	25.6	27.7 (+ 2.1)
Our results	28.3	29.1 (+ 0.8)

Table 7: Reproducing results from Kudo (2018) on IWSLT 15 English-Vietnamese data.

Source	- die Produktion in der Türkei entspricht 1,3 % der chinesischen Produktion;
Target	- Turkey's volume of production amounts to 1,3 % of Chinese production,
NMT Baseline	- the production in slkei is 1.3% of a Chinese **hamster ovary (CHO) cell**
Multilingual	- production in turkei is equivalent to 1.3% of Chinese **Hamster** production;
Reconstruction	- the production in thekei is equivalent to 1.3% of the Chinese production;
Reconstruction + NC	- production in the turkei equals 1.3% of the Chinese production;

Table 8: Example translations for DE→EN. Hallucinated parts are shown in **bold**.

Reconstruction Since reconstruction models are fine-tuned from multilingual models, we report scores for those multilingual models as well. Row 5 of Table 6 shows that our multilingual models perform equally well or better than the NMT baseline. As shown in Row 6 of Table 6, reconstruction outperforms the NMT baseline on out-of-domain data for both language pairs (+0.8 BLEU for DE→EN, +2.3 BLEU for DE→RM), while maintaining (DE→EN) or improving (+0.9 BLEU for DE→RM) in-domain BLEU.

Noisy Channel Reranking We evaluate the performance of noisy channel reranking in four different settings: applied to multilingual or reconstruction systems, both with and without subword regularization. The results are shown in Rows 9 to 12 of Table 6.

For DE→EN, reranking a reconstruction model achieves a good in-domain BLEU (+1.3 over the baseline), and slightly improves out-of-domain translation on average (+0.5 BLEU over reconstruction). For DE→RM in our low-resource setting, reranking with a noisy channel model improves the reconstruction model by +0.4 BLEU, producing the best result overall. The improvement on out-of-domain translation is much larger for the multilingual model (+1.8 over multilingual model without reranking). Combining reranked models (see Rows 11 and 12 in Table 6) with subword regularization does not lead to consistent improvements. Out-of-domain BLEU for DE→RM is slightly better compared to a subword regularization system without reranking (+0.4 BLEU), while all other scores are comparable or worse.

We believe that the success of reranking could be limited for two reasons. Firstly, model weights λ are optimized on in-domain data. Oracle experiments that optimize weights on out-of-domain data show that optimal model weighting differs greatly between domains and could further improve out-of-domain results by 0.5–1 BLEU on average. Secondly, reranking could be held back by the lack of diversity among hypotheses in n-best lists.

6.2 Manual evaluation

In a small manual evaluation, we analyze if methods that improve domain robustness in terms of BLEU also directly address the lack of adequacy in out-of-domain translation (see Section 3.2.1). The results are shown in Figure 2b. For anectodal examples of translations by several models, see Table 8.

Techniques with a bias for fluency We find that subword regularization increases fluency by several percentage points in some domains. However, it fails to improve adequacy which explains why it consequently fails to improve out-of-domain BLEU. Defensive distillation improves translations in a similar way, with a bias for fluency while not consistently improving the adequacy of out-of-domain translations.

Reconstruction having a bias for adequacy We show that reconstruction is limiting hallucination on out-of-domain data, reducing the percentage of inadequate translations by 5 percentage points on average. We also note that there appears to be a tradeoff between adequacy and fluency: while reconstruction does improve out-of-domain adequacy, the improvement comes at the cost of lower fluency.

7 Discussion

Overall, we emphasize that SMT no longer appears to have higher domain robustness than NMT—a widely held belief given the findings of Koehn and Knowles (2017). However, SMT and NMT models achieve comparable domain robustness in different ways: SMT translations are more adequate (since SMT decoding implicitly enforces coverage), while NMT translations are more fluent (since an NMT decoder is simply a language model of the target language conditioned on source context). Therefore, evaluating domain robustness with automatic metrics only can be misleading and hide the fact that models have very different inductive biases, even if their BLEU score is similar.

Our experiments to reduce NMT hallucination and improve adequacy can be summarized as follows. Several methods lead to moderate improvements in translation quality, but only reconstruction combined with noisy channel reranking robustly increased BLEU across domains and data conditions (see Row 10 of Table 6). Other techniques are successful only in certain conditions. For instance, combining multilingual systems with Subword Regularization improves out-of-domain translation only, but not in-domain quality (see Rows 7–8 of Table 6). This suggests that techniques found to work well on in-domain test data cannot be assumed to have a similar effect on out-of-domain data without proper testing.

Our manual evaluation suggests that for NMT systems, an increase in out-of-domain BLEU also means that translations are slightly more adequate. However, NMT models still have a strong bias for fluency (all models under the diagonal in Figure 2b) and their adequacy falls short of the adequacy of SMT systems. Our most successful reconstruction model does indeed improve adequacy, but at the same time decreases fluency to a certain extent. We believe radically different approaches are needed to increase the coverage and adequacy of NMT translations without sacrificing their fluency.

8 Conclusions

Current NMT systems exhibit low domain robustness, i.e. they underperform if they are tested on a domain that differs strongly from the training domain. This is especially problematic in settings where explicit domain adaptation is impossible because the target domain is unknown, or because we are in a low-resource setting where training data is only available for limited domains. We find that hallucinated translations are a common problem for NMT models in out-of-domain settings, which partially explains their low domain robustness. Our results show that several methods yield improved generalization to out-of-domain data. We achieve an improvement in average out-of-domain BLEU of 1.5 (DE→EN) and 2.7 (DE→RM), as well as a reduction in hallucinated translations according to manual evaluation.

We analyzed the fluency and adequacy of translations manually, leading to a discussion of several pitfalls regarding the evaluation of NMT models in out-of-domain settings. Also, we believe that future research will need to address the lack of adequacy without losing fluency. We consider domain robustness an unsolved problem and encourage further research. For this purpose, we share data and code to serve as a baseline for future experiments.[6]

Acknowledgements

We are grateful to Manuela Weibel, Beni Ruef, Florentin Lutz and the *Lia Rumantscha* for providing Rumansh data, to Xing Niu for his help with reconstruction training, and to *Fremde Welten* for their help with manual annotations. MM and AR have received funding from the Swiss National Science Foundation (SNF, grant number 105212_169888). RS has received funding from the European Union's Horizon 2020 Research and Innovation Programme (ELITR, grant agreement 825460).

---

[6] https://github.com/ZurichNLP/domain-robustness

References

Arthur, P., Neubig, G., and Nakamura, S. (2016). Incorporating discrete translation lexicons into neural machine translation. In *Proceedings of EMNLP 2016*, pages 1557–1567.

Ba, J. and Caruana, R. (2014). Do deep nets really need to be deep? In *Advances in neural information processing systems*, pages 2654–2662.

Belinkov, Y. and Bisk, Y. (2018). Synthetic and natural noise both break neural machine translation. In *Proceedings of the 6th International Conference on Learning Representations*, Vancouver, Canada.

Goodfellow, I., Shlens, J., and Szegedy, C. (2015). Explaining and harnessing adversarial examples. In *International Conference on Learning Representations*.

Goodfellow, I. J., Shlens, J., and Szegedy, C. (2014). Explaining and harnessing adversarial examples (2014). *arXiv preprint arXiv:1412.6572*.

Hieber, F., Domhan, T., Denkowski, M., Vilar, D., Sokolov, A., Clifton, A., and Post, M. (2018). The Sockeye Neural Machine Translation Toolkit at AMTA 2018. In *Proceedings of the 13th Conference of the Association for Machine Translation in the Americas (AMTA)*, pages 200–207.

Hinton, G., Vinyals, O., and Dean, J. (2015). Distilling the knowledge in a neural network. *arXiv preprint arXiv:1503.02531*.

Jang, E., Gu, S., and Poole, B. (2017). Categorical reparametrization with gumbel-softmax. In *Proceedings International Conference on Learning Representations 2017*. OpenReviews.net.

Johnson, M., Schuster, M., Le, Q. V., Krikun, M., Wu, Y., Chen, Z., Thorat, N., Viégas, F., Wattenberg, M., Corrado, G., Hughes, M., and Dean, J. (2017). Google's multilingual neural machine translation system: Enabling zero-shot translation. *Transactions of the Association for Computational Linguistics*, 5:339–351.

Kim, Y. and Rush, A. M. (2016). Sequence-level knowledge distillation. In *Proceedings of the 2016 Conference on Empirical Methods in Natural Language Processing*, pages 1317–1327, Austin, Texas.

Kobus, C., Crego, J., and Senellart, J. (2017). Domain control for neural machine translation. In *Proceedings of RANLP 2017*, pages 372–378. INCOMA Ltd.

Koehn, P., Hoang, H., Birch, A., Callison-Burch, C., Federico, M., Bertoldi, N., Cowan, B., Shen, W., Moran, C., Zens, R., Dyer, C., Bojar, O., Constantin, A., and Herbst, E. (2007). Moses: Open Source Toolkit for Statistical Machine Translation. In *Proceedings of the ACL-2007 Demo and Poster Sessions*, pages 177–180, Prague, Czech Republic.

Koehn, P. and Knowles, R. (2017). Six Challenges for Neural Machine Translation. In *Proceedings of the First Workshop on Neural Machine Translation*, pages 28–39.

Kudo, T. (2018). Subword Regularization: Improving Neural Network Translation Models with Multiple Subword Candidates. In *Proceedings of ACL 2018*, pages 66–75.

Läubli, S., Müller, M., Horat, B., and Volk, M. (2018). mtrain: A convenience tool for machine translation.

Lee, K., Firat, O., Agarwal, A., Fannjiang, C., and Sussillo, D. (2018). Hallucinations in neural machine translation.

Li, J. and Jurafsky, D. (2016). Mutual information and diverse decoding improve neural machine translation. *arXiv preprint arXiv:1601.00372*.

Li, X., Michel, P., Anastasopoulos, A., Belinkov, Y., Durrani, N., Firat, O., Koehn, P., Neubig, G., Pino, J., and Sajjad, H. (2019). Findings of the First Shared Task on Machine Translation Robustness. In *WMT 2019*, pages 91–102, Florence, Italy.

Lison, P. and Tiedemann, J. (2016). OpenSubtitles2016: Extracting Large Parallel Corpora from Movie and TV Subtitles. In *Proceedings of LREC 2016*, pages 923–929.

Luong, M.-T. and Manning, C. D. (2015). Stanford Neural Machine Translation Systems for Spoken Language Domains. In *Proceedings of IWSLT 2015*, Da Nang, Vietnam.

Nguyen, T. and Chiang, D. (2018). Improving Lexical Choice in Neural Machine Translation. In *Proceedings of NAACL-HLT 2018*, pages 334–343.

Niu, X., Xu, W., and Carpuat, M. (2019). Bi-directional differentiable input reconstruction for low-resource neural machine translation. In *Proceedings of NAACL-HLT 2019*, pages 442–448.

Ott, M., Edunov, S., Baevski, A., Fan, A., Gross, S., Ng, N., Grangier, D., and Auli, M. (2019). fairseq: A fast, extensible toolkit for sequence modeling. In *Proceedings of NAACL-HLT 2019: Demonstrations*.

Papernot, N., McDaniel, P., Wu, X., Jha, S., and Swami, A. (2016). Distillation as a defense to adversarial perturbations against deep neural networks. In *2016 IEEE Symposium on Security and Privacy (SP)*, pages 582–597. IEEE.

Papineni, K., Roukos, S., Ward, T., and Zhu, W.-J. (2002). BLEU: A Method for Automatic Evaluation of Machine Translation. In *Proceedings of the 40th Annual Meeting on Association for Computational Linguistics*, pages 311–318, Philadelphia, PA.

Post, M. (2018). A call for clarity in reporting bleu scores. In *Proceedings of the Third Conference on Machine Translation: Research Papers*, pages 186–191, Belgium, Brussels.

Scherrer, Y. and Cartoni, B. (2012). The Trilingual ALLEGRA Corpus: Presentation and Possible Use for Lexicon Induction. In *Proceedings of LREC-2012*, pages 2890–2896, Istanbul, Turkey.

Sennrich, R., Haddow, B., and Birch, A. (2016a). Improving Neural Machine Translation Models with Monolingual Data. In *Proceedings of ACL 2016*, pages 86–96, Berlin, Germany.

Sennrich, R., Haddow, B., and Birch, A. (2016b). Neural Machine Translation of Rare Words with Sub-word Units. In *Proceedings of ACL 2016*, pages 1715–1725, Berlin, Germany.

Szegedy, C., Zaremba, W., Sutskever, I., Bruna, J., Erhan, D., Goodfellow, I., and Fergus, R. (2013). Intriguing properties of neural networks. *arXiv preprint arXiv:1312.6199*.

Tu, Z., Liu, Y., Shang, L., Liu, X., and Li, H. (2017). Neural Machine Translation with Reconstruction. In *Proceedings of the Thirty-First AAAI Conference on Artificial Intelligence*, pages 3097–3103.

Vaswani, A., Shazeer, N., Parmar, N., Uszkoreit, J., Jones, L., Gomez, A. N., Kaiser, Ł., and Polosukhin, I. (2017). Attention is All you Need. In *Advances in Neural Information Processing Systems 30*, pages 5998–6008.

Yee, K., Dauphin, Y., and Auli, M. (2019). Simple and effective noisy channel modeling for neural machine translation. In *Proceedings of EMNLP-IJCNLP 2019*, pages 5696–5701, Hong Kong, China.

Yu, L., Blunsom, P., Dyer, C., Grefenstette, E., and Kociský, T. (2017). The neural noisy channel. In *5th International Conference on Learning Representations, ICLR 2017*, Toulon, France.

Low-Resource NMT: an Empirical Study on the Effect of Rich Morphological Word Segmentation on Inuktitut

Ngoc Tan Le   le.ngoc_tan@courrier.uqam.ca
Fatiha Sadat   sadat.fatiha@uqam.ca
Department of Computer Science, Universite du Quebec a Montreal
201, avenue du President-Kennedy, Montreal, QC, Canada

Abstract

Nowadays, very little research for Indigenous languages has been studied. Indigenous languages bring significant challenges for Natural Language Processing approaches because of multiple features such as polysynthesis, morphological complexity, dialectal variations with rich morpho-phonemics, spelling with noisy data and low resource scenarios. Particularly, morphological segmentation for polysynthetic languages is challenging because a word may contain many individual morphemes and training data can be extremely scarce. The current research paper focuses on Inuktitut, one of the Indigenous polysynthetic language spoken in Northern Canada. First, a rich word segmentation for Inuktitut is studied using a set of rich features and by leveraging (bi-)character-based and word-based pretrained embeddings from large-scale raw corpora. Second, we incorporated this pre-processing step into our first Neural Machine Translation system. Our evaluations showed promising results and performance improvements in the context of low-resource Inuktitut-English neural machine translation.

1 Introduction

In the Americas, there are a wide range of linguistic families about 140 linguistic families in the world. About 900 different Indigenous languages spoken in the Americas approximately are reported in (Mager et al., 2018). In Canada, there is a great diversity of Indigenous languages, grouped into 12 language families, that have been central to the history of First Nations people, Métis and Inuit in Canada and continue to play a vital role to this day (Rice, 2011).

This research paper focuses on Inuktitut, one of the Indigenous polysynthetic languages spoken in Northern Canada and the development of a Neural Machine Translation (NMT) for Inuktitut-English. The main objective and motivation of this project is the revitalization and preservation of Indigenous languages and cultural heritage through major tasks in NLP.

However, the development of Indigenous language technology faces many challenges such as polysynthesis with a high rate of morphemes per word, lack of orthographic normalization, dialectal variations and lack of linguistic resources and tool such as corpora (Littell et al., 2018). This first step towards a multilingual NMT framework that will involve several endangered Indigenous languages of Canada, is essential as the only parallel corpus freely available for research is the Nunavut-English Hansard corpus (Joanis et al., 2020).

Inspired by the work of Farley (2012), related on the creation of the first Inuktitut morphological analyzer, we build a neural network-based word segmenter for Inuktitut. The main goal of this research is two folds: (1) to investigate empirically several word segmentation methods on Inuktitut; and (2) to improve low-resource NMT that involves Inuktitut through rich morphological word segmentation.

The structure of the paper is described as follows: Section 2 presents the state-of-the-art on MT involving Indigenous languages. In section 3, we describe our methodology. Then, in section 4, we present our experiments and evaluations. Finally, in section 5, we present our conclusion and some perspectives for future research.

2 Related work

Farley (2012) developed a morphological analyzer for Inuktitut, which makes use of a finite-state transducer and hand-crafted rules. This Uqa·Ila·Ut project (Uqailaut)[1] is a rule-based system that involves regular morphological variations of about 3200 head, 350 lexical, and 1500 grammatical morphemes, with heuristics for ranking the various readings. Inspired by the Uqailaut project of Farley (2012), Micher (2017) applied a segmental recurrent neural network approach (Kong et al., 2015) from the output of this morphological analyzer for Inuktitut.

The development of MT systems for Indigenous languages have followed the trends in the field, with rule-based, statistical-based and neural network-based approaches. Micher (2018) applied the Byte Pair Encoding (BPE) algorithm (Sennrich et al., 2016) pre-processing both the English and Inuktitut sides of the Nunavut Hansard corpus, in the Inuktitut to English direction, reported a BLEU score of 30.35. NMT approaches use neural networks architectures that are fed with very big amounts of parallel texts. However, these resources are currently unavailable or scarce for most Indigenous languages, especially for the endangered such as Inuinnaqtun, except Inuktitut-English (Joanis et al., 2020).

3 Methodology

In this section, we present some existing word segmentation methods for Inuktitut as well as our proposed one.

3.1 Uqailaut morphological analysis

The Uqailaut project, proposed by Farley (2012), is based on a Finite-State Transducers (FST), while applying several techniques and resources such as grammar rules, linguistic knowledge and heuristics. The FST-based morphological analyzer produces one or more morphological predictions for a given word. The heuristics allow to choose the shortest path of the morphological analysis. For example, *'katimajiit'* is segmented as *'kati ma ji it'* (Table 1). The root *'kati'* means *'to accumulate; to gather; to join; to unite'*. And the suffixes are *'ma'* means *'to be in a state of'*; *'ji'* means *'one whose job is; agent'*; *'it'* means *'to be such'*.

Segmentation	Sentence Example
Raw text	ilangit katimajiit : angiqpugut . (Meaning: *some members : agreed* .)
Reference	ila ngit kati ma ji it : angiq pugut .
Uqailaut project (Farley, 2012)	ila ngit kati ma ji it : angiq pugut .
BPE (Sennrich et al., 2016)	ilangit kati@ @ ma@ @ jiit : angiq@ @ pu@ @ gut .
Our proposed approach	ila ngit kati ma ji it : angiq pugut .

Table 1: Illustrations on the Inuktitut word segmentation involving our proposed approach and others

---

[1] http://www.inuktitutcomputing.ca/Uqailaut/info.php

3.2 Byte-Pair Encoding

The byte-pair encoding (BPE), proposed by Sennrich et al. (2016), is an unsupervised word segmentation that aims at splitting word by subword units, which helps cope with rare and unknown words. BPE applies the minimum entropy on the subword units, aka tokens, with the predefined vocabulary size. These tokens look like morphemes, although BPE segmentation model is based on training data rather than on linguistic knowledge. For example, in Inuktitut, *'katimajiit'* (meaning: *members* in English) may be segmented as *'kati@@ ma@@ jiit'* (Table 1). This word should be correctly segmented *'kati@@ ma@@ ji@@ it'*, in the case of a large-scale training data. The symbol @@ represents an in-word morpheme boundary.

3.3 Our proposed approach

Neural network-based approaches have shown their efficiency when applied on word segmentation and enhanced with large-scale raw texts to pretrain embeddings. Adding these linguistic factors allows the neural model to perform better, especially when dealing with data sparseness or language ambiguity (Kann et al., 2018).

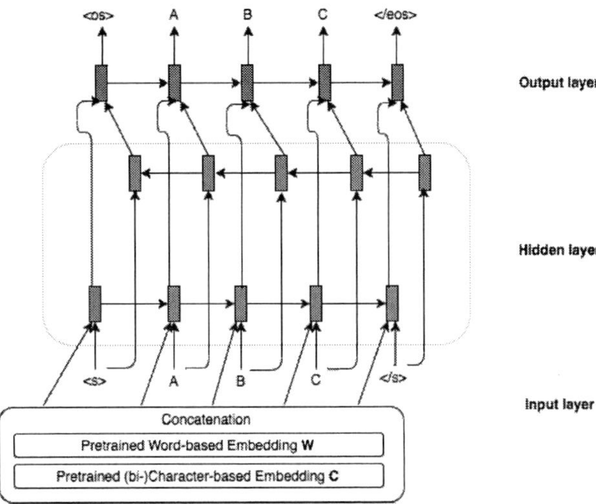

Figure 1: The system architecture of Inuktitut Rich Morphological Word Segmentation based on neural networks

In this research, the word segmentation task is considered as a sequence labeling task. Given an input sequence, W and C that contain all the input words and the input (bi-)characters. At each step, the state consists of a sequence of words, $W = [w_0, w_1, ..., w_m]$, that have been fully recognized, and a sequence of next incoming (bi-)characters $C = [c_0, c_1, ..., c_n]$, as shown in Figure 1. The architecture is composed of three main layers: the input layer, the hidden layer and the output layer. The input layer contains the input word sequence transformation by concatenating pretrained (bi-)character-based and word-based embeddings, with the state $S = \langle W, C \rangle$. On the top of the input representation layer, we use a hidden feature layer h to merge all input features X_W, X_C into a single vector. This layer is built with bidirectional LSTM (*Long-Short Term Memory*) (Hochreiter and Schmidhuber, 1997).

$$h = tanh(W_{hW} \cdot X_W + W_{hC} \cdot X_C + b_h) \tag{1}$$

The output layer o calculates the activation function as an output function and displays the output hypothesis.

$$o = softmax(W_o \cdot h + b_o) \tag{2}$$

4 Experiments

4.1 Data Preparation

We train our NMT model by using the Nunavut Hansard for Inuktitut-English (third edition). As described in Joanis et al. (2020), this corpus contains 1,293,348 sentences, 5,433 sentences and 6,139 sentences for the training, development and testing sets, respectively (Table 2).

Dataset	#tokens	#train	#dev	#test
Inuktitut	20,657,477	1,293,348	5,433	6,139
English	10,962,904	1,293,348	5,433	6,139

Table 2: Statistics of Nunavut Hansard Inuktitut-English parallel corpus 3.0

In order to pre-train the (bi-)character-based and word-based embeddings for Inuktitut, these Nunavut Hansard datasets were used with the *word2vec* toolkit (Mikolov et al., 2013) with a dimension of 50 and 30 for word-based and (bi-)character-based embeddings, respectively, and option $CBOW$ (*Continuous Bag-Of-Words*) by default. We observe there are only 97,785 unique terms for word-based vocabulary, 102 unique terms for character-based vocabulary and 1,406 unique terms for bicharacter-based vocabulary (Table 3). To train our rich word segmenter[2], we annotated 11K sentences, 250 sentences, 250 sentences for training, development and testing, respectively. We used Uqailaut toolkit (Farley, 2012) to annotate the training data.

Embedding type	#terms	#dimension
word-based	97,785	50
character-based	102	30
bicharacter-based	1,406	30

Table 3: Statistics of word-based, (bi)character-based embeddings training by using Nunavut Hansard Inuktitut-English parallel corpus 3.0 for Inuktitut

4.2 Training Configuration

For word segmentation, we adapted the *RichWordSegmenter* toolkit (Yang et al., 2017) to train our Inuktitut word segmenter. The model is composed of 2-layer bi-directional Long Short-term Memory (LSTM) cells, with a dimension size of 50 for the projection layer to encode the input sequences and a dimension size of 200 for the hidden layer. The *Adam* optimizer (Kingma and Ba, 2014) was used to learn the network's weights with a learning rate of 0.001. In the BPE subword segmentation, we used *subword-nmt* (Sennrich et al., 2016) toolkit to create a BPE joint source-target vocabulary with dimension of 30,000.

In the preprocessing step, we used *Moses* (Koehn et al., 2007) tokenizer in all experiments and Moses preprocessing scripts to clean the training data with a threshold of 50 words by sentences and without repetitive sentences. We used Marian-nmt (Junczys-Dowmunt et al., 2018) to train our Transformer-based NMT with the following hyper-parameters settings: 6-layer depth for both encoder and decoder, embedding dimension of 512, 2048 units in hidden

---

[2]Github repository: `https://github.com/NgocTanLE/Inuktitut-English-NMT`

layers in the feed-forward networks, optimizer with SGD, an initial learning rate of 0.0003. We run 50 iterations (#max_epochs) with an early stopping based on the cross-entropy scores for the validation set every 5,000 updates. We used 6-GPUs of NVIDIA GeForce GTX 2080 Ti 12Gb.

Our experiments on NMT using the Transformer-based architecture (Vaswani et al., 2017) are described as follows: (1) the Baseline with only tokenized training data; (2) System 1 with only BPE-preprocessed data; (3) System 2 with our proposed Inuktitut word segmentation ; and (4) System 3 that combines both BPE-segmentation and our proposed word segmentation. In the system 3, the training data are firstly segmented by using our Inuktitut word segmentation. Then these segmented training data are secondly processed in subwords with the BPE-segmentation method.

4.3 Evaluations

Evaluations on word segmentation were performed using different automatic metrics such as *Recall*, *Accuracy* and *F-measure*. As described in Table 4, the model of EXP2, with all pre-trained embeddings, showed better performances than the model of EXP1, that uses only pre-trained word-based embedding, with F-measure of 72.21% and 75.33% (+3.21%) on the *test set* respectively (Table 4).

		Recall	Accuracy	F-measure
EXP1	*dev*	74.52	87.68	80.57
	test	64.34	82.28	**72.21**
EXP2	*dev*	68.94	80.82	74.41
	test	70.57	80.79	**75.33**

Table 4: Results on Inuktitut word segmentation. EXP1: word-based embedding, EXP2: all character-based, bicharacter-based, word-based embeddings

The NMT models were evaluated with the BLEU metric (Papineni et al., 2002), with lowercase and v13a tokenization, similar to Joanis et al. (2020). All the systems outperformed the baseline with gains up to +24.32 for the development set and up to +18.44 for the test set in terms of BLEU scores (Table 5). The performance of our proposed NMT models has significantly improved up to +1.03 and to +7.09 of BLEU scores with Systems 1, 2 and 3, respectively, compared to the NMT system of Joanis et al. (2020).

Experiment	dev set	test set
Baseline (tokenized)	27.98	23.65
(Joanis et al., 2020) (BPE)	41.40	35.00
System 1 (BPE)	42.62	36.03
System 2 (our Inuktitut WS)	49.12	**39.53**
System 3 (our Inuktitut WS+BPE)	52.30	**42.09**

Table 5: Performances on Inuktitut-English NMT in terms of lowercase word BLEU score

Our proposed NMT approach, that incorporates word segmentation for the Inuktitut as a source language, achieved significant improvement over the baseline system, 39.53 versus 23.65 in terms of BLEU score. Moreover, although our Inuktitut word segmentation model is trained on a small annotated corpus, the translation model can show good predictions compared to other models (Table 6). The experimental results have a positive impact on the translation model performance.

System	Sentence Example
[iu] raw	pikkugijauningit quviasuutauninganut arraagunit 15 @-@ nik uiviititut ilinniarvimmik
[en] Reference	congratulations *on celebrating 15 years* of the *francophone* school
[en] Baseline	congratulations *to 15 years* of *french* school
[en] Joanis et al. (2020)	congratulations *to the 15 years* of the *french* school
[en] System 1	congratulations *to the 15 years* of the *french* school
[en] System 2	congratulations *on celebrating 15 years* of the *french* school
[en] System 3	congratulations *on celebrating the 15 years* of the *french* school

Table 6: Illustrations on some translation predictions using different NMT systems

5   Conclusion and Perspective

In this paper, we presented an empirical study for rich morphological word segmentation on Inuktitut in Machine Translation. A neural network-based word segmenter was built for Inuktitut Indigenous language, with the use of a rich features set by leveraging (bi-)character-based and word-based pretrained embeddings from large raw texts. We applied our method to preprocess the Inuktitut source language into an Inuktitut-English NMT system. Our proposed NMT system showed better performance than the state-of-the-art, as presented in Joanis et al. (2020) with only BPE-preprocessed training data, thanks to the rich word segmenter.

The interests for Indigenous languages are growing in NLP community. We noticed that North American languages are the most studied. We observed the past, current NLP researches have been done for morphology and machine translation. The study of Indigenous languages could lead us for a more complete understanding of human languages and advance towards universal NLP models.

Future work will focus on adding more annotated data and additional domain-specific features to improve the accuracy of our model. Moreover, we are working towards a multilingual NMT framework to incorporate more Indigenous languages, more precisely the endangered ones, with the aim of preserving and revitalizing endangered and Indigenous languages, their heritage and culture.

References

Farley, B. (2012). The uqailaut project. *URL http://www. inuktitutcomputing. ca.*

Hochreiter, S. and Schmidhuber, J. (1997). Long short-term memory. *Neural Comput.*, 9(8):1735–1780.

Joanis, E., Knowles, R., Kuhn, R., Larkin, S., Littell, P., Lo, C.-k., Stewart, D., and Micher, J. (2020). The nunavut hansard inuktitut english parallel corpus 3.0 with preliminary machine translation results. In *Proceedings of The 12th Language Resources and Evaluation Conference*, pages 2562–2572, Marseille, France. European Language Resources Association.

Junczys-Dowmunt, M., Grundkiewicz, R., Dwojak, T., Hoang, H., Heafield, K., Neckermann, T., Seide, F., Germann, U., Aji, A. F., Bogoychev, N., Martins, A. F. T., and Birch, A. (2018). Marian: Fast neural machine translation in C++. In *Proceedings of ACL 2018, System Demonstrations*, pages 116–121, Melbourne, Australia. Association for Computational Linguistics.

Kann, K., Mager Hois, J. M., Meza-Ruiz, I. V., and Schütze, H. (2018). Fortification of neural morphological segmentation models for polysynthetic minimal-resource languages. In

Proceedings of the 2018 Conference of the North American Chapter of the Association for Computational Linguistics: Human Language Technologies, Volume 1 (Long Papers), pages 47–57, New Orleans, Louisiana. Association for Computational Linguistics.

Kingma, D. P. and Ba, J. (2014). Adam: A method for stochastic optimization. *arXiv preprint arXiv:1412.6980*.

Koehn, P., Hoang, H., Birch, A., Callison-Burch, C., Federico, M., Bertoldi, N., Cowan, B., Shen, W., Moran, C., Zens, R., et al. (2007). Moses: Open source toolkit for statistical machine translation. In *Proceedings of the 45th annual meeting of the association for computational linguistics companion volume proceedings of the demo and poster sessions*, pages 177–180.

Kong, F., Li, S., and Zhou, G. (2015). The sonlp-dp system in the conll-2015 shared task. In *Proceedings of the Nineteenth Conference on Computational Natural Language Learning-Shared Task*, pages 32–36.

Littell, P., Kazantseva, A., Kuhn, R., Pine, A., Arppe, A., Cox, C., and Junker, M.-O. (2018). Indigenous language technologies in canada: Assessment, challenges, and successes. In *Proceedings of the 27th International Conference on Computational Linguistics*, pages 2620–2632.

Mager, M., Gutierrez-Vasques, X., Sierra, G., and Meza-Ruiz, I. (2018). Challenges of language technologies for the indigenous languages of the Americas. In *Proceedings of the 27th International Conference on Computational Linguistics*, pages 55–69, Santa Fe, New Mexico, USA. Association for Computational Linguistics.

Micher, J. (2017). Improving coverage of an inuktitut morphological analyzer using a segmental recurrent neural network. In *Proceedings of the 2nd Workshop on the Use of Computational Methods in the Study of Endangered Languages*, pages 101–106.

Micher, J. (2018). Using the nunavut hansard data for experiments in morphological analysis and machine translation. In *Proceedings of the Workshop on Computational Modeling of Polysynthetic Languages*, pages 65–72.

Mikolov, T., Yih, W.-t., and Zweig, G. (2013). Linguistic regularities in continuous space word representations. In *hlt-Naacl*, volume 13, pages 746–751.

Papineni, K., Roukos, S., Ward, T., and Zhu, W.-J. (2002). Bleu: a method for automatic evaluation of machine translation. In *Proceedings of the 40th annual meeting on association for computational linguistics*, pages 311–318. Association for Computational Linguistics.

Rice, K. (2011). Documentary linguistics and community relations. *Language Documentation & Conservation*, 5:187–207.

Sennrich, R., Haddow, B., and Birch, A. (2016). Neural machine translation of rare words with subword units. In *Proceedings of the 54th Annual Meeting of the Association for Computational Linguistics (Volume 1: Long Papers)*, pages 1715–1725, Berlin, Germany. Association for Computational Linguistics.

Vaswani, A., Shazeer, N., Parmar, N., Uszkoreit, J., Jones, L., Gomez, A. N., Kaiser, Ł., and Polosukhin, I. (2017). Attention is all you need. In *Advances in neural information processing systems*, pages 5998–6008.

Yang, J., Zhang, Y., and Dong, F. (2017). Neural word segmentation with rich pretraining. In *Proceedings of the 55th Annual Meeting of the Association for Computational Linguistics (Volume 1: Long Papers)*, pages 839–849, Vancouver, Canada. Association for Computational Linguistics.